T0247199

PENGUIN B

SHATTERED HOPES

An international correspondent with over twenty-two years of reporting experience in the region, Romen Bose heads a crisis management and political communications consultancy. He is a close confidant of many Malaysian decision-makers and the upper echelon of the country's political elite, having worked as a political communications consultant for former Malaysian Premier Najib Razak for six years.

Before setting up his own consultancy, Romen was head of Asian social media intelligence at IHS Markit and worked as a senior foreign correspondent with international news agency AFP based in Kuala Lumpur. He was the founding president of the Foreign Correspondents Club of Malaysia and a senior producer with the English service of *Al Jazeera International* when it opened its regional base in Malaysia. Prior to this, Romen was the Indochina Bureau Chief for *Channel News Asia*, Assistant Director for the north-west India region at the Singapore Tourism Board and has also consulted for the United Nations. Romen has also researched and written extensively on the Second World War and its impact on Southeast Asia.

ADVANCE PRAISE FOR *SHATTERED HOPES*

'The book reads like a fast-paced thriller! PH1.0 began with so much hope and promise but ended so shockingly! I particularly enjoyed the climactic first chapter as well as the ones on the grumpy grandpa and Tommy Thomas. By far, the most detailed account of the backstage manoeuvring, clashes, and backstabbing that marked Dr Mahathir Mohamad's second attempt to shape the future of our country.

A blow-by-blow account of how he managed to work his way back into power and try to impose his will and rule on a changed Malaysia. Perhaps the only constant was the distrust between him and Anwar Ibrahim and there are fascinating insights into how Mahathir never intended to hand over power to Anwar as well as a close-up look at the Attorney-General that neither Mahathir nor the Malay rulers wanted in the first place.'

—Joceline Tan, political columnist, *The Star*

'A compelling behind-the-scenes account of a pivotal turning point in modern Malaysian history, deeply reported and full of fascinating detail and colourful characters. *Shattered Hopes* pulls back the curtain on the machinations of politics in Malaysia at a critical time. Required reading for anyone interested in the country and its future.'

—Mike Chinoy,
Former CNN Senior Asia Correspondent

ALSO BY Romen Bose

Final Reckoning: An Insider's View of the Fall of Malaysia's Barisan Nasional Government (2021)

Shattered Hopes

The Promise, Reality, and
Collapse of New Malaysia's
Pakatan Harapan 1.0 Government

Romen Bose

PENGUIN BOOKS

An imprint of Penguin Random House

PENGUIN BOOKS

Penguin Books is an imprint of the Penguin Random House group of
companies whose addresses can be found at
global.penguinrandomhouse.com

Published by Penguin Random House SEA Pte Ltd
40 Penjuru Lane, #03-12, Block 2
Singapore 609216

First published in Penguin Books by Penguin Random House SEA 2024

ISBN 9789815127911

Typeset in Garamond by MAP Systems, Bengaluru, India

www.penguin.sg

To my wife, Brigid, and our daughters Lara, Olive, and Cilla.
And to the memory of my late uncle, Mrinal Kanti Dutta.

Contents

Preface

The initial idea for this book arose during a lunch meeting I was having with my long-time friend and agent, Chris Newson, at the Wolseley in London, in late February 2020, just before the Covid-19 pandemic placed the world under lockdown. As we were discussing a few projects, my phone suddenly began buzzing with alerts and messages as news began trickling in of the sudden power grab by the new Perikatan Nasional (PN) coalition from the reform minded Pakatan Harapan (PH1.0) Government in Malaysia.[1]

Despite my self-imposed exile following the fourteenth General Election (GE14) in 2018, I had been closely monitoring the events in Malaysia through my numerous contacts and friends, who were in and out of the government and power. I was, therefore, aware of the fragility of the then Prime Minister, Mahathir Mohamad's, hold on power.

---

[1] In order to avoid confusion and provide clarity, I have labelled the coalition and government led by former Prime Minister Mahathir Mohamad and which had won GE14 as the Pakatan Harapan 1.0 or PH1.0 coalition and government. This is not to be confused with the Pakatan Harapan 2.0 or PH2.0, known as the National Unity Government formed and led by Prime Minister Anwar Ibrahim in November 2022. Although some of the coalition members remain the same, the PH1.0 Government and coalition was led and directed by Mahathir, while Anwar remained in the political wilderness and was not involved in much of what took place during PH1.0's time in power. This book, on the whole, deals with the PH1.0 Government.

But I must admit that, despite being aware of the various undercurrents and backroom machinations that had begun within Mahathir's circle of cronies and political leaders long before 9 May 2018, I was still surprised at the speed with which a much acclaimed virtuous and multiracial PH1.0 coalition—that was attempting to rid Malaysia of its cronies, corruption, racism, and inequalities—had, in a spate of twenty-two months, not only imploded but been replaced by a group of ultra-nationalists that were the very antithesis of 'A New Malaysia'.

This hope of 'A New Malaysia' was what caused voters to abandon, in droves, the Barisan Nasional (BN) coalition, which had ruled the country since its independence in 1957, in favour of the promises of reform and change made by the PH1.0 coalition of parties.

Knowing my familiarity with the key players and what was transpiring on the ground, Chris immediately suggested that I start working on a book. I, however, wasn't convinced that there was a book to write.

After all, PH1.0 was only in power for twenty-two months, and so, how much really could have happened to warrant a book?

Actually, quite a lot, it would appear.

Recalling the numerous conversations I had during 2018 and 2019 that exposed the privately held bitterness and disappointment of several staunch PH1.0 supporters and senior leaders, it was clear that what had transpired needed to be written down.

This book is not just for posterity but more as a guide for a future generation of Malaysians, on what to do in order to hold on to the trust of the people and more importantly, what not to do so as to prevent the country from being hijacked and led by a coterie of narrow-minded and power-hungry political leaders. To quote former top diplomat and political columnist Dennis Ignatius, who had been an unabashed PH1.0 supporter and activist:

Many have expressed disbelief that one man could be so cunning and manipulative and wonder whether it ascribes too much to the nonagenarian. Mahathir may not, of course, have orchestrated everything but he certainly knew how to light or stoke fires here and there and then exploit the ensuing angst and alarm to further his agenda. Looking at all his statements and actions over his twenty-two months in power, a pattern emerges that suggests he orchestrated the downfall of his own multiracial government in order to build something more to his liking. Having used non-Malays to defeat UMNO in GE14, he cynically planned to defeat the non-Malays by forging an all-Malay coalition that included parties that were defeated in the same elections . . .

. . . (And) in the face of the sustained assault on Pakatan Harapan's legitimacy, non-Malay politicians dithered, too afraid to challenge Mahathir for fear of upsetting the apple cart. Lim Kit Siang protested that, 'lies, falsehoods, fake news and hate speech cannot restore the dignity of any race or nation,' but he, along with other DAP leaders, carefully avoided any direct criticism of Mahathir. Even Mahathir's derogatory use of the term 'foreigners' to describe Malaysia's ethnic minorities evoked no strong reaction from Kit Siang or Guan Eng.[2]

I hope those in power and others seeking it spend time to read this book and understand the message, instead of shooting the messenger. I, of course, remain fully responsible for any and all mistakes and errors and apologize in advance for them. I have also attempted, in good faith, and to the best of my ability, to corroborate and verify the various events, comments, and issues raised in this book and believe that it is a fair commentary and

---

[2] Ignatius, Dennis. 2021. *PARADISE LOST: Mahathir & The End of Hope.* Kuala Lumpur. Page 94.

of public interest. They also form the core of my belief as to what transpired during those twenty-two months. I have, in my possession, copies of all documents cited, most of which have long been available to the public. I have also taken the creative liberty to dramatize certain events and incidents, based on my understanding of what transpired, in order to make it easier for readers to follow how events unfolded. So, I stand corrected should any person, organization, etc., mentioned in this book dispute or disagree with my account of events. I urge them to come forward with documentary evidence and proof, which I will be happy to include in a future edition. Should you wish to reach me with new information, ideas, or comments, my email is romen@hotmail.com.

In writing this book, I must thank my editor at Penguin Random House SEA Thatchaayanie Renganathan for the amazing work she has done yet again on another one of my books and also several of my close friends and fellow journalists (who wish to remain anonymous), who have spent time reading and critiquing my early drafts in order to make them the best they can be. I would also like to thank my good friend Jeyathurai Ayadurai MBE, Jennifer Ayadurai, Francesca Nathan, Savita Kashyap, Ms Jeyaletchumi, my brother Ajoy, and my sister Anita, for all their support and encouragement.

But my biggest thanks go to my amazing and long-suffering wife Brigid for being the kind, compassionate, and caring person that she is, and in putting up with all my shenanigans in getting this book complete. I love you to the moon and back.

I would like to dedicate this book to her and to our daughters Lara, Olive, and Cilla, who will hopefully find their dad's ramblings of interest. I would also like to dedicate this book to the memory of my late uncle, Mrinal Kanti Dutta, whose love of learning and interest in the world around him made him an essential source of reference on almost any topic. I celebrate his memory with a glass of warm water, some Jacob & Co. Cream Crackers and a slice of dried-out toast. He would have appreciated that.

—Romen Bose
London
2 August 2023

Chapter 1

The Day PH1.0 Imploded aka
Akibat Mahathir Merajuk

'*Astaghfirullah!*' he thought to himself, as the car stopped yet again and then crawled along slowly in the congested evening traffic along the suburban highways surrounding the capital, even on a Sunday!

He needed to get to the hotel and get there quick, but it was still miles away.

If he didn't get there soon, if he did not make it on time . . . he didn't want to think of that.

The various factions had all gathered at the hotel, and they were no longer listening to reason. They were enraged and bitter, and they wanted blood.

But once they pushed the button, there would be no going back. Their actions would cause the end of something that so many had sacrificed for and worked so hard to build.

As he looked out the car window, at a blur of buildings and cars, he spotted people strolling about in their Sunday best, dining at restaurants and enjoying a day of rest. He wondered if they realized that everything was about to change.

His colleagues and him, seated in the convoy of cars, had been charged with stopping this from happening, and this he had promised to do. But could he actually deliver?

The young cabinet minister knew the much-touted multiracial and reform-minded government of second-time Prime Minister Mahathir Mohamad was on the verge of imploding, and he was hoping to convince the powers that be to stop it, to cease fire. At least for the moment. But he knew it would not last.

On that Sunday, 23 February 2020, the then recently discovered Covid-19 viral threat—it had yet to become the global pandemic that we now know—was seeing Chinese cities in lockdown and thousands of deaths globally. But Malaysians were more focused on the political drama and intrigue playing out in the corridors of power in Putrajaya and Petaling Jaya. This had people enthralled by various rumours of power grabs and new political alliances.

These strong rumours were boosted by reports claiming the formation of a new Mahathir-led political coalition—wait, wasn't he leading the current coalition government?—that would exclude the Chinese-led Democratic Action Party (DAP) and former Deputy Premier and opposition leader Anwar Ibrahim's Parti Keadilan Rakyat (PKR). And parliamentarians, including the United Malays National Organization (UMNO) lawmakers, had supposedly signed statutory declarations (SDs) in support of Mahathir serving as prime minister until the next general election, instead of passing the baton to Anwar mid-term as had been agreed.

This would mean the end of the PH1.0 Government and, with it, the dreams and hopes for reform, equality, and justice in the country.

Twenty-seven-year-old Syed Saddiq bin Syed Abdul Rahman knew he had only minutes to stop this from happening.

And his involvement had started so innocuously.

A handsome young man with a broad smile and sharp features speaking of his Arabic ancestry, with wavy hair gelled back and a soft voice with a slight lisp, Syed Saddiq was educated at the Royal Military College and the International

Islamic University Malaysia. He was also widely known in the debating community, having won Asia's Best Speaker award at the Asian British Parliamentary Debating Championship three times.

Although he initially supported BN, he became a political icon when, in 2016, he joined twenty-four other youths in a group that called themselves Change Led by the Young Generation (Challenger), which published a statement rejecting the then Premier and BN President Najib Razak's leadership following the 1Malaysia Development Berhad (1MDB) scandal.

Then 'retiree' Mahathir, who had been out of office since 2003, was very impressed by Syed Saddiq's motivation and energy and the admiration was mutual, with Saddiq becoming the head of ARMADA, the youth wing of BERSATU or The Malaysian United Indigenous Party (Parti Pribumi Bersatu Malaysia), the party founded by Mahathir in 2016 following his departure from UMNO. Syed Saddiq also sat on BERSATU's Supreme Council and became a member of Mahathir's kitchen cabinet, constantly seen with, and doing the bidding of, the nonagenarian.

Syed Saddiq was seen, and I believe, remains, the face of modern Malaysian politics.[3]

Charismatic and with a disarming wit, Syed Saddiq's belief in multiracialism, multilingualism, integrity in governance, and commitment to Malaysia's vision of becoming a developed nation meant he was head and shoulders above many of his political contemporaries in seeking to better the lives of all Malaysians, especially the country's burgeoning youth.

Syed Saddiq deeply respected Mahathir and the former Premier's twenty-two-year contribution to the building of modern Malaysia, but Saddiq had differing views on race, strongly subscribing to the need for a more multiracial and corruption-free

---

[3] This, despite the fact that Syed Saddiq was found guilty on four charges of criminal breach of trust, misappropriation of property, and money laundering in November 2023. He is currently appealing the conviction.

Malaysia, which had often put him at odds with his erstwhile mentor. More importantly, I believe he knew that despite his best efforts, the promised power transfer to Anwar was not going to happen.

As part of the agreement with Pakatan Harapan (PH) in the flush of victory following GE14, Mahathir had promised to step down as PM within two years and hand over power to Anwar. Although that time was now almost up, and despite his numerous statements on the transition of leadership, Mahathir had still not made it clear exactly when he intended to leave office.

Anwar's supporters were now pressing Mahathir for a handover date, suggesting the two-year anniversary of the historic GE14 elections which would fall in May 2020, but the ninety-four-year-old Prime Minister refused to be drawn.

Two months earlier, in Doha, Mahathir had implied a delay in the power transfer, saying he might have to stay in power after 2020 to fix issues he had inherited from the previous government before handing over power to Anwar.

Following weeks of reports that a new Mahathir-led Pakatan Nasional coalition—eventually renamed Perikatan Nasional or PN—was being formed, with a bid by the pan-Islamic party PAS to push through the parliament a motion of confidence in Mahathir to serve his full term instead of handing over power, Anwar had gone to see 'the old man' at the Prime Minister's Office in Putrajaya.

Following a 'cordial' meeting, Anwar told the gathered media the much-anticipated transfer would be determined during a meeting of the ruling PH1.0 coalition on 21 February 2020.

'I tend to believe that he will continue leading the country until the end of the Asia Pacific Economic Cooperation (APEC) Summit (in November 2020),' said Anwar.[4] He said Mahathir

---

[4] Mustafa, Muzliza, 'Anwar Ibrahim: Malaysia's Transition of Power to be Determined This Month', 13 Feb 2020. Accessed at: https://www.benarnews. org/english/news/malaysian/malaysia-politics-02132020170744.html.

assured him that he was not involved in the signature campaign to get lawmakers to endorse Mahathir completing his full term, and Mahathir had even told Anwar 'emphatically' that he would step down as promised.

However, I believe Syed Saddiq knew this was one of his mentor's gambits to buy time, because Mahathir wanted to ensure that there was a 'Grand Malay Alliance' that was in power and which would necessarily exclude DAP, Anwar as well as Anwar's faction from power.

Laying his heart bare to aides and close friends who had gathered at his place, Syed Saddiq reportedly said that although he was ambivalent about Anwar, the young politician didn't really believe in the concept of 'Malay power at any cost' and was more interested in maintaining the Pakatan Harapan ethos and cooperation with DAP as well as PKR.

However, he knew Mahathir wanted to ensure Anwar and DAP were not in the government and that the current politicking was all part of that.[5]

Mahathir had the numbers in parliament and a plan for a late February or March 2020 parliamentary session would likely see the Malaysian Islamic Party or Parti Islam Se-Malaysia's (PAS) motion of confidence in Mahathir or a motion insisting that Mahathir continue until the end of his term as PM.

If this happened, it would be game over for Anwar as the majority of MPs would then be on Mahathir's side, and there was no way there would be a transfer of power to Anwar anytime soon.

And privately, Syed Saddiq acknowledged what only Mahathir's inner circle knew and that was the fact that Mahathir was really not 'officially' involved in the current machinations.[6]

This was because Mahathir had orchestrated the whole thing 'using numerous levers, proxies and it was a game of push and

---

[5] Interview with PMO Source 2, Putrajaya, 11 Sep 2022.

[6] Ibid.

pull'. 'Although Mahathir was not directly issuing instructions etc., the stars had started to align in the direction of giving Mahathir the majority he needed in parliament to carry on as PM till the end of his term,' Syed Saddiq reportedly told his people.[7]

The reality was that Mahathir had given instructions to 'various individuals' to carry out his wishes, and Mahathir's involvement was buried within layers; so it was impossible to directly point fingers at Mahathir and thus, 'Tun had plausible deniability in all of this'.[8]

The group was told that a large number of MPs from UMNO, PAS, BERSATU, the National Trust Party (AMANAH), the Sarawak Parties Alliance (Gabungan Parti Sarawak or GPS), and the Heritage Party (WARISAN) had signed statutory declarations in support of Mahathir, and Mahathir had more than 112 MPs on his side. Even former premier Najib Razak had signed an SD although Najib's SD came with conditions.

So, Mahathir's plan was now for MPs in parliament to call for a motion of confidence at the next parliamentary sitting. As part of the alleged plan, certain individuals like PAS President Abdul Hadi Awang, AMANAH President Mohamad Sabu (Mat Sabu), former UMNO Defence Minister Hishammuddin Hussein, and others were to make statements and say 'certain things' in parliament, alluding to the need for a motion of confidence in Mahathir to serve his full term as the prime minister.

However, the plan was fraught with danger because Mahathir had used several different individuals as proxies and had hidden his involvement under so many layers that neither did he have complete control over what would happen, nor did he have any guarantee or assurance by the people carrying out the plan that it would be fully executed or would succeed.

---

[7] Zoom interview with BERSATU leader 6, 10 Nov 2020.

[8] Ibid.

Hisham had reportedly been rounding up support within his party. Economic Affairs Minister and PKR Deputy President, Azmin Ali, was doing the same in PKR. Mat Sabu was bringing AMANAH's support, and Hadi Awang would ensure PAS support. Mahathir had allegedly also gotten others who guaranteed GPS and WARISAN support for the motion.

The aides were allegedly told that Mat Sabu was very loyal to Mahathir and would even be willing to work again with PAS if Mahathir insisted, as the mood for Malay unity was very strong and this was something that 'any informed Malay MP would realize'. As such, it would be political suicide not to support any move that aimed to strengthen 'Malay unity'.

However, the confirmation for the plan and its likelihood of success would only be known when the list of speakers was released just ahead of the parliamentary session as that would show if the right people had chosen to speak out and whether or not support for Mahathir had been fully sewn up.

But one of the worrying factors was the total silence from DAP, despite the fact that DAP was aware that something big was brewing.

Syed Saddiq would have liked to have told his friends in DAP about the plan but that would have been breaking Mahathir's confidence, and Saddiq had been sworn to secrecy.

Syed Saddiq appeared worried that the DAP would continue to fully support Anwar, and in that case, it would be thoroughly embarrassing for DAP to not support a motion of confidence for their own PM.[9]

Syed Saddiq knew it was going to be a rocky few months following the parliamentary session because, if Mahathir won, Anwar was not going to take this lying down and was almost certain to fight back. And it was unclear whose side DAP would take in that instance.

---

[9] Zoom interview with BERSATU leader 6, 10 Nov 2020.

And if Mahathir lost, it was unlikely that the 'old man' would accept the decision, and thus an even bigger battle would commence.

BERSATU Deputy President, Muhyiddin Yassin, who was supposedly trying to keep Mahathir in power, had created the new Pakatan/Perikatan Nasional coalition's operations room in the Publika offices of former BN Minister Hamzah Zainuddin and from there, his kitchen cabinet along with Azmin, carried out backroom canvassing of support from Malaysian lawmakers on both sides of the aisle as PH1.0 coalition partners, DAP, and the pro-Anwar elements of PKR that were the bulk of the party became more and more isolated within their own government.

Tensions were running very high when the PH1.0 Presidential Council met late in the evening of 21 February 2020. In what could only be described as heated exchanges, Anwar's supporters pushed for Mahathir to step down according to the original deadline of two years following the May 2018 general elections—GE14—while Mahathir's supporters, led by Azmin Ali and Syed Saddiq, urged Mahathir not to agree to a timeline as he would then be a lame-duck Prime Minister.

In the end, Anwar and his supporters agreed that Mahathir would choose the date on which to resign after the APEC Meetings in Malaysia in November 2020.

Syed Saddiq allegedly told his team, 'Tun has the numbers—from PAS and UMNO for a confidence motion to pass. But on the surface—in order to save Anwar's face—at the meeting, the understanding was we can't afford to have a lame-duck PM, so we must allow Tun to decide when and where to resign.'[10]

The following day, PAS announced that it was cancelling its move to table the motion of confidence as the PH1.0 Presidential

---

[10]   Zoom interview with BERSATU leader 3, 15 Mar 2020.

Council had decided 'to leave it to the PH chairman to decide on when the succession to his prime ministership will take place'.[11]

At the meeting, there had been three options on the table, i.e., Mahathir handing over power in May 2020, after the APEC Summit, or at the end of his term as PM. But, in the end, everyone agreed to 'the middle ground of resigning after APEC in November'.[12]

However, this didn't necessarily mean that Mahathir would step down in November. Mahathir had said, 'I will step down after APEC that's scheduled in November,' and this could be interpreted in two ways—that he would step down in November after APEC, or that he would step down sometime after APEC.

Following the meeting, Anwar and the other PH1.0 leaders believed that Mahathir would do the right thing.

Speaking to the media, he said, 'Dr Mahathir should be given latitude because both of us and the Pakatan Harapan council have decided that the change would be smooth, peaceful and orderly, and we still continue to work as a team.'[13]

How wrong they were.

Because for months now, Mahathir had already begun accepting defectors from UMNO into BERSATU as part of the highly sensitive and secret Operation Hijrah, and his deputy Muhyiddin had courted parties like PAS with the intention of forming the Grand Malay Alliance—that had translated into the Pakatan/Perikatan Nasional or PN coalition.

---

[11] Mahsinah Abdullah, Sharifah, 'Pas cancels move to table vote of confidence', 22 Feb 2020, *NST Online*, accessed at: https://www.nst.com.my/news/politics/2020/02/568015/pas-cancels-move-table-vote-confidence.

[12] Zoom interview with BERSATU leader 3

[13] Sivanandam, Hemananthani, 'Anwar: Don't pressure Dr Mahathir and me over power transition', thestar.com, 20 Feb 20, accessed at: https://www.thestar.com.my/news/nation/2020/02/20/anwar-don039t-pressure-dr-mahathir-and-i-over-power-transition.

But the demand for Mahathir to pick a date for the handover and now pinning it down to a specific point in time angered Muhyiddin's faction within BERSATU and the various other coalition parties in PN, causing Mahathir's allies to move up their Malay unity government game plan but with disastrous consequences for Mahathir.

Because, the irony was, after the 21 February meeting, Mahathir had finally decided in his mind that he would have to hand over power to Anwar.

But Mahathir didn't want Anwar.

While Azmin had always been his choice—after secretly defecting to Mahathir's side with his breakaway faction of MPs from PKR—to take over BERSATU and then become his successor as PM, Mahathir was now seriously disillusioned with him, following Azmin's lacklustre ability in reviving the economy and the sex scandal that had almost deep-sixed his career just months earlier.

And although Muhyiddin was effectively Mahathir's deputy and had been the individual building the PN coalition—that would see Anwar and DAP thrown out of power—Muhyiddin was willing to work with UMNO, and this was something Mahathir could not abide by. Moreover, since late 2019, Muhyiddin had also been campaigning to be Mahathir's replacement as prime minister and the nonagenarian felt that Muhyiddin was getting too ambitious.

So, by the end of the 21 February meeting, when Mahathir said he would be handing over power to Anwar, he had actually meant it.

Because, by then, Mahathir felt that he had no other option.

But it was too late.

The Frankenstein of his making was now on the loose, and although he tried, he could no longer control the movement.

Sunday, 23 February 2020, dawned on the politically charged capital, with the key parties of the new Grand Malay Alliance holding extraordinary meetings.

As the BERSATU Supreme Council met, UMNO and its Muafakat Nasional partner PAS met in Janda Baik, UMNO's Supreme Council met in Kuala Lumpur, as did GPS lawmakers. Azmin's splinter faction from PKR also met, with a 'dinner' for all the factions arranged at the fateful Sheraton hotel in Petaling Jaya for later that evening.

And the agenda for all these meetings was the plan to declare the formation of PN that day itself and the end of the PH1.0 Government.

The UMNO–PAS faction was keen on seeing a united Malay front while the rest of UMNO wanted to get rid of DAP, which they viewed as the key agitators behind the PH Government's vengeance against Najib, Zahid, and all other UMNO leaders. Muhyiddin and Azmin felt there was no choice but to throw out DAP and PKR immediately if Anwar was to be stopped. Now, Muhyiddin had the support of the various Malay parties, so all he needed was Mahathir's final approval. He thought that was going to be a mere rubberstamp.

But, given Mahathir's sudden change of mind, this approval was not going to come easily.

At the BERSATU Supreme Council meeting that morning, Mahathir was briefed that Anwar's faction was trying to meet with the King to convince him that Anwar commanded the majority of support of MPs and the King should call Anwar for an audience.

Muhyiddin then briefed Mahathir on their ability to formally create PN that day itself with the new coalition consisting of BERSATU, UMNO, PAS, a third of PKR's MPs, GPS, and Warisan. Together, they held 134 parliamentary seats and all these lawmakers had signed a statutory declaration to support Mahathir as PM and form PN, including Najib, who signed it with conditions.

Muhyiddin and several other leaders then urged Mahathir to pull BERSATU out of the PH1.0 coalition and for Mahathir to present the 134 SDs to the King and get the ruler to dissolve the PH1.0 Government in favour of the new PN coalition.

This was the plan that Mahathir had been encouraging and supporting for so long. And yet, now, Mahathir disagreed. He told the leaders he needed to make sure that it was really the case that Anwar was 'declaring war', in which case Mahathir would have no choice but to form the new coalition and have a Cabinet reshuffle.

Otherwise, BERSATU just 'needed to reassure the King that Mahathir had the numbers and to ask the King to ignore the Anwar faction's drama and moves'.[14]

Moreover, Mahathir was still having doubts about forming a coalition government with UMNO as he would have to accept Zahid and Najib, the leaders whom he had toppled in the first place.

As such, Mahathir asked for an appointment with the King and told Muhyiddin to hand deliver the 134 SDs to the palace in order to prove that he commanded more than a simple majority of MPs in parliament. Mahathir refused to go to the palace, saying he would be at home but would monitor the situation, and if there was a need, would go to the palace to stop Anwar.

Regardless, the majority of the BERSATU Supreme Council wanted to pull out of the PH1.0 coalition immediately. However, at the meeting, they agreed to leave the announcement of the decision to pull out in Mahathir's hands and to give him a week in which to decide.

But privately, Muhyiddin disagreed.

For him and Azmin, the threat from Anwar was imminent and they had to act now. And they began to realize that Mahathir was actually contemplating handing over power to Anwar; something he had said privately many times before that he did not want to do.

So, the leaders of the new PN coalition, namely Muhyiddin, Azmin, Zahid, Hadi, Abang Johari Openg, and Shafie Apdal

---

[14] Zoom interview with BERSATU leader 6, 10 Nov 2020.

turned up at Mahathir's home following the meeting, to try and convince him to set up the new coalition.

They told him they would all be headed to the palace for the submission of the SDs as a show of force against Anwar and to brief the King that Mahathir was still in control and could form a new PN Government, if needed. And they would then hold a 'dinner' marking the event at the Sheraton Petaling Jaya Hotel, where they could potentially announce the new government's formation.

However, Mahathir still disagreed. He said he was happy for them to go to the palace as a show of force, but Mahathir would not turn up at the Istana or at the Sheraton dinner.

By now, the media had gotten wind of the moves, and there was huge speculation that a new government with a new prime minister was about to be formed. A large contingent of media had gathered outside the palace gates, awaiting 'a big announcement', amid reports that several PH ministers had packed up all their personal belongings in their offices ahead of an expected announcement.

Meanwhile, in the Istana Negara's receiving room, Muhyiddin yet again spoke to Mahathir on the phone, to try one last time to get his approval to form PN, informing him of the presence of all the PN leaders at the Istana, but Mahathir still demurred. 'If you want to get rid of Anwar, do it after I leave office,' Mahathir told him.[15] Mahathir then called the King to personally convey his intention not to proceed with the PN takeover.

Demoralized, some of the PN leaders led by Azmin decamped to the Sheraton Hotel. But the momentum for the formation of PN remained strong. After much discussion, the various other leaders present decided to take matters into their own hands and declare the formation of PN later that evening.

The thinking was that if they made the formation of PN and its announcement a *fait accompli*, then Mahathir would have no choice but to take charge of the new government. So, the

---

[15] Zoom interview with BERSATU leader 6, 10 Nov 2020.

call went out to the other coalition leaders who had left after the Istana meeting to turn up at the Sheraton.

But, unfortunately for them, the news of this call to arms also reached Syed Saddiq, who—together with BERSATU Women's wing chief Rina Harun and Mahathir's son Mukhriz, who was also BERSATU Deputy President—met at Mahathir's home in Sri Kembangan at around 8.30 p.m. to brief the party Chairman.

The three told Mahathir that the situation had gotten out of control and what was an initial show of force had taken a momentum of its own and Muhyiddin Yassin, Hadi Awang, and Zahid Hamidi were now headed for the Sheraton Hotel, where they were planning on actually trying to form and announce the formation of a Pakatan or Perikatan Nasional coalition.

Mahathir, who had been reading the newspapers and attending to household chores, appeared surprised and told them that he was opposed to forming the new coalition this quickly and in such a rushed manner and that the BERSATU Supreme Council had given him a week in which to decide what to do. More importantly, the current plan of action was only supposed to 'show Anwar that he cannot force my hand'.[16]

Mahathir reportedly said that he did not want to form a new coalition as yet, and it had to be done following proper planning and calculations. He said that there should be no press conference at the Sheraton Hotel as the whole Istana event was only meant to be a show of force. Anything that was said at a press conference could be viewed as an act of war by the other PH1.0 coalition partners, and Mahathir wanted to avoid this as he still needed the current PH coalition to govern the country. Mahathir said he did not want to see the government collapse in this manner as chaos would ensue.[17]

---

[16] Zoom interview with BERSATU leader 7, 10 Feb 2021.

[17] Zoom interview with BERSATU leader 3, 15 Mar 2020.

Mukhriz reportedly told Mahathir that it appeared as if Muhyiddin had gotten ambitious and was keen to push ahead with the coalition idea as Muhyiddin would be able to secure a key position in the new coalition.

Syed Saddiq reportedly added that Azmin was also very keen for the new coalition because Mahathir had now made it very clear he would hand over power to Anwar, and that if this actually did happen, it would be the end of Azmin.

Therefore, Azmin needed to push for this new coalition as it was almost guaranteed that Azmin would then be able to take over as PM soon. This was why the various groups were converging at the Sheraton Hotel, in the hopes that their actions would convince Mahathir to push ahead with the new coalition.[18]

Mahathir was very unhappy about this turn of events and ordered Syed Saddiq and Rina to rush over to the Sheraton Hotel and personally convey to the various party leaders that they needed to stand down and that Mahathir would not support any announcement or decision made at the Sheraton Hotel that night. And he also ordered that no press conference be held.[19]

So, by 9 p.m., Syed Saddiq and Rina were now in separate vehicles rushing towards the Sheraton Hotel, in the hopes that they could reach it before Muhyiddin and the others took to the stage and made the announcement.

By the time they reached the hotel, it was surrounded by large numbers of supporters dressed in red BERSATU t-shirts chanting, 'Hidup Tun'. Inside, the hallways were packed with journalists and cameramen, along with hundreds of supporters and lawmakers from the various coalition parties.

Syed Saddiq pushed his way through the throngs of supporters and went straight to the ballroom, where the dinner was being held and into the anteroom, where all the VIPs were located.

---

[18]   Ibid.

[19]   Ibid.

There, standing next to Rina, he addressed Muhyiddin and the rest of the plotters, telling them Mahathir did not want to proceed with the formation of PN as yet and that Mahathir had been given time by the BERSATU Supreme Council to make a decision as to when to do it, but that it was not going to happen that night. And there was to be no press conference.

Grudgingly, in the face of Mahathir's open and clear refusal to form PN that night and his inability then to rebel openly against his party chairman, Muhyiddin and the other leaders were forced to accept and obey Mahathir's decision and instructions, with all those assembled leaving the hotel without speaking to the masses of journalists waiting outside. The situation had been defused. For now.

But the momentum was still growing.

The next morning, Anwar, his wife and Deputy Premier Wan Azizah, coalition partner AMANAH's president Mohamad Sabu, and DAP Secretary General Lim Guan Eng held an urgent meeting with Mahathir at Sri Kembangan to seek clarification on what had happened the day before.[20]

Mahathir reassured them that he was not behind the plotting and that he was not involved in the plans for a new coalition. Mahathir told Anwar that he could never work with UMNO. But he did not tell them that he had been briefed on what the plotters were planning to do at the BERSATU Supreme Council meeting, nor that he was fully aware of the possible creation of the new coalition, given that he would be heading it.

Following the meeting, Anwar told the media he was satisfied with Mahathir's explanation and that the status quo had been maintained.[21]

[20] Muzamir, Muhammad Yusri, 'Pemimpin PH jumpa Dr Mahathir', *Berita Harian Online*, 24 Feb 2020, accessed at: https://www.bharian.com.my/berita/politik/2020/02/658588/pemimpin-ph-jumpa-dr-mahathir.

[21] Shukry, Anisah, Azmi, Hadi, Liau, Y-Sing, 'Anwar Hails "Good Meeting" With Mahathir Amid Malaysia Rumors', *Bloomberg News*, 24 Feb 2020,

However, Muhyiddin and a large number of leaders within BERSATU were livid with Mahathir's decision not to back the new coalition the day before. They felt that Mahathir would be handing over power to Anwar imminently and something had to be done now to force Mahathir's hand.

So, after speaking with BERSATU leaders, Muhyiddin went to Mahathir's home to tell him that the Supreme Council members wanted the withdrawal announcement to be made now.

Muhyiddin left a few minutes later to prepare BERSATU's announcement pulling out of the coalition. BERSATU was only pulling out of PH but still supported Mahathir as PM. That was part of the plan as the pull-out would only cause the PH1.0 coalition to collapse while Mahathir would still have the confidence of the majority of lawmakers to carry on as PM.

The plan was for Mahathir to now see the King and dissolve the Cabinet, following which Mahathir could set up his new PN government that did not include Anwar's PKR and the DAP, without having to call for fresh elections.

But I believe that in a fit of pique that his own party was now forcing him to do what he had planned and conspired to do for months, and the fact that he had now lost complete control of his party, Mahathir decided to resign as Prime Minister, as Chairman of BERSATU and Chairman of the PH1.0 Coalition.

He felt outplayed and outmanoeuvred, and so he felt his resignation would be like a poke in the eye not only to his party but also stymie any chance of Anwar or UMNO taking power as he believed that he still had a majority of lawmakers backing him and that all sides would eventually clamour for his leadership again.

Mahathir consulted his lawyers Gopal Sri Ram and Gobind Singh Deo—who was also a senior DAP leader and a cabinet minister in Mahathir's government—who advised him on the

---

accessed at: https://www.bloomberg.com/news/articles/2020-02-23/anwar-says-there-are-attempts-to-form-new-malaysian-government.

legality of his plans, and the three then headed for the Istana where Mahathir would formally submit his resignation.[22]

Although King Al-Sultan Abdullah Ri'ayatuddin Al-Mustafa Billah Shah tried to convince Mahathir not to resign, he would have none of it.[23] So, the King appointed Mahathir as interim Prime Minister until a new PM was chosen.

With BERSATU pulling out of PH and Azmin's announcement shortly after that he and ten other lawmakers would leave PKR, the PH1.0 Government ceased to exist.

Now the mad scramble for power began.

The King would interview all 221 MPs over the next two days to determine who had the support of the majority of lawmakers. The BERSATU Supreme Council rejected Mahathir's resignation saying they were fully behind Mahathir and PH1.0 also voiced their strong support for Mahathir.

But Mahathir's price for coming back as PM was as head of a new unity government where the new coalition's party presidents would not automatically be in Cabinet, nor have a say in the government and that Mahathir would decide who would be ministers. As such, no coalition would have control, as all political power would be vested in Mahathir alone.

When the King interviewed the parliamentarians, UMNO and PAS lawmakers withdrew their support for Mahathir because the deal for them to support Mahathir was based on the formation of a new government that didn't include DAP. So UMNO and PAS pushed for fresh elections.

And following Mahathir's televised announcement of his new unity government plan on 26 February 2020, the remaining PH1.0 lawmakers withdrew their support for him as they could not accept

---

[22] Interview with PH leader 5, Kuala Lumpur, 15 Jul 2023

[23] Idris, Ahmad Naqib, 'King tried to advise Dr Mahathir against resigning', *The Edge Malaysia online*, 18 May 2020, accessed at: https://theedgemalaysia. com/article/king-tried-advise-dr-mahathir-against-resigning.

that their parties would lose all control in the new administration, and Mahathir would have free reign. As a result, the remaining PH1.0 parties threw their support for PM behind Anwar.

When the King met Mahathir on 27 February 2020, he told him that there was no prime ministerial candidate with a clear majority. So, three days after Mahathir's resignation, Malaysia still had no government. Mahathir then announced that there would be a special sitting of parliament on 2nd March to resolve the impasse, failing which new polls would be called.

However, the following day, Speaker Mohamad Ariff Yusof said there would be no such session as the request did not adhere to parliamentary standing orders.

The Conference of Rulers had also met that day and following that, it was announced that the King would meet with heads of the various political parties to nominate their choice for prime minister.

Unwilling to accept Mahathir's call for a unity government that would see DAP and Anwar back in office, Muhyiddin, with the backing of other BERSATU leaders, had begun back-channel talks with UMNO, PAS, and Azmin's faction.

UMNO and PAS did not want to see DAP in any future government, and Azmin wanted Anwar and PKR out of any new government. So, they were happy to back the initial proposal of creating PN and the appointment of a new PM, who they now agreed would be Muhyiddin instead of Mahathir.

Syed Saddiq had been attempting to convince BERSATU leaders to stick by Mahathir and not agree to Muhyiddin as PM or to a new coalition. He even had the party's youth wing issue a statement on 28 February, saying it would continue to back the party's supreme council's decision in its meeting on 24 February to support Mahathir as prime minister. But by nightfall, it all appeared to be in vain.

'As a sign of respect,' Muhyiddin said he met with Mahathir on the night of 28 February, to ask for the latter's support.

'. . . (Mahathir) was prepared to support me if I managed to obtain a majority support from MPs,' he later said.[24]

However, the following morning, now aware of BERSATU's imminent takeover plans, the remaining PH parties tried to consolidate their position. In order to prevent a takeover by BERSATU, UMNO and PAS, the PH presidential council announced they were willing to back Mahathir once again as their PM candidate. Mahathir then accepted the nomination, saying that he had a majority of support and could be appointed as the next PM following the King's assent.

But as this was transpiring, Muhyiddin, along with party leaders from UMNO, PAS, Gabungan Parti Sarawak (GPS), Parti Bersatu Rakyat Sabah (PBRS), and the Homeland Solidarity Party (STAR) sought an audience with the King to show him that they had the majority support to form a government. Although Anwar later rushed to the palace to inform the King of PH's nomination changes, it was too late. The Palace issued a statement that evening stating that Muhyiddin would be the country's next PM.

And that was the end of PH1.0

On his twitter feed that night, Syed Saddiq posted:

I am sorry for failing you.
I tried. I really tried to stop them.
Sorry Malaysia
As the Malaysian Youths, we must stick to our Principles & fight in what we believe in.
What's the purpose of being surrounded by Power, but being cursed with an empty soul.[25]

---

[24] 'Muhyiddin: I am no traitor, it was Dr M who started Bersatu's exit from Pakatan', *Malay Mail Online*, 30 Oct 2022, accessed at: https://www.malaymail.com/news/malaysia/2022/10/30/muhyiddin-i-am-no-traitor-it-was-dr-m-who-started-bersatus-exit-from-pakatan/36378.

[25] Syed Saddiq, Twitter post, 1 Mar 2020, accessed at: https://twitter.com/SyedSaddiq/status/1233968197641965568.

Strangely, after the initial outcry, there did not appear to be much sympathy for Mahathir and his move to collapse the government. As Ignatius noted,

> Mahathir saved our democracy only to do it irreparable harm. He had everything going for him: a popular mandate, a parliamentary majority, a genuinely multiracial coalition behind him, tremendous goodwill and the outlines of a common agenda for reform. He could have used such a formidable position, something that was surely the envy of politicians elsewhere, to build a great nation, to break from our destructive racist past and from religious extremism to build a better, more stable, and progressive nation.[26]

But as you will read in the following chapters, the nonagenarian went back to being the 'Mahathir of old', in playing racist games and giving new life to his racist ideologies. U-turning on promises, he ended up not only abandoning PH1.0's promises of equality in favour of Malay supremacy, but in shattering any hope for A New Malaysia.

> He, more than anyone else, must be held responsible for the end of Malaysia Baru, for the end of the hope we had. More than that, the policies he crafted and pursued over his unbearably long years as prime minister crippled the nation. It is a legacy that will haunt us long after he is gone.[27]

After twenty-two months of machinations, a legitimately elected government that was to bring greater equality, an end to

---

[26] Ignatius, Dennis, Paradise Lost: *Mahathir & The End of Hope*, Dennis Ignatius, Kuala Lumpur, 2021. p. vi.

[27] Ignatius, Dennis, Paradise Lost: *Mahathir & The End of Hope*, Dennis Ignatius, Kuala Lumpur, 2021. p. vi.

corruption, spur economic growth, jobs, prosperity, and progress for the country ended up imploding only to be replaced by a shaky, ultra-Malay coalition that would itself disintegrate after just eighteen months.

Today, many still ask how did such a coalition of hope shatter and turn into one of such deep despair? It is not an easy question to answer, and academics and analysts will argue about the cause and reasons behind it for decades to come.

But, I believe, this is what really happened.

Chapter 2

Compromises on the Road to Putrajaya

I think Mahathir had been a bitter and unhappy man for a very long time.

And I think it began just months after his anointed successor, Abdullah Ahmad Badawi, also known as Pak Lah, took over as Malaysia's fifth Prime Minister (PM5) in 2003.

Pak Lah had refused to give in to Mahathir's demands to spend money the country did not have—on completing the former premier's remaining mega-projects in the country and building a crooked bridge across the causeway with Singapore, that nobody wanted or needed except for the crony businessmen who had been hired to build it, and who would now lose out on the hundreds of millions that they would have made on the inflated project costs.

So, Pak Lah had to go.

And after the punishing loss of its two-thirds majority in parliament and control of five states in the twelfth general election on 8 March 2012, and with various promises and deals struck, Pak Lah did go several months later. He left the scene quietly with a Tun-ship and a nice home on the hillsides off Carcosa Negara.

Although Mahathir was initially critical of his next anointed successor, Najib Razak for his loyalty to Pak Lah (and Mahathir had even gone so far as to get Muhyiddin Yassin to try to topple

Pak Lah and to take over as PM), he finally agreed to the transition of power that took place in April 2009, with Najib becoming PM6 and Muhyiddin his deputy.

But Mahathir was not happy.

Because not only did Najib not complete the mega-projects and the crooked bridge, but he also became friends with Mahathir's enemy in the South—Singapore. Najib then resolved the contentious railway land issue that had been outstanding for over two decades between the two countries and even made Malaysia money in the process.

Not only that, Najib also scrapped the dreaded Internal Security Act (ISA) that allowed indefinite detention without trial—which Mahathir had previously used against his political enemies—and Najib would have removed the Sedition Act from the books if Mahathir and his supporters hadn't threatened an internal coup within the United Malays National Organization (UMNO).

Despite having left office for many years, Mahathir still held significant influence over a large number of proxies who owned thousands of companies that provided the political and election funding for UMNO. Through this, I believe, Mahathir felt that he would be able to control any incumbent UMNO president.

But Najib did not want to be beholden to Mahathir. He had been persuaded by a businessman who had very good contacts with the Saudi royal family to accept funds from them. Following the Arab Spring, Saudi Arabia had been funding many Muslim nations. At a meeting arranged by the businessman, King Abdullah bin Abdulaziz Al Saud told Najib he was keen to help Malaysia become the model of a stable and modern Islamic country, with the funds the King was donating (similar to funds he had donated to King Juan Carlos I of Spain) to be used at Najib's own discretion and thus removing any control Mahathir had over the party and president.

The businessman was also involved in a new sovereign fund that the federal government had inherited from the state of Terengganu and would ostensibly fund development projects in the country and sort out the monopoly of power-producers in the country.

In Mahathir's eyes, however, the final nail in Najib's coffin was the 2013 UMNO General Assembly, where Najib had quietly supported his cousin Hishammuddin Hussein for the Vice President's post, instead of supporting Mahathir's son, Mukhriz. This meant that not only had Mahathir's dreams of his legacy projects been destroyed but his dynastic ambitions had also been thwarted as Mukhriz would not be in line for the party's top leadership positions and, by default, would not have a shot at becoming PM7 or 8.

This, I believe, infuriated Mahathir to no end, and it was clear to him then that the sixth Prime Minister had to be dethroned.

In any other circumstance, this would have been a tall order. By 2012, Najib had been well ensconced as PM and had the support and loyalty of a large majority of the party and the electorate that kept UMNO and Barisan Nasional (BN) in power.

But little did Najib realize that Mahathir would not have to wait long to watch Najib fall.

This was because the businessman who had introduced Najib to the Saudi royals, and who was involved with this new sovereign fund, was none other than Low Taek Jho, better known as Jho Low.

And the fund, of course, was 1Malaysia Development Berhad, or 1MDB.

I believe that Jho would have gotten away with the world's biggest financial fraud, and no one would have been the wiser, not even Najib, if it hadn't been for Xavier Andre Justo.

Justo, who had previously worked in the banking industry, was offered a job at PetroSaudi, a little-known company, which had a 2009 deal with 1MDB. The sovereign wealth fund had provided funds to PetroSaudi that was to be invested in the oil industry. Although 1MDB invested billions of dollars, 'PetroSaudi relied on artificial assets in the form of oilfields in Turkmenistan'.[28]

Moreover, Petrosaudi's Patrick Mahony and Tarek Obaid were alleged to have received nearly $200 million in commissions. Following a dispute with Mahony and Obaid, Justo left the company in April 2011 and demanded Fr2.5 million in compensation. In the meantime, Justo claimed that a friend in Petrosaudi's IT department had given him a copy of the company's server, which had over 227,000 emails, with a large number allegedly showing how 1MDB was being looted by PetroSaudi in cooperation with Low and senior Malaysian government officials.

Justo threatened to release the emails if he wasn't paid.

PetroSaudi refused to pay.

So, Justo went in search of people who could help him expose PetroSaudi's dealings, and he met with Clare Rewcastle-Brown, the editor of the *Sarawak Report* blogsite and even handed over a copy of the emails to media tycoon Tong Kooi Ong and Ho Kay Tat, the editor of *The Edge Media Group*, on the promise that he would be paid US$2 Million for the information.

But Tong and Ho double-crossed Justo. They didn't pay him and, instead, used his data to begin working with *Sarawak Report* and other international news organizations like *The Wall Street Journal* to expose the scandal.[29]

---

[28] '1MDB confirms our suspicions were right', jebatmustdie blog, 17 Jun 2015, accessed at: https://jebatmustdie.wordpress.com/2015/06/17/1mdb-confirms-our-suspicions-were-right/.

[29] In 2015, Tong and Ho admitted to cheating Justo of the US$2M. 'Justo is obviously an angry man, and understandably so, as we did not pay him what he wanted,' they said. 'Yes, we misled him. But that was the only way to get hold of the evidence to expose how a small group of Malaysians and foreigners cheated the people of Malaysia of US$1.83 billion. 'The Edge owner and editor admit they 'misled' Justo over US$2m payment for stolen data', Malaymail.com, 24 Jul 2015, accessed at: https://www.malaymail.com/news/malaysia/2015/07/24/

And the rest is history.

Interestingly, only in 2019 did Tong finally pay Justo what he was owed—following Justo's 2016 failed lawsuit against Tong for compensation—for 'help in exposing the wrongdoings at 1MDB'.[30]

And despite being portrayed as an altruistic whistle-blower, in an interview with Al Jazeera in 2019, when asked whether he would have given the data back to PetroSaudi (which would have prevented the 1MDB scandal from coming out) if he had been paid, Justo said he was unsure.

'I don't know, I just wanted to recover my money,' he said.

'That's . . . that's a beautiful question. If I want to make me a glorious guy I will tell you of course I would have given the data. I don't know. You can't go back in history.'[31]

Despite the enormous size of the 1MDB scandal and the ensuing fallout—with salacious pictures of lavish parties, yachts, champagne lifestyles, multi-million-dollar penthouses, and artworks—Mahathir realized that this would not be enough to overthrow Najib, as there was no direct link between Najib and the looting of 1MDB.

So, while the *Sarawak Report* and *The Wall Street Journal* were publishing weekly articles exposing all kinds of shenanigans that Low and his conspirators had allegedly been involved in, and three

---

the-edge-owner-and-editor-admit-misled-justo-over-us2m-payment-for-stolen-d/939069.

[30] 'Tong finally pays Justo RM8 million for the stolen data on 1MDB', Malaysia-today.net, 31 Jan 2019, accessed at: https://www.malaysia-today.net/2019/01/31/tong-finally-pays-justo-rm8-million-for-the-stolen-data-on-1mdb/.

[31] 'Would I have exposed 1MDB scandal had PetroSaudi paid me? 'I don't know', says Justo', Malaymail.com, 8 Feb 2019, accesses at: https://www.malaymail.com/news/malaysia/2019/02/08/would-i-have-exposed-1mdb-scandal-had-petrosaudi-paid-me-i-dont-know-justo/1720859.

of the country's top civil servants were planning a coup against a sitting prime minister, Mahathir convened his war cabinet.

Key loyalists like Mahathir's former political secretary and lawyer Matthias Chang and former UMNO Division chief Khairuddin Abu Hassan helped strategize a campaign to get the 1MDB scandal on the front pages of the world's newspapers and media in a bid to embarrass and shame Najib and UMNO/BN. These veteran political players, who were at the top of their game when Mahathir stepped down, were easily able to help propel the scandal not only in the media but also to help the US Department of Justice and various other regulatory authorities in the UK, Austria, Hong Kong, and Singapore in their investigations into the scandal.

But this was still not enough. Mahathir knew that his best bet was to galvanize the opposition and get enough votes in order to oust Najib and BN at the polls.

By 2016, Mahathir had once again resigned from UMNO, and now he set up a new party, Parti Pribumi Bersatu Malaysia, also known as BERSATU. The party was formed as a nationalist Malay-based opposition party to UMNO/BN, with Mahathir as Chairman and former Deputy Premier Muhyiddin Yassin as President. BERSATU was meant to replace UMNO as the party that represented Malaysia's Malays and many UMNO members, who had been expelled from UMNO for one reason or another, became founding members.

However, Mahathir was quick to realize that it would be an uphill challenge to get the Malay heartland to switch their allegiance from UMNO to BERSATU overnight and that in order to topple UMNO/BN, Mahathir also needed a large proportion of non-Malay votes. So, to defeat Najib at the polls, Mahathir would need to work together with the then opposition, Pakatan Harapan coalition, which at that point consisted of the Chinese-led Democratic Action Party (DAP), National Trust Party (AMANAH), and Parti Keadilan Rakyat (PKR) in the peninsula.

PH, through DAP veteran Lim Kit Siang and his son, Guan Eng, along with former businessman turned politician Tony Pua and PKR's Rafizi Ramli, had carried out online attacks on the 1MDB issue. However, there was no real coordination among all the various opposing factions.

And, at that time, almost all Malaysians would have thought that Mahathir working with DAP would be an impossible dream.

After all, it was Mahathir who as UMNO President led the rhetoric against the DAP, accusing them of Chinese chauvinism and of being a party that Malays could never ever support. This was a message that Mahathir had drilled into the Malay mindset in the twenty-two years that he had been prime minister. He had indoctrinated UMNO members to hate the DAP.[32]

But most importantly, it was Mahathir who had detained Lim and his son under the ISA, not once but twice. And up until 2013, Mahathir was still slandering Kit Siang, calling him 'an extreme racist' and claiming that 'Lim and the DAP have been "poisoning" Chinese minds in the GE13 polls campaign by telling them the community are victims of discrimination by a Malay government'.[33]

So, it was impossible to conceive that Lim Senior and Junior could even contemplate making a deal with the devil. The late former DAP Chairman and legal giant Karpal Singh would never have countenanced such a move. But father and son claimed that it was their interest in saving Malaysia that led them to work with Mahathir. Many still question whether this was their real intention. I personally believe it was nothing more than political expediency.

---

[32] 'Dr M indoctrinated us to hate DAP, says Zahid', *Free Malaysia Today*, 28 Dec 2022, accessed at: https://www.freemalaysiatoday.com/category/nation/2022/12/28/dr-m-indoctrinated-us-to-hate-dap-says-zahid/.

[33] 'Dr M says 'racist' Kit Siang wants to pit Chinese against Malays', TheMalaysianInsider.com, 2 May 2013, accessed at: https://bitly.ws/3gLH2.

Back in 2008, despite massive outcries among its membership, the two Lims had pushed through plans to form the Pakatan Rakyat coalition that included close cooperation with the ultra-religious Parti Islam Se-Malaysia (PAS), only to see the implosion of the coalition in 2015 given PAS' extreme stances on issues.

And once again, despite many within the party pointing out that Mahathir, just like PAS, had always been the enemy and remained a clear and present danger to non-Malays, the two once again pushed through another 'realignment' that supposedly 'focused on the future to chart a new course of history'[34]. And this would, once again, blow up in their faces in a spectacular fashion.

I believe the then DAP leadership made three assumptions that proved to be seriously flawed. Firstly, they believed that Mahathir had become a reformed man, or as the Malays say, *bertaubat*. Secondly, they believed that through working with Mahathir, the DAP, its leadership and by extension, the Chinese, would finally wield almost equal political power within the country. And thirdly, that Mahathir would actually deliver on his promises of reforming the racist system of administration and transferring power to those who should rightfully lead a PH Government, namely Anwar Ibrahim.

After his sacking as deputy prime minister in 1998, Anwar Ibrahim had been the glue to hold the opposition parties together through Barisan Alternatif and successor Pakatan Rakyat and Pakatan Harapan coalitions. Anwar was the unofficial leader of the Pakatan Harapan coalition, which included PKR, DAP, and AMANAH. The past twenty years had been a long journey for the opposition and the challenge facing the two Lims and Mahathir was to convince Anwar to work with Mahathir, despite all that Mahathir had done to Anwar.

---

[34] 'Building a New Malaysia for All', DAPMalaysia.org, accessed at: https://dapmalaysia.org/en/building-a-new-malaysia-for-all/.

Anwar was completely unaware that Mahathir and the two Lims had been in discussions while he was continuing to serve his second prison sentence in Sungai Buloh. Mahathir and the two Lims, along with Anwar's then very close confidante and PKR Deputy President Azmin Ali, saw the possibility of forming a new coalition with Mahathir as its head.

The coalition would not only have the support of the majority of non-Malays in the country but, with Mahathir, would also be able to bring along a significant number of Malay votes that, for once, could possibly give the opposition enough votes to win in the next general election.

There was no love lost between Anwar and Mahathir, given how Anwar had been railroaded on sexual and corruption charges, not once but twice, and when that did not seem enough, was targeted with a videotape purporting to show him involved in a sex scandal.

So, it would not do, to only have Mahathir propose this to Anwar. Someone closer to the jailed leader would need to convince him. And that person would be Azmin. Azmin had worked for Anwar since 1987 and had gone into the wilderness with Anwar when Mahathir had sacked him as Deputy Premier in 1998, with both Anwar and Azmin going on to establish PKR.

Anwar and Azmin were close, but Mahathir had never really wanted to work with Anwar. What Mahathir was doing now was allying himself with Anwar to remove Najib. Mahathir was privately of the view that if he could cultivate Azmin, eventually, Azmin would be able to replace Anwar and that Azmin, rather than Anwar, would take over as PM8.

But, before any of this could happen, Mahathir needed to strike a deal with Anwar and topple Najib's regime. So, it was decided that it would be Azmin who would try and convince Anwar to join forces with Mahathir.

On 5 September 2016, Anwar was brought from his prison cell in Sungei Buloh to the Kuala Lumpur High Court for a hearing on his bid to challenge the National Security Council (NSC) Act 2016.[35]

As Anwar was brought into the court room from his holding cell, he was caught completely off guard. There was Mahathir waiting for him, along with the PKR boys and Azmin.

Azmin immediately went over to Anwar and brought Mahathir along.

Anwar was stunned.

This was the man who had tried to destroy him many times and someone he hadn't spoken to in eighteen years. Yet here he was, the 'devil incarnate', and he wanted to shake hands. Anwar couldn't refuse to shake hands, even if it was with the man who had tried to decimate his political career and had jailed him. Malay culture dictated he had to be polite to his elders. Anwar shook Mahathir's hand and smiled.

Azmin then began his attempt to influence and convince Anwar, trying to explain to Anwar that there was a need to forget the past and to work together against the common enemy—Najib.

Did Anwar have a choice? Not really.

Although his family members were against him having any kind of cooperation with Mahathir, Anwar was cajoled again and again by Azmin and the two Lims, and convinced that this was the only way that the opposition would be able to win, that he would be able to get out of jail, and that once the PH1.0 coalition won, he would soon be able to take over as PM8. According to some in Anwar's inner circle, 'Mahathir appeared to be kow-towing to Anwar, in a bid to convince him that he had changed'.[36]

---

[35] 'Mahathir meets Anwar in Malaysia's High Court for first time in 18 years,' *The Straits Times*, 5 Sep 2016, accessed at: https://www.straitstimes.com/asia/se-asia/mahathir-meets-anwar-after-almost-20-years.

[36] Interview with PH leader 5, Kuala Lumpur, 15 Jul 2023

Many opposition leaders felt that Mahathir had yet to genuinely embrace his dark past. He had not apologized for the gross violations of human rights during his twenty-two years as prime minister—his indefinite detention and muzzling of political opponents and the enrichment of crony businessmen during his administration. Mahathir, however, insisted that his sons were self-made billionaires, and that no element of nepotism was practised. Yet in 1999, PKR Youth Chief, Mohd Ezam Mohd Noor, revealed secret documents of a meeting chaired by Rafidah Aziz, the then International Trade and Industry Minister, that documented her approving shares to Mahathir's son. Rafidah admitted that Mahathir forced her to ensure that the sitting committee approve the shares to his son. Ezam was later slapped with a two-year jail sentence under the Official Secrets Act (OSA).[37]

Despite these huge misgivings among many leaders within PKR and DAP, the two Lims and Azmin continued their cooperation with Mahathir, who again visited Anwar in 2017[38], and within months of that meeting, PKR, DAP, and AMANAH 'realigned with forces linked to Tun Dr Mahathir, and made him chairman of Pakatan Harapan on 14th July 2017'.[39]

A large number of Malaysians decided to give Mahathir the benefit of the doubt. Seeing him at the Bersih rally and hearing him talk about unity and reform persuaded many voters that he had changed from days of old. And most wanted a change after the years and years of corruption and nepotism in the BN administration.

---

[37] 'PH's unrealistic election manifesto,' *Free Malaysia Today*, 12 Mar 2018, accessed at: https://www.freemalaysiatoday.com/category/opinion/ 2018/ 03/12/phs-unrealistic-election-manifesto/.

[38] 'Mahathir meets Anwar at court to discuss opposition coalition', *The Straits Times*, 10 Feb 2017, accessed at: https://www.straitstimes.com/asia/se-asia/ mahathir-meets-anwar-at-court-to-discuss-opposition-coalition.

[39] 'Building a New Malaysia for All', DAPMalaysia.org, accessed at: https:// dapmalaysia.org/en/building-a-new-malaysia-for-all/.

In the midst of negotiating with PH, Mahathir was also trying to forge an alliance with PAS, which shared Mahathir's ultra-Malay views, with BERSATU President Muhyiddin Yassin put in charge of parallel negotiations with the Islamic party.

The connections and trust Muhyiddin built with PAS leaders would stand him in good stead just two short years later.

Meanwhile, Muhyiddin was already lobbying in 2017 for support to have him as PH's PM7 candidate, instead of Mahathir, with Azmin as deputy prime minister (DPM). There was much controversy within PH regarding the proposal, but it was decided that Mahathir would be PH's candidate, despite significant opposition from Azmin's faction, as this meant that Azmin would not be in position to become PM8 but would have to wait longer to become PM.[40]

By January 2018, PH had announced that Mahathir would be their seventh prime ministerial candidate with Wan Azizah as the deputy prime ministerial candidate, and Anwar would then be made the eighth prime minister if the coalition won. And by April 2018, all the component parties within PH agreed to use PKR's symbol as the coalition's common logo for GE14.

Despite the outward show of unity, many within PKR and DAP were uncomfortable and reluctant to support Mahathir and did not want him to become PM7. However, most agreed to go along because no one believed that PH would actually be able to topple UMNO/BN.

Even Mahathir didn't think PH would win.

Which was why he agreed to PH's *Buku Jingga* or manifesto of promises. Although he privately disagreed with many of the promises made and knew that they were untenable, he publicly went along with it—in order, I believe, to appear as a reformed

---

[40]   Liew, Chin Tong, 'The strange case of Muhyiddin Yassin, part 1', TheMalaysianInsight.com, 14 May 2020, accessed at: https://www. themalaysianinsight.com/index.php/s/245567.

and trusted leader—and because he didn't believe that he or his new coalition would ever have to deliver on them.

Yet, just like many in the British public who were duped into believing British politician Boris Johnson's promises—that were never delivered—ahead of the Brexit referendum just two years earlier in 2016, the Malaysian public also believed that Mahathir would deliver on the PH's manifesto promises of abolishing PTPTN loans for students in higher learning institutions and the elimination of highway tolls.

PH promised to deliver on ten of its pledges within its first 100 days in office. Instead, it fulfilled only two—the abolition of the Goods and Services Tax (GST) and the review of mega projects. Worse, instead of abolishing fuel subsidies, it ended up reintroducing them and failed to eliminate the unnecessary debts that had been forced on Felda settlers.

So it came to be that the man who had conceptualized, created, and enforced a racist, corrupt, and scandal-ridden system of government for over two decades and who had never apologized for, nor recanted, his actions in destroying lives and demolishing the judiciary while his cronies plundered the country's wealth was now the head of a coalition set to save Malaysia and topple that system he built and still defended, in order to put him again back in charge, this time, of a new, reformed government free of racism, corruption, and scandal.

Really?

As I have said before, often, truth is stranger than fiction.

Much has been written about the night of 9 May 2018, when the BN government was decimated at the polls. But what only a few know is the way in which this transfer of power took place.

As the horrendous—for BN—results began filtering in to Najib's home during that evening, Mahathir, Azmin, and the two Lims, along with the majority of opposition leaders, had gathered at the Sheraton Hotel in Petaling Jaya, which had become the PH1.0 election operations centre.

However, Anwar's wife, Wan Azizah was conspicuous by her absence.

This was because following the-then secret assessment that BN had collapsed, Najib had made phone calls to Anwar's prison bed, to negotiate forming a minority coalition government with PKR.

There are conflicting accounts of the content of the secret phone calls between the two politicians that night. Although Anwar denied that any deal was discussed, sources close to Najib claim otherwise.

They say Najib did not want to hand over power to Mahathir who, he and most leaders within UMNO believed, would seek to not only destroy BN but also all the coalition's leaders and take down the country at the same time.

So, Najib was keen to hand over power to Anwar's faction, who would likely be 'fairer and more even-handed' and would not seek vengeance, but justice.

Najib's proposal was for PKR to leave the PH coalition, with Wan Azizah to be sworn in as PM7 and the UMNO Deputy President Zahid Hamidi as her deputy premier.

However, sources allege that the King was hesitant to appoint Wan Azizah and was more willing to consider Muhyiddin as PM, which was allegedly conveyed to Wan Azizah when she met him in the early hours, following polling day. They say that the *Agong*[41] preferred to appoint Muhyiddin rather than Mahathir. However, Muhyiddin refused the alleged offer by PKR and the King to be the compromise PM. He firmly declined, saying the PM should be Mahathir and no one else.[42]

So, Anwar was in a bind. He knew that Mahathir could not be trusted to transfer power to him and a deal with BN would really mean he would be PM8. But then again, a deal with BN would

---

[41] A shortened title referring to the Malaysian King, who is normally known in Malay as 'Duli Yang Maha Mulia Yang di-Pertuan Agong'.

[42] Source interview notes, Kuala Lumpur, April 2023.

also mean betraying all the Malaysians who had voted for a new and reformed Malaysia. This was something he could not do.

Mahathir had been busy all evening calling and lobbying the various senior government officials, including the Chief Secretary to the Government of Malaysia—who was the head of the civil service and the heads of the security services—to take instructions from him, even though he had yet to be sworn in as PM7. The country's top civil servants conceded to Mahathir's demand.

The 10th of May, the day after GE14, was supposed to be a regular working day, but Mahathir had promised before the election that if PH won there would be two days of public holiday following election day. By late evening on 9 May, the head of the civil service declared two days of public holidays, even before the Election Commission had officially announced who would form the government and long before the Palace would swear in Mahathir as PM7.[43]

Mahathir had also gotten wind that Najib was trying to negotiate a minority coalition deal with Anwar. Mahathir was furious, according to some near him. Mahathir then spoke urgently with Guan Eng and AMANAH leader Mat Sabu to insist that Anwar toe the line. These PH leaders, along with Azmin, then spoke with Anwar, all agreeing that the only course of action was to go with Mahathir and hope that Mahathir would deliver, not only on his promises to the *Rakyat*[44], but also his pledge to hand over power quickly to Anwar and the rest of PH.

When a defeated and dejected Najib made his concession speech in front of UMNO leaders and the media on the morning of 10 May, he noted that, 'no single party has won a simple majority, so the government could not be formed. The King would need to decide who should be PM.'

---

[43] Bose, Romen, *Final Reckoning: An Insider's view of the fall of Malaysia's Barisan Nasional Government*, Penguin Books, 2021, p. 282.

[44] A Malay term for 'ordinary citizen' or 'general public'.

However, Mahathir immediately claimed victory and called for the PM to be appointed at once, stressing that Najib's role as an interim government is 'now over'. 'We need to form government now, today,' he said, 'there is no government now. The interim government has ceased to exist, as of last night.' He claimed that PH had won the vote, and the coalition had agreed to back him as prime minister.[45]

I had spoken to one of my sources who was close to the royal family to find out what had transpired following Najib's concession. The following is his version of events, which I have not been able to independently verify, and I am happy to stand corrected.

It seems the then King Muhammad V, based on the initial confusion of the electoral results, was minded to delay any swearing-in by a few days, even after Mahathir sought an audience with the King following Najib's concession speech.

Mahathir went to see the King at 5 p.m. in the hopes of being sworn in, but the King allegedly refused to swear him in, saying that no single party had a majority of seats in parliament, and so the King would take some time to make a decision. However, not to be deterred, Mahathir argued that the country urgently needed a prime minister and Mahathir's lawyers showed the *Agong*'s lawyers signed SDs from PKR, AMANAH, and DAP supporting Mahathir as the next PM.[46]

The *Agong* reportedly continued to demur.

However, Mahathir had another trick up his sleeve. Not only had he managed to convince the Chief Secretary of his position, he was also quick to realize that he needed the police and military too if he was to take immediate power. As such, Mahathir not only worked on the Chief Secretary to the Government (KSN)

---

[45] Trowell, Mark, KC, *Anwar Returns, The Final Twist: The Prosecution and Release of Anwar Ibrahim*, Marshall Cavendish International Asia, 2018, p. 53.

[46] Bose, Romen, *Final Reckoning*, p. 283.

during the wee hours of the morning but also reached out directly to the Inspector General of Police (IGP) and Malaysia's Chief of Defence Forces (PAT), allegedly demanding their loyalty as the rightful prime minister of the country. My source was on the phone with a senior royal accompanying the King when the KSN, IGP, and PAT requested an audience with him, while Mahathir waited in the outer chambers. He said that all three heads of service allegedly urged the King to decide quickly on who would be the next PM. The IGP reportedly said that the ground situation was quite tense and that there was an urgent need for certainty and stability. Thus, it was important to swear Mahathir in. Both the IGP and PAT allegedly implied that violence could break out across the country if Mahathir was not sworn in, and that they could not guarantee being able to quell the violence in that situation. All three heads also allegedly informed the King that they were loyal to the King and the government of the day, and that they were willing to serve Mahathir as the next prime minister.

As such, my source said the *Agong*, after interviewing the leaders of the four parties in the PH coalition who backed Mahathir, did not have much choice but to swear in Mahathir during the night of 10 May 2018, in order to avoid any chance of potential violence and given that the country's top three service heads were also willing to work with Mahathir as head of the new PH1.0 Government. So, Mahathir was appointed as Malaysia's seventh Prime Minister at 9.30 p.m. that night.

At Mahathir's swearing-in ceremony, the King reportedly indicated to Guan Eng that he was willing to pardon Anwar immediately. According to author and lawyer Mark Trowell KC, who has written extensively on Anwar's legal battles, 'the King gave no public explanation for the immediate pardon'.

However, Anwar, in 2022, told parliament that he had not asked the King for a pardon. 'The one who took the initiative at the time was the King,' Anwar said.

'He called me when I was at the rehab centre . . . and said, "Anwar, I will give a full pardon because I followed the developments in your trial (and there was) clear travesty of justice."'[47]

So, as Trowell noted:

> . . . at 11.30 a.m. on the morning of 16 May 2018, Anwar left the Cheras Rehabilitation Hospital for an audience with the King, Sultan Muhammad V, at noon. He walked along the outside balcony with his wife by his side. She touchingly held her arm around his waist as they walked towards the waiting vehicles. Their daughter, Nurul Izzah, joined them. Several police officers walked in front of them as they reached the waiting SUV, to be confronted by a throng of supporters and media. He paused, standing on the vehicle's sill to speak, but the shouts of support were too great. So, with a wave, he slipped quickly into the rear seat and was whisked away to meet the King.
>
> Anwar was met by Prime Minister Mahathir at the palace. The pardon granted to him was unconditional, without any admission of guilt. After a one-hour audience with the King, Anwar and his entourage left the palace and headed for his residence in Segambut Dalam. When he arrived home, the media contingent that had gathered there was even bigger than that at the hospital. The convoy of vehicles had difficulty driving up the street to enter the compound because of the number of supporters and media.
>
> At a press conference at his home, Anwar told the media that he would not serve in the new government for the time

---

Mahmud, Aqil Haziq, 'King gave me royal pardon because there was "travesty of justice": Malaysia PM Anwar', channelnewsasia.com, 20 Dec 2022, accessed at: https://www.channelnewsasia.com/asia/anwar-ibrahim-royal-pardon-malaysia-pm-parliament-3157206.

being, as he needed 'time and space' to rest with his family and to travel overseas to fulfil teaching and speaking engagements. 'I will be kept informed, but I don't need to serve in the Cabinet for now,' he said, after being asked if he would have a role in the new Cabinet.

That night, Anwar made a comeback speech at Padang Timur in Petaling Jaya. Several thousand people turned up to hear him. The ground was muddy and soggy from an afternoon downpour. With PKR banners waving and vuvuzela horns tooting, the boisterous and happy throng dressed mostly in Pakatan Harapan light blue t-shirts shouted 'Reformasi' to welcome the man who until ten hours before had been in custody (. . .) When Anwar arrived at around 9.30 p.m., he was mobbed by supporters and media. There were warm-up speeches, but the crowd had come to see Anwar (. . .) 'I give my support to Tun Dr Mahathir. We must give strong support to him and the Cabinet. I would not support him if I was not confident that he would bring change to the country,' Anwar told the crowd.

Anwar told them that those appointed to Cabinet must be given time to do their job. 'We must point out their weaknesses. If we see them living lavishly, we terajang (kick) them. But not Tun Mahathir, the others,' he joked.[48]

Ironically, it would be Anwar who would end up being 'kicked', once again, by Mahathir.

---

[48] Trowell, Mark, KC, *Anwar Returns*, p. 56.

Chapter 3

We Won. It's a New Malaysia.
So, What Do We Do Now?

By 14 May 2018, Mahathir was firmly ensconced in the Prime Minister's office on the fifth floor of the Perdana Putra building in the country's administrative capital of Putrajaya.

The office and its furnishings were not new to Mahathir and brought a nostalgic smile to his face, because he was the first occupant of these suite of offices in April 1999, as the country's fourth Prime Minister, before stepping down in 2003 in favour of his then deputy Abdullah Ahmad Badawi.

Now as PM7, Mahathir was back again at the helm of power in Putrajaya.

However, he was now serving as Prime Minister in vastly different circumstances.

When Mahathir was last in this seat of power, he had a plan and a vision for Malaysia. It was called Vision 2020. And it had the full backing of the country's civil servants and buy-in from the vast majority of Malaysians, from schoolchildren all the way to the *Neneks* and *Atuks* in the kampung.

And this plan, along with the Government's policies and objectives, was developed, fine-tuned, and executed by the serried ranks of civil servants attuned and comfortable with the long-serving Mahathir and the continuing BN leadership.

This time round, however, there was no vision, and there was definitely no plan. This was because Mahathir and the Pakatan 1.0 leadership never expected to win the elections. So, there was no government in waiting, there was no PH1.0 policy platform, there were no lists of senior civil servants and policy experts that the new government could immediately plug into the system, and there was no political machinery set to take over the reins of administration. There was effectively no incoming PH1.0 administration.

For several months following PH1.0's takeover of the government, a large proportion of office spaces and cubicles within the Prime Minister's Office in the Perdana Putra building and in minister's offices throughout Putrajaya remained empty. This was not because there was a surfeit of space, but because there just were not enough new PH appointees to take up the various posts and positions within the government.

And the dearth of appointees was also due to the fact that a significant number of PH appointees did not have suitable academic or other qualifications that would qualify them for higher civil service pay scales or remuneration; and most were unwilling to accept a lower pay scale.

This meant that many of these appointees had to go without pay for close to a year or more after GE14, while ministers, and eventually Mahathir himself, fought battles with the Treasury and Civil Service Commission officials, trying to get his people paid.

As for the civil servants, they were terrified. For years, the opposition had accused them of being the 'running dogs' of the government, creating the impression that the majority of civil servants were card-carrying members of BN/UMNO or sympathizers at the very least.

And now, many opposition supporters who would take on key governmental roles, like the incoming Attorney General, appeared to have 'drunk their own Kool-Aid' in believing their own propaganda—so much so that he reportedly brought in large numbers of lawyers from private practice into the Attorney General's Chambers (AGC), effectively side lining the incumbent, hardworking, and independent legal officers in favour of former partners and lawyers linked to him. It was true that there were some 'bad apples' and officials who were allied to the previous administration. But to treat almost all civil servants as the enemy was reprehensible.

It was also an awkward time for Mahathir, and the fact that he was leading the new government as a leader from a minority party made things even more bizarre. Mahathir was unable to dictate everything as he had done when he was PM4. Now, he had to contend with his coalition partners who controlled more seats in parliament than his own party. As such, Mahathir had to now consider their views and opinions (which he did but only for a while) like in the setting up of the PH1.0 Cabinet. Mahathir told aides he had wanted only twenty cabinet ministers, but the other PH1.0 leaders were seeking more ministerial positions. Instead, twenty-eight ministers were finally appointed.

Many may not be aware that PKR had actually boycotted the first meeting to decide on Cabinet posts following GE14, because the party's leadership was not happy with the idea of appointing Mohamad Sabu as Defence Minister and Lim Guan Eng as Finance Minister, as they felt both these powerful portfolios should have been given to PKR instead.

Moreover, Anwar had also objected to having the controversial former Finance Minister, Daim Zainuddin, appointed as chairman of the Council of Eminent Persons (CEP) that was supposed to help implement PH1.0's 100-day election promises and review the country's existing or proposed mega-projects and international business deals.

However, Mahathir overrode all these objections and pushed his plans through.

Within weeks of taking over, Mahathir was already showing signs of his age. He often looked and felt extremely tried and frequently visited the hospital for various health checks and to treat the ailments of a nonagenarian.

Mahathir was also having a hard time controlling the Malay ground because of several issues.

This included Mahathir's comments that PH1.0 would consider giving official recognition to the Unified Examination Certificate qualification, which was offered through the Malaysian Independent Chinese Secondary Schools, and which had been opposed by ultra-conservative Malay groups. The Malays were also unhappy with the appointment of a non-Malay Attorney General, the sudden termination of the Chief Justice, and the appointment of VK Liew as the minister in charge of Law.

Mahathir was also fully aware that the government needed to do something about the deteriorating value of the Ringgit, the expected hike in electricity tariffs in 2019, the fact that the much touted removal of the Goods and Services Tax (GST) had not reduced the prices of goods, the high fuel prices, and the absence of any sign of an increase in job opportunities for Malaysians. Mahathir told his people that he was aware that Malaysians were getting impatient to see results but that he was finding it difficult to provide quick results in the current scenario.

Politically, Mahathir knew that he needed more seats in parliament than that captured by PH, especially if ever there was a vote of no confidence pushed against him. As such, Mahathir and his people had begun talks with the Malaysian Islamic Party—Parti Islam Se-Malaysia (PAS). And Mahathir accepted a meeting with PAS chief Abdul Hadi Awang. According to witnesses, Hadi was very quiet and only asked 'fundamental questions' like 'if DAP will control (the government), *macam mana* Islam?' to which Mahathir responded, 'Don't worry'. When the Islamist leader asked about the government's intransigence in paying or increasing oil royalties, long a bugbear of the PAS-controlled northern states, Mahathir reportedly told him that the federal government would return the royalty directly to the state governments. Hadi clearly didn't expect that response and appeared to have gone back satisfied.

His close officials confided in friends that Mahathir was having a hard time with parties like DAP and with certain requests, such as the one to make Lim Kit Siang Speaker of Parliament.

However, they claimed that Mahathir managed to 'buy' the party's loyalty by giving them key Cabinet posts and appointing Lim Guan Eng as Finance Minister, despite creating unhappiness among factions within the party by ignoring some of the other senior leaders in favour of younger—and less influential—ones, whom he could potentially control.

Mahathir knew he had to work with the DAP, but that did not mean he would give significant power to the Chinese-led party despite his promises before GE14. Aides said the old man's belief in Malay hegemony would not allow him to cede any real power to non-Malays. So, even though Guan Eng was given the finance portfolio, Mahathir stripped the ministry of control of the powerful and lucrative GLC sector, which was then given to Azmin Ali, with Guan Eng thus having limited control over his own ministry.

In a media interview just months after his government's collapse in 2020, Mahathir confessed as much:

> I think you are insulting me if you think DAP can control me. I was the one who had control. Before this, the prime minister had no role in drafting budgets. Only the finance minister (. . .) When he did the budget, I asked him to show me the draft first. Only after I was satisfied, then we took it to Parliament . . .
>
> . . . He also performed many other actions, but he only implemented them after discussing with me. Lim could not simply bring matters into the cabinet without me looking into whether it is appropriate or not.[49]

---

[49] Hariz, Mohd, 'It's an insult if you think DAP can control me - Dr M', *Malaysiakini*, 13 Sep 2020, accessed at: https://www.malaysiakini.com/news/542444.

Thus, despite doing a deal with Mahathir and expecting to be an equal partner in government, the DAP ended up with very little power, while Mahathir still controlled things.

Appointing the New Attorney General

However, the two Lim's were able to prevail in their one and only nominee for Attorney General, Tommy Thomas.

Thomas was one of Lim's counsel from when he was charged with using his position as then Penang Chief Minister to allegedly gain gratification for himself and his wife in 2015.

Within the opposition leadership, it was well known that Guan Eng and Kit Siang were strongly lobbying for Thomas as the PH1.0 Government's Attorney General, despite his serious lack of experience.

Previous AGs had either risen through the ranks of the chambers or were former chief judges, who had the expertise, breadth of experience, and management skills required to lead such a big legal organization. Thomas had none of these, and the lack of such experience and skills showed in Thomas' later actions.

It was obvious that the strong lobbying by the Lims had worked when Kit Siang called Thomas on the Saturday following GE14:

> That evening, Lim Kit Siang telephoned. He made a cryptic remark, 'Congratulations, you will be doing national service. All legal reforms are in your hands.' Although Kit Siang did not specifically mention the post of Attorney General, I had a fair idea what he was referring to.[50]

---

[50] Thomas, Tommy, *My Story: Justice in the Wilderness*, 2021, p. 231.

And a few days later,

> Tun stated that he was appointing me Attorney General, but he
> was meeting resistance from the Yang di-Pertuan Agong. Tun
> said that he was adamant to see my appointment through and
> I was to leave the matter with him.[51]

Sources close to the Palace said Malaysia's then King and many of
his brother rulers did not think Thomas was suitable for the post
and were unhappy that Mahathir only suggested one name for the
position of AG, instead of the customary three names. Mahathir
was clearly not giving them a choice in the matter.

The Palace had kept delaying Thomas' appointment because,
I believe, the King thought that Thomas was neither qualified nor
loyal enough to the country to be given such a critical position.

After all, as Thomas noted in his book, he had left Malaysia in
1988 in favour of emigrating to Canada but then returned in 1991
when things didn't work out.[52]

And he was also the very vocal legal representative of one
of Malaysia's most hated individuals, Chin Peng, the former
Secretary General of the Malayan Communist Party. Chin Peng,
who had fought to liberate Malaya from the Japanese during
the Second World War, had been held partly responsible for the
violent deaths of over 10,000 people in his bid to overthrow the
colonial and then the Malaysian Government as well as the Malay
rulers, which led to the Malayan Emergency that lasted from 1948
to 1960, and which continues to inform the racial enmity and
mistrust among some Chinese and Malays even today.

The King was also aware of Mahathir's vengeful streak and
that the prime minister was not a fan of the royalty, as seen by
the actions that he had taken against them when he was PM4.

---

[51] Ibid.

[52] Ibid., p. 152.

As such, the Palace was sympathetic to former PM Najib's plight given Mahathir's need for blood. Aides said there was concern that Thomas would willingly do Mahathir's bidding in politically persecuting Najib, by moving to charge him, even without proper investigations or charge sheets being brought to bear.

Moreover, in his conversations with his brother rulers on WhatsApp, there was also a concern that Thomas had a serious lack of understanding and appreciation for the Shariah aspects of the law.

However, Mahathir was not to be deterred in his bid to get his man appointed as Attorney General. So, within days of Mahathir's meeting with the King, the Prime Minister's spin doctor—and one of his bagmen during his previous premiership—Kadir Jasin, along with the man lobbying for Thomas' appointment Lim Kit Siang, began to subtly build pressure against the Palace for delaying Thomas' appointment. In the end, the rulers held a special meeting, wherein they were forced to accept Thomas' appointment. However, many PH1.0 leaders were acutely aware that forcing the hand of the rulers would not augur well for the fledgling government.

Mahathir was also facing challenges within his own party.

BERSATU members were fully aware that the then ninety-three-year-old Mahathir was the party's only hope (at least at that time) for staying in power, given that the party's Deputy President and former Deputy Prime Minister Muhyiddin Yassin was reportedly in recovery from stage 2 cancer and his prognosis was not clear at that point.

Most of BERSATU's senior leadership were also former UMNO members who had resigned or were thrown out or dismissed from the party for unprofessionalism or violating party discipline. With the exception of Mahathir, his son Mukhriz, Syed Saddiq, and to some extent Muhyiddin, the party did not have any strong senior leaders who could engage the foreign or local media easily in English, nor were they able to debate very well, unlike DAP and AMANAH.

There was also a serious lack of young women leaders (BERSATU Puteri) in the movement. Young women leaders were very rare and those that were members, were absorbed under Sri Kandi (Wanita) which did not have many members in the first place. Given the merger and relative inexperience of the Puteri members, these women were side-lined and not taken seriously. The situation became so bad that Syed Saddiq asked Mahathir of the possibility of either setting up an exclusive Puteri wing or having the young women integrate with Bersatu's male youth wing, ARMADA, to prevent these young women members from becoming disillusioned and leaving the party. The issue was never resolved.

Internal party analysis indicated that following GE14, most Malays were jittery about BERSATU because many felt they were poorly represented by the limited number of BERSATU lawmakers and that BERSATU had yet to stem the perceived erosion in Malay rights and privileges. Some of Mahathir's closest aides said they were surprised to hear, just months after PH1.0's victory, negative comments about Mahathir by Malay PH voters, condemning Mahathir for being too lenient with the DAP. So, one of its biggest problems was one of credibility as the Malays had yet to join the party en-masse.

Many Malays felt that with Anwar eventually coming in as PM, PKR would be a better bet for support, as BERSATU only had Mahathir and Mahathir would be gone after two or three years; Anwar was likely to be around for a much longer period.

And to many members, the party appeared to be moving too slowly in getting these better-quality leaders. BERSATU needed young talented leaders to move forward, and Mahathir had promised that young people would be in top government positions within a very short period. He appeared to signal this by appointing Maszlee Malik, who joined BERSATU just a week before elections, as Education Minister. However, Maszlee's continual *faux pas* in managing his ministry and his stubbornness in accepting instructions even from the prime minister, forced Mahathir to remove him. This showed just how difficult it was to get talented professionals to sign up.

And another reason it was hard to get new leaders was that whenever an attempt was made to try to recruit talent from outside the party, these potential members would be instantly rejected by current members who were less talented and feared they would be sidelined by the newer, more capable members. As such, the party was stuck.

Funding was also another critical issue that confronted the party. BERSATU and its various wings had survived on a budget of RM200,000 since its inception in 2016, and RM150,000 of that money had come from crowd funding. All party leaders and candidates had to use their own money to pay for political and election expenses, and many stayed at their friend's houses during campaigning to save cost. However, now that they were in government, the hope was that this would no longer be an issue. But the reality was that most did not know how or from where the party would be able to get funds.

There were also many reports that ARMADA members were seen 'busy trying to get government projects and cutting deals for their own benefit but at the same time trying to stay away from having to do any work and off the Malaysian Anti-Corruption Commission's (MACC) radar'.[53] They were seen pushing for contracts despite the governments then austerity measures.

A large number of ARMADA members were also reportedly using their political influence and power to secure deals and contracts. It got so bad that within the ministries, many civil

---

[53] Interview with PMO Source 2, Putrajaya, 11 Sep 2022.

servants were wary of these BERSATU members, especially ARMADA members.

Party insiders admitted that in some cases, these members used proxy companies to execute a ministry project but had failed to receive payment. This was because government servants were reluctant to approve these projects and some didn't process the paperwork or payments, even though instructions had come down from the minister's office. This was because BERSATU members were alienating civil servants with the way they were trying to ride roughshod over the existing procedures, systems, and SOPs in the ministries, with some referring to ARMADA members as 'Mat Rempit[54] with suits'.

Even party members felt that PKR and DAP's youth wing were much more professional and had many more well-educated professionals compared to ARMADA, with many referring to BERSATU as 'UMNO 2.0'.

Although BERSATU had negotiated with the rest of the PH component parties to contest for fifty-two seats, it only won thirteen seats in GE14. So, party insiders believed that there was still a lot of room to appoint new candidates for GE15. Syed Saddiq told aides he was confident that a large number of UMNO seats would be wrested away in GE15, given UMNO's almost complete collapse following GE14.

However, BERSATU was still concerned because even though UMNO may not have been the largest opposition block, PAS could potentially be, given its strength in the states of Kedah, Pahang, Terengganu, and Kelantan.

So, BERSATU was very open to accepting UMNO members, including division chiefs and lawmakers. However, there was a process that had to be followed. These UMNO MPs/politicians had to declare themselves as independent first, then after a three-

---

[54] 'Mat Rempit' is a Malay term for an individual (usually a youth) who participates in hooliganism and illegal activities.

month cooling-period, they could join BERSATU. With the membership pie shrinking following DAP, PKR, and AMANAH's heavy recruitment drive, there was no other option.

Multiracial Membership Ambition

Despite the venality and unprofessionalism of many within its rank and file, in the flush of PH's victory, there were still many who held on to PH's values of multiracialism, reform, and equality. BERSATU did this through the idealistic and energetic Syed Saddiq, who at that point in time, really believed BERSATU could and would be the future for all Malaysians.

As ARMADA chief, Syed Saddiq had been pushing—even before GE14—to introduce multiracial membership within Bersatu. However, Mahathir had insisted that BERSATU must remain a pure Malay party before GE14, in order to attract the Malay heart-landers to the party.

However, now that elections were over, Syed Saddiq told his close allies within PH that BERSATU was supposedly working towards becoming multiracial, within one or two terms.[55]

Syed Saddiq said this was why he was trying to recruit as many young leaders as possible, in order to push for this idealistic aim. Saddiq believed that as the rural Malay voter base became smaller and smaller, more and more people would begin to accept multiracialism as a solution to Malaysia's racial woes.

Another one of his aims, he told colleagues, was to lower the voting age to eighteen, in order to open the floodgates of multiracial thinking youths. And he talked about setting up an automatic registration process for accepting new members into the party. Syed Saddiq said the support base among non-Malays was huge, so BERSATU could not miss an opportunity to win them over by staying exclusively Malay.

---

[55] Zoom interview with BERSATU leader 5, 12 Sep 2020.

During the seat negotiations prior to GE14, the urban and Chinese seats went to DAP, some urban and Malay seats went to PKR, rural Malay seats went to BERSATU, while overlapping urban and rural seats went to AMANAH.

His political calculation, according to his colleagues, was that BERSATU was unlikely to get additional seats in GE15 if huge urban constituencies were broken down under a new delineation process, which was to be done by an independent body.[56]

As an example, the federal constituency of Petaling Jaya had 150,000 voters and the constituency of Bangi had 170,000. If these seats were broken up into smaller constituencies, Syed Saddiq believed that BERSATU would not get any of these new seats if it remained a party just for Malays. As such, he believed that BERSATU would be wiped out eventually.

However, what Syed Saddiq did not realize at that time was the fact that the majority of BERSATU's leadership only paid lip-service to the concept of multiracialism as they were mainly ultra-Malays who, like their party chairman and president, believed in Malay hegemony. Therefore, they listened to Syed Saddiq's attempts, appeals, and plans with smiles on their faces, as an adult would to placate a stubborn child, but they would never be able to accept a new, more equitable power sharing model with the DAP or any other party representing the Chinese community. They followed in the footsteps of their chairman, who would pay lip service about reform and better race relations but would then continue with his antiquated and racist policies to govern the country.

Syed Saddiq really believed Mahathir would accept a multiracial party and by extension a country based on multiracialism, and he believed he saw indications of these in the way Mahathir was dealing with his PH1.0 coalition partners.

Soon enough, he would realize how very wrong he was.

---

[56] Ibid.

Chapter 4

Dark Days Part I: Persecuting Anyone We Don't Like

Strangely, the first acts of Mahathir's PH1.0 Government were not aimed at uniting the country or looking at how to improve the lot of Malaysians. The first moves were aimed purely at seeking political revenge over the vanquished Barisan Nasional (BN) coalition, and this took not only the form of attempting to file a blitz of charges against BN politicians but also the unceremonious dismissal of senior civil servants, heads of government-linked companies, and individuals who Mahathir and his team felt were loyal to Najib and the former BN government.

In most commonwealth countries that have a Westminster-style of democracy, a general election that saw a change of the ruling party, would result in a change in individuals holding political appointments, but the civil service would remain unchanged as they are not political in nature but meant to continue running the country's administration regardless of its political masters. Of course, one can understand that there may be a need to change some wayward officials whose political allegiances were openly displayed.

I think that most people would agree that the majority of Malaysia's civil service were politically neutral in carrying out their roles and duties although the fact that BN had been the country's

political masters for sixty-one years prior to GE14 meant that
many of the policies implemented by these civil servants had
benefitted the government of the day, namely BN. This did not
mean that the civil servants were 'BN stooges or lackeys'.

Mahathir's and PH1.0's reign of terror began with the
Malaysian Anti-Corruption Commission (MACC) calling in
almost all of Najib's former aides, officials, advisers, and friends
for 'interviews' at its Putrajaya headquarters. At its height, the
agency became a revolving door of who's who in Malaysia, as
politicians, business tycoons, civil servants, bankers, and even
socialites were dragged in for interrogation and questioning in a
bid to get as much dirt as could be found on the collapsed BN
Government and their leaders.

The Inland Revenue Board of Malaysia, also known as
Lembaga Hasil Dalam Negeri (LHDN), which ordinarily carried
out spot audit checks on taxpayers, suddenly began 'routine
checks' on all individuals believed to be close to Najib and the
BN government.

Prior to GE14, Mahathir had accused Najib of abusing
his authority by getting LHDN to investigate Mahathir's close
associates and opposition politicians. And yet, just months into
the PH1.0 Government, Mahathir's administration was doing
just that.

I believe the philosophy behind Mahathir and his Attorney
General Tommy Thomas' actions was to charge, embarrass, and
try destroying Najib, Zahid, and as many United Malays National
Organization (UMNO) and BN politicians and associates as
they could, regardless of whether there was any real evidence
against them.

The idea was to show the voters that they were right in
voting in PH1.0 as those responsible for economic and political
crimes against Malaysia would now be made to pay. PH1.0 leaders
believed the people were baying for blood and that is what they

intended to give them. So, instead of going down the path of South Africa's Truth and Reconciliation Commission, in order to move forward with a united country, the plan here was something more akin to the Spanish Inquisition.

The first salvo was fired less than seven days after Mahathir took power, with late night raids on Najib's home and residences. They even raided the home of Najib's eighty-five-year-old mother, Rahah Noah, the widow of Malaysia's revered second Prime Minister Abdul Razak Hussein, where they found nothing.

But at Najib's residences, police seized handbags, jewellery, and cash worth $273 million. Of that amount, Police said $28.6 million was found in cash during the raid.

Video footage and pictures of the boxes of handbags, jewellery, and bags of cash being carted out of the Pavilion residences were plastered across local, regional, and global newspapers and television screens, giving the impression that Najib had allegedly used 1MDB funds to enrich himself.

But the reality was that the cash actually belonged to UMNO and had been kept by the party president as an election war chest in the safes at the Prime Minister's Office in Putrajaya. After being forced to immediately vacate the premises following the election loss, Najib had to hastily arrange for the party funds to be temporarily stored at a safe location and chose to do so at an apartment owned by a close business associate and family friend. That was the cash that was 'found'.

And the handbags, jewellery and other high value items seized from Najib's residences belonged to him and his family, and had been accumulated over a lifetime. The MACC was unable to establish any link between any of these items and the funds allegedly siphoned from 1MDB.

In the end, after a four-year long court battle, the High Court, on 14 November 2022, ordered the government to return *all* the goods and cash, finding insufficient evidence linking the assets to unlawful activities.[57]

But back in May 2018, Mahathir was able to use the spectacle of the raids as 'proof' and create the impression in the mind of all Malaysians that Najib was guilty of corruption.

It was a trial by the media and the guilty narrative built was all that mattered.

I believe that this was the way Mahathir and his team viewed the situation, and this included PH1.0's newly-minted Attorney General Tommy Thomas.

However, even before Thomas was appointed, Mahathir had it in for Thomas' predecessor, Apandi Ali, a former Federal Court judge, who had taken on the Attorney General's role in July 2015.

Apandi had replaced Gani Patail, who had been removed following his alleged involvement, with the then Bank Negara Governor Zeti Akhtar Aziz and MACC Commissioner Abu Kassim Mohamed in an alleged coup to topple then Prime Minister Najib Razak.

Mahathir took against Apandi when the former judge announced in January 2016 that based on the available evidence at that time, there was no criminal offence committed by Najib in relation to the 1MDB scandal.

As many within the Attorney General's Chambers (AGC) knew, Apandi, a veteran legal service officer, never made decisions on high profile cases without great deliberation and consultation. Upon becoming Attorney General, Apandi formed a special panel within the AGC to advise and help him decide on all cases of significant public interest and scrutiny.

---

[57] 'Malaysia court dismisses govt bid to forfeit millions in assets linked to ex-PM Najib', *Reuters*, 14 Nov 2022, accessed at: https://www.reuters.com/world/asia-pacific/malaysia-court-dismisses-govt-bid-forfeit-millions-assets-linked-ex-pm-najib-2022-11-14/.

So, in the case of Najib, Apandi formed a panel consisting of various AGC Division heads, including that of the criminal division, and senior officials from the MACC, to sit down, examine in detail the investigation paper (IP) from the enforcement agency, in this case the MACC, and then discuss and decide, by way of consensus, whether there was enough evidence against the accused and whether to proffer charges or send the IP back to the agency for further investigations.

As all senior officials in the AGC knew, Apandi abided by the chamber's longstanding rule that there had to be '99 per cent evidence to secure a conviction before the AGC would proceed to charge an individual'. At that point of time, the panel decided that the evidence had not met the chamber's threshold to file charges against Najib, sending the IP back to the MACC for further investigations. As Apandi had told his senior officials, 'We must abide by the chamber's founding principle, if the evidence is 50/50, or some have the attitude of charge first, then investigate and find the evidence later, that is not my way.'[58]

Once the panel had completed examining the MACC's IP and if it found that it had met its threshold, the AGC would then draft the charge sheet and work with the enforcement agency to begin legal proceedings.

However, in Najib's case, what the panel found mystifying was the fact that the initial IP—which would normally be sent back to the enforcement agency a few times before the document could meet the AGC's threshold for prosecution—and which normally only contained the details of the investigations and conclusions, also included charge sheets against Najib that had been drafted by the MACC, something that was not within the agency's legislated role and which had been drafted even before the MACC's investigations had been complete.[59]

---

[58] Interview with AGC Source, Putrajaya, Aug 2023.

[59] Ibid.

It was clear that some individuals or groups were attempting to influence the MACC, which was normally unbiased and the champion of integrity within the government, in its investigations into Najib and wanted him to be found guilty by providing 'unwanted and unasked for help to the AGC by drafting the charges', and without even bothering to complete its own investigations first.[60]

Although it appeared as if the agency was convinced of Najib's guilt, it became evident a few months later that it was all part of the machinations of certain individuals to topple Najib at any cost.

In Apandi's own words:

One evening in January 2018, Dato Sri Gopal Sri Ram came to my house after a couple of calls wanting to speak to me personally and privately.

Since he was a former brother judge, I obliged.

He had indicated that he wanted to persuade me further to unfreeze the accounts of a certain firm as the lawyers who had engaged him needed to be paid and it was from that said account that they were to be paid from.

He had earlier sent in a representation to the AGC as I was the AG at that time but after consultation with the officers in the criminal division, I wrote to him with a negative response.

He arrived at my house with a young Chinese lawyer, and upon sitting down, he launched into his long argument of why I shouldn't have responded negatively but I countered him and explained that everything I had put in the reply was carefully thought out and argued amongst us in chambers.

Then suddenly, he said, that that was only an excuse to see me and that he had a bigger agenda at hand.

'Tun M sent me to see you.'

---

[60] Ibid.

He continued, 'He wants you to arrest Najib at his office, you go tomorrow at 2 p.m., we have arranged for the police in Putrajaya to do what is necessary on your instructions. We have also arranged for a magistrate to issue the remand order when he is brought before him or her.'

'Brother, you will be a hero in the eyes of the people, and you will be the first AG to arrest a sitting prime minister.'

'Don't worry, we have laid the ground plans, all I need now is for you to agree.'

Then I asked him, 'On what grounds is he supposed to be arrested?'

He said, 'Brother, people out there are frustrated and unhappy, the fact that you arrest him, never mind the reason, will make people happy.'

Gopal Sri Ram was persuasive, and he had wanted a response immediately.

I said to let me sleep on it.

He then left with the young Chinese lawyer he brought with him.

At that time, my family and I were also under attack in social media, not only from the opposition but also from within the government of the day and cyber troopers.

There is no reason for me to save anyone when I was 'everyone's enemy'.

Gopal Sri Ram can deny this but I would like to caution that at that material time I was the AG, and my house was fitted with CCTV (one specifically for the hall) and not to mention my bodyguards and the police personnel who was manning the guardhouse in front of my house—CCTV will not lie and I, too, have witnesses.[61]

---

[61] Ali, Tan Sri Apandi, 'A prelude to a chapter in my memoirs,' 10 Jun 2020, Facebook.com, accessed at: https://www.facebook.com/mohamedapandi.ali/posts/2755017934626211.

So, if Apandi was to be believed, it was now obvious that a former PM and his lawyer, who later became the key prosecutor against Najib in the various 1MDB corruption and abuse of power cases—a conflict of interest perhaps?—were asking a sitting Attorney General, to take an illegal and extrajudicial action against an elected head of government, effectively plotting treason.

This was now a second coup in three years which had failed, and both masterminded by the same individual.

It was clear that Apandi was not going to play ball with Sri Ram and Mahathir by illegally arresting a sitting Prime Minister.

So, Apandi had to go.

Just a day after winning GE14, Mahathir claimed that Apandi had hidden evidence of wrongdoing in the 1MDB scandal.

And on 12 May 2020, Mahathir 'declared' that the country did not have an Attorney-General.

'We have placed certain restrictions on a number of people who may be involved in wrongdoings or making wrong decisions. So, at the moment, we do not have an Attorney General,' Mahathir said at a press conference.[62]

And this was despite the fact that the Attorney General's post is not a political appointment and that the government's top legal officer—the Attorney General—is appointed by the King.

The Attorney General's dismissal under the constitution is the same as in the dismissal of judges of the superior courts—it is done via a recommendation to the King, from a duly appointed tribunal consisting of at least five judges who are current or former Federal Court judges.

The Attorney General cannot be summarily dismissed by the Prime Minister. These provisions are clearly listed in Article 145(5 and 6) and Article 125 of the Federal Constitution. As such, Apandi was still the Attorney General.

---

[62] Tong, Geraldine, 'Dr M says no AG, Apandi says no comment', *Malaysiakini*, 12 May 2018, accessed at: https://www.malaysiakini.com/news/424494.

Mahathir's statement and actions were not surprising given how fast and loose he had played with, and effectively destroyed, the country's independent judiciary in 1988 (see Appendix 2).

So, on the afternoon of 14 May 2018, the then KSN (Chief Secretary/Head of Civil Service) Ali Hamsa called Apandi into his office and gave him a letter, saying that, 'Mahathir has decided for you to go on "garden leave"[63] for thirty days.' And before those thirty days were over, in a letter dated 5 June 2018, they terminated him.

However, what Mahathir failed to realize or appreciate—and this appears to have happened a few times during his twenty-two-month rule—is that in addition to Apandi's dismissal being a violation of Article 145(6), the Attorney General's appointment was a contractual appointment based on contract law.

When Apandi was first appointed Attorney General in 2015, he had insisted that the appointment be based on a three-year contract, outlining his salary, perks, etc. The contract was subsequently renewed by the government in early 2018. So, when Mahathir decided to unceremoniously terminate Apandi, Mahathir caused the government to be in breach of the contract it had signed. Apandi had not violated his part of his contract, but Mahathir had violated the government's part of the contract.

As such, in October 2018, Apandi sued the government for this breach, and in April 2023, both parties settled the matter out of court with the government paying Apandi what I believe was a hefty compensatory amount. Although the terms of the settlement remain a secret, the fact that the government shelled out such an amount was a clear indicator of which party was wronged.

Mahathir remains bitter over the issue, claiming Apandi doesn't deserve any compensation because he had been 'derelict

---

[63] 'Garden Leave' refers to a practice where an employee who has just been terminated or who has resigned serves out the rest of his notice or period of service away from work and the office, while still remaining on the payroll.

in his duties' and because he 'did not study the case thoroughly before declaring that Najib had no case to answer'.[64]

However, what Mahathir appeared to have conveniently forgotten was the fact that under the Federal Constitution, it is at the Attorney General's discretion to prosecute or not. As stated by then Lord President Tun Mohamed Suffian in 1974:

> . . . the supreme law clearly gives the Attorney General very wide discretion over the control and discretion of all criminal prosecutions. Not only may he institute and conduct any proceedings that he has instituted, and the courts cannot compel him to institute any criminal proceedings which he does not wish to institute or to go on with any criminal proceedings which he has decided to discontinue (. . .) Still less then would the court have power to compel him to enhance a charge when he is content to go on with a charge of a less serious nature. Anyone who is dissatisfied with the Attorney General's decision not to prosecute, or not to go on with a prosecution or his decision to prefer a charge for a less serious offence when there is evidence of a more serious offence which should be tried in a higher court, should seek his remedy elsewhere, but not in the courts.[65]

It was these same laws that, according to the Government Task Force investigating Mahathir's anointed Attorney General (who

---

[64] Chan, Dawn, 'Dr M: Apandi had been derelict in his duties, secret payment to him unjustified', *New Straits Times Online*, 22 Aug 2023, accessed at: https://www.nst.com.my/news/nation/2023/08/945926/dr-m-apandi-had-been-derelict-his-duties-secret-payment-him-unjustified.

[65] Ariana Azhari, Aira Nur, Lim, Wei Jiet, 'Separating the Attorney General and Public Prosecutor: Enhancing Rule of Law in Malaysia', Institute for Democracy and Economic affairs (IDEAS) policy paper 34, Dec 2016, accessed at: https://www.ideas.org.my/wp-content/uploads/2021/04/PI34-Separating-the-Attorney-General-and-Public-Prosecutor.pdf.

replaced Apandi), allowed Tommy Thomas to get away with 'rampant abuse of his powers'[66] because 'he was armed with the prosecutorial powers and no person can threaten to prosecute him on any of his decisions'.[67]

Mahathir was clearly interested in neither what the Attorney General's Chambers had been doing nor in Apandi's advice on the upcoming Batu Puteh case (see Chapter 7), which would, as a result, have disastrous consequences for Malaysia.

He just wanted Apandi gone.

Palace sources said that the then King, who had followed the Attorney General's dismissal through the media, was sympathetic towards Apandi. They said that the King was in touch with Apandi, who told him that he was under intense pressure to resign following Mahathir's announcement. Apandi, being a Kelantanese, asked his Sultan and King, what he should do. The King told him, 'Stay put, don't resign.'

But in the end, following Mahathir's actions—which have been outlined in Chapter 8—the King was forced to sign the warrant dismissing Apandi.

But that was not enough. The tax department was then set upon Apandi and an arbitrary travel ban was imposed on him from 14 May 2018 to August 2019, when he won his case against the unlawful action at the Appellate and Special Powers Division of the High Court. But it was of little comfort as he had been unfairly deprived of attending his youngest son's graduation ceremony in the UK in June 2018.

Another non-politician, but a key target on Mahathir's list and that of several DAP leaders, was the CEO of 1MDB, Arul Kanda.

---

[66] Page 167, Laporan Pasukan Petugas Khas: Siasatan ke atas dakwaan-dakwaan dalam buku bertajuk 'My Story: Justice in the wilderness' Tulisan YBHG. Tan Sri Tommy Thomas bekas Peguam Negara, 2022.

[67] Ibid.

Educated at Malaysia's Royal Military College, Arul had obtained a law degree from the London School of Economics and a master's in corporate and commercial law from University College London. Although qualified as a barrister, Arul started his career by entering the cut and thrust world of investment banking, first in the city of London and eventually in the Middle East. In the aftermath of the global financial crisis, Arul developed a specialization in financial restructuring of large and complex debts, playing a pivotal role in the restructuring of the heavily indebted Dubai World conglomerate as well as other large corporates in Abu Dhabi, Saudi Arabia, and Kuwait. Arul was headhunted for the top job at 1MDB, stepping into one of the country's hottest political potatoes, to jumpstart stalled projects like TRX and Bandar Malaysia, to monetize EDRA—the power generation arm of 1MDB—and to restructure and refinance the debt-mired firm.

Arul had turned up long after the alleged brazen looting of the sovereign wealth fund by businessman Low Taek Jho and his cronies between 2009 and 2013. Arul's job was to restore confidence in the company, help it to list, and get it back on an even keel. However, at that time, Arul was completely unaware of the financial fraud—and of its enormity—that had taken place.

Mahathir and the DAP leaders, namely Lim Guan Eng and his protégé Tony Pua, insinuated that Arul had been brought in by Najib to cover up the scandal. This could not have been further from the truth, given that it was Arul who had urged Najib to get the Auditor General to investigate 1MDB in 2016, as details of the extent and complexity of the scandal began emerging. Guan Eng and Pua had been very critical of 1MDB and they blamed Arul for the abuse and mismanagement that had taken place at the firm.

So, when Guan Eng became Finance Minister—whose portfolio included 1MDB—and Pua was appointed his Political Secretary following GE14, the scene was set for a showdown with Arul.

Just days after Lim was sworn in, the Finance Ministry called Arul, who had been on garden leave since January 2018 ahead

of a long-planned departure from the company, for a meeting to brief the new Finance Minister.

Witnesses said it was a very cold meeting, with Guan Eng demanding to know the state of the company. When Arul told him that he had been on garden leave since January, was unaware of the latest developments, and did not have access to any of the company papers, Guan Eng became enraged.

He then questioned Arul as to how he could make speeches on the 1MDB roadshows claiming the company was doing well. According to a source present at the meeting, Arul said that his comments during the 1MDB roadshows mainly dealt with the company's rationalization plan and future prospects. He said that with the implementation of the business rationalization plan, the MOF now owned all of 1MDB's assets and was paying off its debts, and so the company was in decent shape. At this point, Guan Eng blew up, allegedly accusing Arul of being a liar, and ranted and raved, with other officials in the room barely able to get a word in. In another emotional pique, Guan Eng immediately ordered the sealing off of the 1MDB offices, which meant that the staff there could not get into their workplace. This also meant there was no formal handover of documents and equipment.

Following the meeting, Guan Eng made his displeasure public:

> I have found Arul to be utterly dishonest and preposterous. Prior to the change in government, he toured the country preaching 1MDB's financial viability and soundness of investments.
>
> Today, Arul is singing a completely different tune from the songs he sang to the Public Accounts Committee as recorded in the Hansard.
>
> I have immediately instructed MOF legal counsels to review Arul's position as 1MDB president.[68]

---

[68] Ramasamy, Manirajan, 'Arul Kanda mulls legal action against Guan Eng', *New Straits Times Online*, 24 May 2018, accessed at: https://www.nst.com.my/news/nation/2018/05/372592/arul-kanda-mulls-legal-action-against-guan-eng.

However, the reality of the situation was that Arul had not committed any wrongdoing. But I believe Guan Eng wanted a scapegoat. He wanted to show the public that he was taking action against those who had cheated and plundered the nation's coffers. And Arul was an easy target, even if he hadn't committed any crime.

Unable to pin anything on Arul—because there was nothing there—all Guan Eng could do was dismiss Arul as the company president.

So, Arul was fired from his job just two days before his contract was to expire on 30 June 2018, to ensure that he would not get any of the contractual benefits due to him on the conclusion of his stint.

But then, I believe Guan Eng felt he had stumbled onto the 'smoking gun' with which to nail Arul, when it was found that the Auditor General's report on 1MDB that had been submitted to parliament's Public Accounts Committee in 2016 had been allegedly doctored.

Auditor General officer Nor Salwani Muhammad told her boss, Madinah Mohamad, that the previous Auditor General Ambrin Buang had supposedly been 'ordered' to amend the report, and he had ordered Salwani to destroy all copies of the original report, but that she had kept a copy 'under her chair'.[69]

So Madinah wrote to the Mahathir Cabinet about it, and in what appeared to be one of the fastest investigations and prosecutions in Malaysian judicial history, within a few weeks, Najib was charged with using his position as the then Prime Minister to instruct for the final audit report on 1MDB to be amended before it was presented to the parliamentary Public Accounts Committee (PAC), while Arul was charged with abetting Najib in making the amendments to the report.

---

[69] Ho, Kit Yen, 'Ex-auditor general tells court she was shocked predecessor told to amend 1MDB audit report', *Free Malaysia Today*, 30 Mar 2022, accessed at: https://www.freemalaysiatoday.com/category/nation/2022/03/30/ex-auditor-general-tells-court-she-was-shocked-predecessor-told-to-amend-1mdb-audit-report/.

Then followed four long years of the trial, where it was made very clear by Ambrin that he was in no way forced or coerced by Najib to make changes to the report. And it was also found that the four significant changes to the report had not even been suggested by Arul. So, on 3 March 2023, the High Court threw out the case, without calling for Najib or Arul's defence.[70] But during this period of uncertainty, Arul's reputation and life had been left in tatters. His passport had been confiscated, his bank accounts had been frozen, and yes, he had also been investigated by the tax authorities.

Arul had done the nation a service by taking on the thankless job of being 1MDB's head and trying to rebuild the company. But instead of receiving his contractual end of term salary and benefits, he became a political pawn and was treated as an enemy of the state.

As for Nor Salwani, for her role in 'saving' what was proven to be worthless 'evidence' and exposing the non-existent tampering of the audit report, she was awarded a Datukship by the PH1.0 government.

The appointment of PH politician and lawyer Latheefa Koya as head of the MACC—despite PH's condemnation of political appointees in key government positions prior to GE14—saw the anti-graft body move full-speed to investigate the BN leadership and file civil forfeiture suits and compound notices against forty-one individuals and entities to recover RM270 million in alleged 1MDB funds given to them by Najib.[71]

---

[70] Ho, Kit Yen, 'Najib, Arul Kanda freed of 1MDB audit tampering charges', *Free Malaysia Today*, 3 Mar 2023, accessed at: https://www.freemalaysiatoday. com/category/nation/2023/03/03/najib-arul-kanda-freed-of-1mdb-audit-tampering-charges/.

[71] The BN entities included Puteri UMNO, Perak, and Penang UMNO liaison bodies, fifteen UMNO divisions, Selangor and Kedah MCA liaison committees, Parti Rakyat Sarawak, Kedah Gerakan, Kedah Parti Progresif Penduduk Malaysia (PPP), and the Malaysian Indian Congress.

Some individuals and entities, fearing reputational damage, legal costs, and further persecution, made deals with the Malaysian Anti-Corruption Commission and Attorney General's Chambers for returning the funds despite the fact that the money had been given to them for legitimate and legal purposes, and they'd had no idea if the funds had really come from allegedly illegal activities.

But by February 2023, the Attorney General's Chambers had finally withdrawn its appeal on forfeiting funds totalling RM194 Million from nine entities including UMNO and Wanita MCA after both the High Court and Court of Appeal dismissed these forfeiture applications, noting that there was 'insufficient evidence that the monies seized were the subject matter or evidence relating to the commission of an offence or proceeds of unlawful activities'. The court also determined 'there was no link between the monies in the bank accounts of the respondents and the funds allegedly misappropriated from 1MDB'.[72]

Back in January 2020, however, despite seeing signs that the PH1.0 Government was about to unravel and that there was now a distinct possibility that all these acts of vengeance perpetrated by the government could come to light, Thomas insisted the MACC prosecute former Federal Land Development Authority (FELDA) chairman and senior UMNO leader Shahrir Samad for failing to declare RM1 million, received from Najib, to the tax authorities, even though the MACC's investigation papers on his case were still incomplete.[73]

---

[72] Khairulrijal, Rahmat, 'Govt withdraws appeal to forfeit RM194 million linked to 1MDB', *New Straits Times Online*, 7 Feb 2023, accessed at: https://www.nst.com.my/news/crime-courts/2023/02/877374/govt-withdraws-appeal-forfeit-rm194-million-linked-1mdb.

[73] *Bernama*, 'Ex-AG insisted MACC charge Shahrir though probe incomplete, court told', *Free Malaysia Today*, 23 Dec 2022, accessed at: https://www.freemalaysiatoday.com/category/nation/2022/12/23/ex-ag-insisted-macc-charge-shahrir-though-probe-incomplete-court-told/.

As a result, Shahrir went through three years of 'hell'. MACC assistant superintendent Nurzahidah Yacop, who was the agency's investigating officer tasked with the case, shockingly admitted in court that she had never looked into the RM1 million that Shahrir received from Najib, even though the UMNO leader insisted eight times during investigations in 2019 that the money was to replace his pension. On 5 January 2023, the High Court cleared Shahrir of all charges after the Attorney General's Chambers withdrew the case against him.

Thomas had also ordered the January 2019 prosecution of former Tabung Haji Chairman and former UMNO Supreme Council member Abdul Azeez Abdul Rahim on three counts of accepting bribes amounting to RM5.2 million and ten charges of money laundering worth RM140 Million in relation to road projects in the states of Perak and Kedah, for offences allegedly committed between September 2010 and April 2018.

By September 2022, the Court of Appeal had struck off four of the money laundering charges and the MACC, upon the eventual completion of its investigations—which should normally be done *before* charges are filed—found no wrongdoing on Azeez's part. On 9 December 2022 the High Court discharged and fully acquitted him.[74]

Persecuting Najib and Zahid

Mahathir and Thomas' main target remained Najib and Zahid.

On 18 October 2018, Zahid was arrested by the Malaysian Anti-Corruption Commission, and faced forty-seven charges involving multiple counts of criminal breach of trust, corruption,

---

[74] Palani, Tarani, 'Former Tabung Haji chairman Abdul Azeez gets full acquittal in graft, money-laundering case', *The Edge Malaysia*, 9 Dec 2022, accessed at: https://theedgemalaysia.com/article/former-tabung-haji-chairman-abdul-azeez-gets-full-acquittal-graft-moneylaundering-case.

and money laundering related to the misuse of RM114 million of funds in Yayasan Akalbudi—a charity he had established to eradicate poverty. In total, Zahid faced eighty-seven charges. But in September 2022, he was acquitted of forty of the bribery charges, and in a very controversial move following UMNO becoming a member of the current Unity Government coalition and Zahid's appointment as Deputy Premier, the other forty-seven charges were dropped by the Attorney General's Chambers in September 2023.

Najib, however, was not as lucky, with the government filing five charges of corruption and nine counts of criminal breach of trust against him.[75] He also faced one charge of receiving RM42 million in bribes and three counts of criminal breach of trust and was subsequently charged with three more counts of related money-laundering charges.

Najib was also slapped with twenty-one counts of receiving, using, or sending illicit funds as well as four counts of corruption involving US$681 million that appeared in his personal bank accounts. The charges were linked to his alleged role in 1MDB deals, including a US$2 billion joint venture with PetroSaudi International, a RM10.6 billion bid for Tanjong Energy Holdings, and RM2.1 billion of funds from Tanore Finance's account at Falcon Private Bank in Singapore.

Najib was also jointly charged with the then Treasury Secretary General, Irwan Serigar, in relation to RM6.6 billion of government payments to International Petroleum Investment Company (IPIC)—an Abu Dhabi sovereign wealth fund—as well as money linked to rail and pipeline projects that involved Chinese companies. Najib also faced six counts of criminal breach of trust

---

[75] Bloomberg, 'A long list of charges against Najib as 1MDB trial kicks off on Tuesday', *The Straits Times*, 11 Feb 2019, accessed at: https://www.straitstimes.com/asia/se-asia/a-long-list-of-charges-against-najib-as-1mdb-trial-kicks-off-on-tuesday.

for his alleged role. In addition, he was also charged with receiving a total of RM47 million of proceeds from illegal activities, resulting in three money laundering charges. And finally, Najib faced one count of corruption for allegedly tampering with the Auditor General's 1MDB report.

I am not going to get into details regarding all the charges and what transpired over the last five years in relation to these charges against Najib, as much of it has been documented and reported. However, the way in which it was pushed through the courts and the judicial process has left many a question as to whether Najib has received justice so far.

Instead, I will touch on the RM42 million SRC case and the RM6.6 Billion IPIC case to illustrate my point. Readers may want to read Appendix 2 of this book before proceeding further, as that will help provide a background as to the happenings around Malaysia's judiciary prior to and during Najib's trial.

The SRC International Sdn Bhd Case

Najib was slapped with three criminal breach of trust charges as a public servant and agent of the government, namely the prime minister, finance minister, and SRC International adviser emeritus, for misappropriating RM27 million and RM5 million in December 2014 and another RM10 million in February 2015. The funds were part of two loans from the Retirement Fund Incorporated or Kumpulan Wang Persaraan (Diperbadankan) (KWAP) and were loaned to SRC with a total worth of RM4 billion.[76]

He was also charged with one count of abuse of power as prime minister and finance minister, in using his position to commit bribery involving RM42 million through his participation

---

[76] Yatim, Hafiz, 'SRC Trial: Najib found guilty of all charges', *The Edge Malaysia Online*, accessed at: https://theedgemalaysia.com/article/src-trial-najib-found-guilty-all-charges.

or involvement in the decision to provide government guarantees for the KWAP loans to SRC.

I followed the rushed four-year saga of Najib's SRC trial—in comparison, Anwar's sodomy II trial took six and a half years—and believed in the independence and integrity of the Malaysian judiciary and in the honourable men and women who would interpret and deliver justice based on the laws of the land.

I was not surprised when Thomas appointed the late Gopal Sri Ram—yes, Mahathir's lawyer who had allegedly asked the then AG Apandi to arrest Najib—as the lead prosecutor in the case. But I was shocked that despite such a glaring conflict of interest, the courts refused to remove Gopal Sri Ram from leading the prosecution in the various cases against Najib, saying that there was no evidence to show Gopal Sri Ram was biased.[77] But as British Law Lord, Lord Hewart noted in 1924, 'Justice must not only be done, but must also be seen to be done.' Given the doubts cast on Sri Ram, wouldn't it have been prudent to have removed him from the case?

I was also taken aback when the Court of Appeals dismissed[78] new evidence allegedly showing that the husband of former Bank Negara Malaysia (BNM) Governor Zeti Akhtar Aziz, was allegedly in cahoots with Jho Low in the 1MDB scandal, a relationship the Malaysian Anti-Corruption Commission effectively confirmed in

[77] Anbalagan, V, 'Sri Ram can prosecute Najib's 1MDB audit report trial, says Federal Court', *Free Malaysia Today*, 7 Dec 2022, accessed at: https://www.freemalaysiatoday.com/category/nation/2022/12/07/sri-ram-can-prosecute-najibs-1mdb-audit-report-trial-says-federal-court/.

[78] Hamdan, Nurbaiti, 'Court of Appeal dismisses Najib's appeal for discovery of documents on Zeti's family, Jho Low', *The Star Online*, 8 Dec 2022, accessed at: https://www.thestar.com.my/news/nation/2022/12/08/court-of-appeal-dismisses-najib039s-appeal-for-discovery-of-documents-on-zetis-family-jho-low.

November 2021[79] when it said that as part of its recovery of 1MDB assets, Singaporean authorities had repatriated US$15.4 million to the Malaysian Government that had been seized from a company owned by Zeti's husband.[80]

Given Singapore's robust banking, investigative, and legal systems, I don't think they would have seized and repatriated funds if they did not have proof that it was related to funds siphoned from 1MDB.

Mind you, Zeti's reassurances was why Najib did not seem panicked when I spoke to him a day after the *Wall Street Journal* exposed the 1MDB scandal in 2015.[81]

As he told me then, he had been assured by Zeti that it was fine to open bank accounts in his own name and to have the US$643.41 million transferred in it. Yet, despite giving Najib these assurances back in 2012, Zeti then in 2018 publicly denied knowing anything about it. She said, 'In fact, on 3 July 2015, I was called to the Prime Minister's Office. He made a request for me to issue a statement that he had done nothing wrong in his account. I informed him that I cannot issue such a statement because I did not have knowledge of transactions that had occurred in his account.[82]'

Funnily enough, I believe the Malaysian Anti-Corruption Commission had investigated Zeti in 2018 and 2019 and had even submitted a report to the Attorney General's Chambers—the

---

[79] 'MACC confirms RM64.4mil recovered 1MDB funds held by Zeti's husband', Themole.my, 20 Nov 2021, accessed at: https://www.mole.my/macc-confirms-rm64-4mil-recovered-1mdb-funds-held-by-zetis-husband/.

[80] 'How much did Zeti know about husband's bank account in Singapore?' *The Edge Malaysia Online*, 8 Mar 2021, accessed at: https://theedgemalaysia.com/article/how-much-did-zeti-know-about-husbands-bank-account-singapore.

[81] Please read Chapter 5 of my book, *Final Reckoning*, for more details.

[82] 'Najib requested me to state he did nothing wrong, reveals Zeti on RM2.6b', *Malaysiakini*, 3 Jul 2018, accessed at: https://www.malaysiakini.com/news/432536.

guys who were already prosecuting Najib—showing that not only was Zeti fully aware of the money flowing into Najib's account but that her husband was allegedly hiding his and their children's ill-gotten gains in Singapore.[83]

Therefore, I believe Zeti had lied about the various 1MDB-linked fund transfers. Whether it was from 1MDB, KWAP, or SRC made no difference. If she lied about this, then one has to call into question BNM's involvement and awareness of the other fund transfers.

The biggest question that I thought the judges would be asking was, 'Why did Zeti not make Najib aware of any "suspicious" transactions?' I would think US$643.41 million would qualify as a suspicious transaction. I believed that they would also ask whether she was fully aware of these transactions but kept quiet because she knew her husband was being paid handsomely by Jho Low. Or was it because, when the scandal broke, she realized the only way to save herself was to deny any knowledge of the transactions?

I would have thought this would have been enough to instil doubt, leading the judges to see that Najib would have very likely been unaware of any impropriety in regard to the funds coming into his account—whether from SRC or not—as he relied on the promises of the then central bank governor, and other trusted advisers who we now know were also on Jho Low's payroll, whose duty was to warn him if anything improper had occurred, and who had now been shown to have lied about her knowledge and actions regarding the siphoned 1MDB-related funds.

A further shock came when the Federal Court said the Court of Appeal was correct in dismissing this new evidence. The Chief Justice laid down circumstances where further evidence could be adduced, namely that the evidence must not have been made

---

[83] 'MACC confirms RM64.4mil recovered 1MDB funds held by Zeti's husband', Themole.my, 20 Nov 2021, accessed at: https://www.mole.my/macc-confirms-rm64-4mil-recovered-1mdb-funds-held-by-zetis-husband/.

available during the trial proper, that it is relevant and credible, and that it would have raised reasonable doubt in the minds of the jury or trial judge in arriving at a decision for the case.

Okay, I am not a lawyer, I know, but isn't an alleged MACC report effectively proving that the head of Malaysia's financial regulator at the time of all these transactions—including that of the SRC funds—had lied about her involvement and knowledge of the transactions—and who knows what else?—would thus not be considered 'relevant and credible'? And would this not have raised a reasonable doubt in the mind of anyone as to whether there was a greater conspiracy linking the 1MDB and SRC charges against Najib?

And shouldn't the judges also have asked themselves why the prosecution—who I believe were made aware of the MACC report back in 2018 and 2019—did not make the report public, but rather chose to quietly drop Zeti as a prosecution witness without giving any explanation?

It was also bizarre when the Bar Council held a protest to condemn the MACC's investigation into the SRC International case trial Judge Mohamad Nazlan Mohamad Ghazali, following allegations of an unexplained sum of RM1 million in his bank account.

It was found out then that Nazlan had failed to disclose his role, involvement, or knowledge in the setting up of SRC International although he had served as the General Counsel and Company Secretary for the Maybank Group in 2006, which had set up SRC International.

In a summary of his High Court judgement, Nazlan allegedly stated that 'the approval for the establishment of SRC by the accused (Najib) provided the true starting point for the involvement of the accused in the company'.

However, anonymous whistle-blowers had sent Najib a cache of minutes of Maybank meetings and emails—that if proven authentic—could prove Nazlan not only served as the General

Counsel for Maybank but had also allegedly attended the meetings where the bank had recommended the setting up of SRC in the first place. As such, Nazlan was privy to matters which went to the heart of Najib's defence in the SRC trial.

Interestingly, some of the documents also indicated that the Malaysian Anti-Corruption Commission, during its investigations of Nazlan, had asked the judge about his involvement in the various Maybank meetings.

In his July 2022 affidavit to adduce the new evidence, Najib said he had been 'made to understand that when asked by the MACC officer of his (Nazlan's) knowledge and involvement, Justice Nazlan had initially denied having any knowledge . . . only after being confronted with email threads and documents by the MACC officers (did Nazlan admit) that he was indeed involved'.[84]

So, now, not only was there strong evidence that the then Governor of the central bank had allegedly lied about her involvement in the 1MDB linked funds transferred into Najib's accounts, but that the High Court judge who had convicted Najib on seven charges of abuse of power and misappropriation of RM42 million funds—belonging to SRC—had himself also allegedly been caught making untruthful and contradictory statements to investigators about his involvement in the setting up of SRC and the deliberations on a RM4.17 billion loan to 1MDB.

In 2018, the Bar Council had demanded that the initial SRC trial judge Mohd Sofian Abd Razak recuse himself as he was the younger brother of the Pahang State Executive Councillor and Benta UMNO State Assemblyperson—Mohd Soffi Abdul Razak. Bar President George Varughese said then that 'the rule of law

---

[84] Khairulrijal, Rahmat, 'Najib claims he had inside info on MACC probe on judge', *The New Straits Times Online*, 15 Jul 2022, accessed at: https://www.nst.com.my/news/crime-courts/2022/07/813606/najib-claims-he-had-inside-info-macc-probe-judge.

demands that justice must not only be done but it must manifestly be seen to be done'.[85]

However, when it was shown that the current SRC trial judge was intimately involved in the setting up of SRC and appeared to have been untruthful to investigators, what action did the Bar Council take?

It is convenient to say that one was not aware of the situation at the time of the trial, but now that you are aware of it, shouldn't you take action?

Shouldn't they be demanding a mistrial because the Bar Council believes that 'justice must not only be done but it must manifestly be seen to be done' in this instance as well? Or does this adage apply only when it is convenient for them?

But really, it was the Federal Court's decision on 16 August 2022 not to allow Najib's newly constituted legal team more time to go through the evidence and prepare for his case—despite just being handed all this new evidence to sift through and prepare—that really took the cake.

Here, there was potential evidence that the country's top financial regulator lied about her knowledge, role, and involvement in the 1MDB related funds that went into Najib's account, and there was also potential evidence that the trial judge who convicted Najib was allegedly caught being untruthful to investigators about his involvement in the very company that Najib was accused of stealing from.

And none of these details were provided to Najib—even though I believe the prosecution would have likely seen the MACC report on Zeti—and it was only because of anonymous whistle-blowers who wanted to see justice prevail that these documents had come to light. So far, no one has questioned or even impeached the authenticity or credibility of any of these

---

[85] 'Bar wants judge in Najib case to recuse himself', *Malaysiakini*, 5 Jul 2018, accessed at: https://www.malaysiakini.com/news/432898.

documents. And, still, Najib was refused a few weeks more to prepare for proper submissions before the Court?

I may not be a lawyer, but even I understand the concept of natural justice. This was not it.

So, it came as no surprise that the Federal Court found Najib guilty on 23 March 2022.

After rejecting evidence allegedly showing that the then head of the country's top financial regulator had allegedly lied about her knowledge of 1MDB/SRC international/KWAP linked-funds going into Najib's bank account and their refusal to give Najib's new defence team even a few weeks to prepare their case, it was not shocking that the Federal Court judges, led by the Chief Justice, then rejected Najib's application for a new trial or to admit new evidence that allegedly showed that not only had the judge who convicted Najib been found to have ben untruthful but was also heavily conflicted because of his involvement in the setting up of SRC International, the company from which Najib was alleged to have stolen money.

The Chief Justice, then, did not only disallow Najib's counsel to dismiss himself from the case—after having been denied more time to prepare new submissions—but insisted that he remain Najib's counsel on record so that the court could push through the appeal process, when in reality, it effectively left Najib without legal representation and meant that he would not be able to put forward his defence before the court.

And I suppose it was not surprising that a copy of the Federal Court's judgement affirming Najib's guilt had been leaked widely, hours before it was delivered in court.

A day later, the Federal Court's Registrar said the leaked copy was a working draft that had been doctored and it was 'a deliberate act to affect the operation of the court and the administration of justice'.[86]

---

[86] Achariam, Timothy, 'Federal Court chief registrar condemns leaked draft of Najib's judgement', *The Edge Malaysia Online*, 23 Aug 2022, accessed at: https:// theedgemalaysia.com/article/federal-court-chief-registrar-condemns-leaked-draft-najibs-judgement.

But what was surprising was the fact that the various international judicial and human rights organizations remained silent.

They were all fully aware of the new evidence Najib was attempting to introduce, which included an alleged twenty-six-page MACC report—that has now been leaked online—that showed SRC trial Judge Nazlan Ghazali had allegedly been untruthful about his involvement as Maybank's legal counsel in the setting up of SRC International and showed the judge's alleged conflict of interest in Najib's case.

A translation of the summary of the alleged leaked MACC report states:

4. (. . .) there is an offence under Section 220 of the Penal Code (para 2.1 and 2.2 in p/s 24).

5. This refers to the violation of judicial ethics, which YA Mohd Nazlan has violated if he did not declare his interest and role in this case before exercising his judicial functions and responsibilities (conflict of interests).

6. A judge must not only reduce the risk of judicial conflict but rather as that great maxim of the Judiciary states, 'Justice must not only be done, but must also be seen to be done'.[87]

Zaid Ibrahim, a former law minister (who had previously been one of Najib's political opponents), a founding partner of one of the country's most respected law firms, and recently one of Najib's lawyers, said, 'I have seen material and the papers to state categorically that the fresh evidence that he (Najib) was seeking to admit would have had a nuclear effect on the issue of Justice

---

[87] 'Penglibatan ya dato' mohd nazlan bin mohd ghazal! Dan yb tengku zafrul bin tengku abdul aziz dalam meluluskan dan melakukan rasuah berjumlah rm6.17 billion terhadap urus niaga pengambilan ekuiti penuh tanjung energy holding s/b oleh lmdb energy', MACC Investigation Report, Jun 2022, p. 26.

Nazlan Ghazali's conflict of interest and apparent bias in being the Trial Judge and passing Judgment and sentence on Dato' Sri Najib.

'It is beyond belief that the highest Court in the land would deny Dato' Sri Najib the right to adduce relevant material and necessary evidence to ensure that the truth is established and justice is done. The application was to show how manifestly egregious was the conflict of interest on the part of Justice Nazlan,' he added.[88]

Idrus Harun, the Attorney General at that time, was unable to verify the authenticity of the leaked MACC report and claimed the MACC papers were not with the Attorney General's Chambers even though he told the media in May 2022 that the AGC was in the midst of examining the MACC papers before taking their decision.

As Zaid noted, 'It falls on MACC now to confirm or deny the authenticity of the (leaked documents). It also falls on the Attorney General to speak the truth, the whole truth, and nothing but the truth. Silence is no longer an option and will lead to a travesty of justice. I call on the Attorney General's Chambers and the Malaysian Anti-Corruption Commission to come forward with the truth once and for all. I am also keen to know what the great defender of justice, the Bar Council, will say to this.'

On 23 February 2023, Minister in the Prime Minister's Department (Law and Institutional Reform) Azalina Othman Said noted that the MACC, which had begun investigations against Nazlan in April 2022, had submitted a report against Nazlan on

---

[88] 'Press Statement by Datuk Zaid Ibrahim', MalaysiaToday.com, 19 Aug 2022, accessed at: https://www.malaysia-today.net/2022/08/19/press-statement-by-datuk-zaid-ibrahim/.

21 February 2023 to the Chief Justice, in relation to violations under the Judges' Code of Ethics 2009.[89]

On 24 February 2023, just three days after the MACC report was submitted, Chief Justice Tengku Maimun ruled that the MACC's investigation into Nazlan was done 'without following protocol',[90] when ruling on a suit brought about by three lawyers to challenge the investigation by MACC into claims of an unexplained sum of more than RM1 million in Nazlan's bank account.

Many in legal circles questioned why lawyers Haris Ibrahim, Nur Ain Mustapa, and Sreekant Pillai brought the lawsuit in the first place, when it ought to have been instituted by the Attorney General in his constitutional position of being the guardian of public interest.

What *locus standi* did the three lawyers have in the matter? And does this mean that anyone can now bring lawsuits, frivolous or otherwise, against the Malaysian Government claiming public interest? Isn't that the remit of the Attorney General?

Thus, was it an orchestrated move to try to derail the MACC investigations?

Tengku Maimun was quoted as saying that, 'investigative bodies like MACC must consult the Chief Justice before (initiating) the probe. Their failure to inform shows that there was a lack of bona fide on their part'.[91]

'The announcement (made by MACC through the media) is enough to damage the judicial institution,' she added.

---

[89] 'Azalina: MACC submits probe report on judge Nazlan to CJ', *Malaysiakini*, 23 Feb 2023, accessed at: https://www.malaysiakini.com/news/656202.

[90] Ho, Kit Yen, 'MACC's probe against Nazlan didn't follow protocol, says apex court', *Free Malaysia Today*, 23 Feb 2023, accessed at: https://www.freemalaysiatoday.com/category/nation/2023/02/24/maccs-probe-against-nazlan-didnt-follow-protocol-says-apex-court/.

[91] Ibid.

'Investigative bodies cannot publicize an investigation against a superior court judge of their own accord without the Chief Justice's approval.'

Tengku Maimun also ruled that the public prosecutor must also consult the Chief Justice 'during the course of giving instructions for investigations and in respect of his decision to prosecute'.

'While investigative bodies are constitutionally entitled to investigate, and the public prosecutor has the discretion whether to charge or otherwise, these powers must be exercised in good faith,' she said.

'If the investigation is done for collateral purpose, then it is liable to be set aside.'[92]

Once again, I am not a lawyer, but as an educated person, I am very unclear as to what this 'protocol' is, and where it is to be found in the Federal Constitution, MACC Act, or any other Malaysian law.

Secondly, where in the Federal Constitution, MACC Act, Criminal Procedure Code, Penal Code or otherwise, does it say that the Public Prosecutor must also consult the Chief Justice during the course of giving instructions for investigations or in respect of his decision to prosecute a superior court judge?

And where does it say in the MACC Act or any other Malaysian law that investigative bodies like the MACC must consult the Chief Justice before initiating a probe?

How does this show a lack of being bona fide when the agency is just doing its job?

And does the ruling on a violation of protocol—which appears to be unwritten and is not a violation of any law—take away from the proven facts of the investigation and recommendations made in the report?

More importantly, as the MACC has filed a report against a Superior Court judge with the Chief Justice, why has no

---

[92] Ibid.

tribunal—as outlined under the law—been set up to investigate and submit its recommendations on Nazlan?

The MACC has retracted neither its media statement nor its report against Nazlan.

The International Petroleum Investment Company (IPIC) Case

In October 2018, Najib and Irwan were jointly charged with six counts of misappropriating RM6.6 billion in public funds involving payments to Abu Dhabi's state-owned oil firm IPIC.

Thereon followed numerous trial management meetings and postponements of the trial, so much so that in March 2022, four years after the two were charged, the trial had yet to begin. Lawyers representing the two applied to the court for a Discharge Not Amounting to an Acquittal (DNAA) given the unexplained delays, but the judge dismissed it on the grounds that the Attorney General's Chambers (AGC) was ready for the trial.[93]

However, it was only in September 2023 that it became clear why the AGC had yet to proceed with the trial.

A leaked September 2019 internal AGC memo[94] from the head of the AGC's IPIC Prosecution Team Jamil Aripin to the-then Attorney General Tommy Thomas noted that:[95]

---

[93] *Bernama*, 'Court dismisses application by Najib, Mohd Irwan for DNAA', TheMalaysianReserve.com, 3 Mar 2022, accessed at: https://themalaysianreserve.com/2022/03/03/court-dismisses-application-by-najib-mohd-irwan-for-dnaa/.

[94] Khairulrijal, Rahmat, 'AGC declines to comment: 12-pg leaked memo of evidence against Najib, Irwan CBT 'grossly insufficient' heard in court', *The New Straits Times Online*, 15 Sep 2023, accessed at: https://www.nst.com.my/news/crime-courts/2023/09/955581/agc-declines-comment-12-pg-leaked-memo-evidence-against-najib-irwan.

[95] 'In the Kuala Lumpur High Court Case no: WA45-10-12/2018, Public Prosecutor v 1. Mohd Najib bin Abdul Razak, 2. Mohd Irwan Serigar bin Abdullah,' Internal memo Attorney General's Chambers, From: Datuk Jamil

The consent to charge was signed and issued by YBhg. Tan Sri (Thomas) under Section 58 of MACC Act 2009 on 23 October 2018 (Appendix S). There were 5 Investigation Papers (IPs) given to the team. We note that in the IPs that the investigation was carried out under Section 23 of the MACC Act 2009. It appears that there was no thorough study made as there were only 2 minutes in the IPs before both accused persons were charged. On top of that, there was not even a minute in the IPs on the direction or instruction to charge contrary to the standard practice of good prosecution.

. . . Moreover, based on the explanation given by the Investigation Officers (IOs) from the Malaysian Anti-Corruption Commission (MACC), the IPs were originally opened for investigation for an offence of gratification or abuse of power under section 23 of MACC Act 2009. In other words, there was no proper consideration and evaluation to gather the evidence of an offence under Section 409 of Penal Code as in the present charges.

On 8 April 2019, during a meeting between the YBhg. Tan Sri AG (Thomas) and the Deputy Public Prosecutors related to 1 MDB-related cases, the IPIC team leader had raised the views of Cik Normazli Abdul Rahim, the Treasury Solicitor (TS) of the Ministry of Finance, (noting) that (despite what Normazli had claimed) the six charges could not stand.

YBhg. Tan Sri AG's response was that 'why are we charging then?' The reply by Tn. Kamal Baharin Omar, MACC's Deputy Head of Legal and Prosecution was that **the decision to charge was solely based on the TS's (Normazli's) recorded statement** at that material time. However, based on our study on the TS (Normazli's) statement and three interviews as well as documents, it does not support the six charges.

---

bin Aripin, Head of IPIC Prosecution Team, To: YBhg. Tan Sri Tommy Thomas Attorney General, 10 Sep 2019, pp. 1–4.

... Based on the team's study on the Investigation Papers, statement of witnesses and the interviews in particular with the present TS and former TS (To'.Puan Azian binti Mohd Aziz), the team (seven DPPs and five IOs) are unanimous in taking the stand that the six charges are **non-starters as it does not meet the minimum requirement or threshold for CBT charges to be brought to Court and to secure a prima facie case against Najib and Irwan.**

... Based on the perusal of 138 witness statements, there **is no statement at all** favourable to the Prosecution's case.

The memo then goes on to list the weaknesses in all six charges with Aripin concluding that he and his team were of 'the considered view that based on maximum evaluation of available evidence, there(sic) are grossly insufficient to prove not even a prima facie case for the six charges, let alone to secure a conviction beyond reasonable doubt'.[96]

So, despite realizing a year after filing such serious charges against Najib and Irwan that the prosecution had no case whatsoever against the two, Thomas allowed the Attorney General's Chambers to continue to prosecute the case for another four years.

And given that the charges were a 'non-starter', it was of no surprise that the prosecution kept dragging its feet for so long.

As the famous human rights leader Dr Martin Luther King Jr. wrote in a letter from his Birmingham jail in 1963: 'Justice too long delayed is justice denied.'[97]

The current Attorney General's chambers have said they are investigating the matter but have stopped short of confirming

---

[96] Ibid., p. 12.

[97] Maxena, Jeannetta, 'Justice Too Long Delayed Is Justice Denied', ICMA website, 24 Feb 2023, accessed at: https://icma.org/blog-posts/justice-too-long-delayed-justice-denied.

the memo's authenticity, with Deputy Premier Zahid Hamidi urging the current Attorney General to drop the charges if the memo is real.[98]

Given the shenanigans in two of the most important cases filed against Najib, one must question whether Najib has received justice or was he the victim of political persecution from the highest levels of the PH1.0 Government?

---

[98] Fadli, Mohamad, 'Drop Najib's IPIC charges if "leaked" memo is real, Zahid tells AGC', *Free Malaysia Today*, 28 Aug 2023, accessed at: https://www.freemalaysiatoday.com/category/nation/2023/08/28/drop-najibs-charges-if-leaked-memo-is-genuine-zahid-tells-agc/.

Chapter 5

Dark Days Part II: So, What Do We Do With UMNO?

Now that his plan to dispose of the United Malays National Organization's (UMNO's) key leaders was underway, Mahathir had to figure out what to do with the party that he had helmed for twenty-two years but which had turned its back on him in 2016.

Mahathir wanted revenge on UMNO and its leaders, but he also knew that he needed UMNO's support base, as well as its rank, as he did not command majority support within the PH1.0 coalition or in the country. In May 2018, that support belonged to the Democratic Action Party (DAP), Parti Keadilan Rakyat (PKR), Heritage Party (Warisan), and the various other smaller component parties in PH1.0. So Mahathir had to counter DAP and PKR's control over the PH1.0 coalition, in which his party was only a minority partner.

Mahathir also most definitely did not trust Anwar, whose control over the electorate he knew he had to remove, if his fledgling Malaysian United Indigenous Party (BERSATU) party had any hopes of surviving beyond Mahathir's second tenure as prime minister.

Following GE14, UMNO was in turmoil, to say the least. With massive defections of lawmakers to PH1.0 that left the party rudderless, given its unpreparedness for life on the Opposition benches, it fell upon Zahid Hamidi, as the party's new president, and Mohamad Hasan (Tok Mat) as his deputy, to stanch the bleeding of its MPs and to help turn the party around.

Zahid had to figure out a plan of action that would lead UMNO/BN back to the path of power but that was not an easy task given that the party and coalition had lost the confidence of a significant majority of Malaysians.

Regardless, analysis of the results showed that vast swathes of the Malay heartland still remained with UMNO but that it had lost much support to Parti Islam Se-Malaysia (PAS) and BERSATU. As such, UMNO could see a way back to power if it was able to work a deal with PAS and then BERSATU. After all, relations between PAS and UMNO had been warming up for some time following Najib's implementation of the 'PAS Move' in 2014 to find common ground between both parties, and if UMNO had done a deal with PAS prior to GE14, UMNO would have, in all likelihood, still been in power.

Now, what was needed was a uniting of the Ummah, because with UMNO, PAS, and BERSATU working together for Malay unity, they could easily outmanoeuvre DAP and PKR. But in order to get BERSATU onboard, Zahid knew he would have to deal with Mahathir, who appeared more in the mood to destroy UMNO than save it.

So, a secret meeting was arranged on 14 September 2018, between Mahathir, Zahid, Tok Mat, and the three UMNO VPs. Zahid was hoping to convince Mahathir of the need for the pact, but Mahathir was in no mood to listen.

The problem was that Zahid had a chequered history with Mahathir. In the 1990s, Zahid was a firebrand leader of UMNO Youth, when Anwar Ibrahim was the party's Deputy President and the country's Deputy Premier. Zahid was never liked by Mahathir and was not favoured to win in the UMNO Youth chief elections. But win he did, much to Mahathir's displeasure.

Following Mahathir's expelling of Anwar from UMNO on 1 September 1998 and his sacking from the Cabinet the following day, Zahid, who was closely aligned to Anwar, helped organize and lead street demonstrations in the capital to protest Anwar's removal.

A day after Anwar's 20 September 1998 detention under the draconian Internal Security Act (ISA), which allowed for indefinite detention without trial, Zahid was also arrested under Section 73(1) of the ISA for causing a threat to national security. While under detention, Zahid was forced to resign as head of UMNO Youth and was released nine days later into political wilderness.

Shunned by large sections of the party, Zahid worked his way back up through UMNO and was eventually elected to the party's supreme council in 2000, but only became a cabinet minister in 2004, after Mahathir had retired and his chosen successor, the then Prime Minister Ahmad Abdullah Badawi took over. Zahid became deputy prime minister and UMNO deputy president in 2015, following the then Prime Minister Najib's removal of Muhyiddin, and took over as UMNO President on 11 May 2018, following the disastrous GE14 results for BN and UMNO.

So, it was not surprising that witnesses said Mahathir greeted the delegation very coldly and looked disinterested as Zahid began speaking.

Zahid explained his proposal to get the three parties to work together so as to put aside the various political differences among the Malay parties and thus strengthen the position of the Malays, which he said, was now severely weakened in terms of political power, what with the non-Malays seen as having the upper hand and the power to have a greater say in shaping the government's agenda and the country.

But Mahathir appeared thoroughly incensed with Zahid proposal. Aides said they had never seen Mahathir so angry before, as he blew up at Zahid and the rest of the UMNO delegation. It was 'as if Mahathir was a father or still UMNO President as he

was was livid and scolded them throughout the entire meeting'
said one source.[99]

In a forty-five-minute tirade, Mahathir dressed them down
for siding with Najib and for 'destroying UMNO and for bringing
ruin to the Malays' in what they did. He called them 'stupid' and
'*bangang*'[100] for firstly having lost the support of the Malays so
badly that it ruined the country and secondly for coming up with
this proposal as if the slate could be wiped clean just for the sake
of Malay unity.

Mahathir said that there was no way BERSATU or the PH1.0
coalition would accept this 'ridiculous' proposal even though it
had the support of all UMNO and PAS MPs.

Mahathir called UMNO '*busuk*' and '*jijik*',[101] saying that he
would never accept UMNO ever again in its current form or as a
partner in any way.

The BERSATU President said that the only way forward
would be for everyone in UMNO to join BERSATU as ordinary
members first.

But before that, Mahathir said that the entire UMNO
leadership had to declare their assets and allow MACC to carry
out full-fledged investigations into their wealth and assets.
Mahathir said that only if nothing was found would they qualify
to join BERSATU.

The group then discussed the upcoming Port Dickson
by-elections—which Anwar was contesting so that he could be
a MP and as such be eligible to be elected as prime minister—
and it was clear from Mahathir's reaction to all those present in
the room that he didn't want Anwar to win the by-election as
Mahathir privately could not accept Anwar becoming the next

---

[99]   Source interview, Putrajaya, Oct 2018.

[100] Malay for 'stupid'.

[101] Malay for 'foul' and 'disgusting' respectively.

prime minister, although he had publicly voiced his support for Anwar.

Following the meeting, Mahathir told his aides that Tok Mat should consider running against Anwar in Port Dickson and win against Anwar as there was a need to try and stop Anwar from becoming prime minister.

However, it was clear from the discussions on the by-elections that Tok Mat was fearful of contesting as he was afraid that former Federal Land Development Authority (FELDA) chief and UMNO warlord Isa Samad would try and sabotage his campaign.

Mahathir viewed Zahid's attendance of PAS' Muktamar a month before as a bid by UMNO to try build support and get greater leverage against Mahathir by building a coalition of all those opposed to Mahathir. However, Mahathir didn't believe that this would be effective as none of the parties had enough money to launch a proper offensive against Mahathir.

But more importantly, Mahathir was of the view that UMNO and PAS were likely to become irrelevant soon enough, with many of their members and leadership likely to defect to BERSATU or AMANAH in the coming weeks and months.[102]

And Mahathir planned to ensure that the defections happened through a secret, high-level operation being run by Muhyiddin and Zainuddin Hamzah—a former UMNO cabinet minister who had defected to BERSATU following GE14—known as Project Hijrah.

By November 2018, a roadmap of how this would happen was drafted. The idea was for Mahathir to encourage the mass exodus of UMNO MPs as well as senior leaders, beginning in January 2019, although it would not be done in one fell swoop.

The plan called for the leaving UMNO announcements for small groups of MPs to happen fortnightly, with press

---

[102] Ibid.

conferences of UMNO MPs who were jumpingship taking place every other week.

Mahathir had a team of people 'marking' UMNO MPs who were 'qualified' to join BERSATU, and they were busy scanning the background of these potential recruits. Once these lawmakers were determined to be 'clean', Mahathir would approach them and get their commitment to switch. He would then set a timetable and schedule when each MP or leader would jumpship, with the frequency and number gradually increasing until UMNO imploded.

However, the major problem that Mahathir's team faced was the fact that a majority of these UMNO MPs and leaders did not qualify to join BERSATU because they had been tainted by allegations of scandal and corruption and had to be cleared of this perception in order for them to join BERSATU.

So, in reality, even though Mahathir said he would not take any tainted UMNO members, realpolitik would force him to accept many such allegedly tainted individuals if he had any hopes of significantly increasing the number of BERSATU lawmakers in the parliament.

As a result, the team had to find ways and means to work around the fact that a large number of these MPs were tainted and to see what could be done so that they could be brought over to BERSATU without its PH1.0 coalition partners and the public objecting to it.

Mahathir's plan was to de-register UMNO as soon as possible so that its MPs would have no choice but to join BERSATU or face life in the political wilderness.

However, Zahid was a survivor. And he and the rest of the UMNO leadership would not take this lying down. The fledgling UMNO president knew he needed to get his party and coalition back into power and this was something he was totally focused on. And then the opportunity struck. And it would eventually culminate in what most people now know as the 'Sheraton Move'.

Chapter 6

Race Politics and Black Shoes

The problem with Mahathir's racist policies and a Malay supremacist-based ideology was the simple fact that often, high calibre and talented non-Malays were ignored and bypassed in favour of mediocre choices, which ended up proving why such blunt discriminatory policies did not work. And this was shown to a large extent in not only how Mahathir and his ministers made political appointments but in how these appointees then carried out their duties.

A prime example was Muhyiddin Yassin, who, as president of Mahathir's BERSATU party, had been appointed Home Minister following PH1.0's win at GE14. Even as a former Deputy Premier in Najib's administration, Muhyiddin's credentials as an ultra-Malay were well-known, especially when in 2010, he claimed he was 'Malay first', rather than, 'Malaysian first'.[103]

Within weeks of taking over the ministry, senior party members within BERSATU were alarmed at the way their members, who Muhyiddin had handpicked and appointed to key posts in the home ministry, were behaving.

A then BERSATU Supreme Council member noted that the overwhelming majority of senior officers in the minister's

---

[103] 'Muhyiddin: I'm Malay first', Youtube.com, 31 Mar 2010, accessed at: https://www.youtube.com/watch?v=_rxiJSs7aYE.

(Muhyiddin's) office were political appointees from BERSATU with almost no civil servants in the office.

And none of these officers understood their job scope, nor did they know the practices and administrative policies of the ministry as most of these officers were too busy engaging in their own political agendas instead of running the ministry.

The officers spent most of their time trying to get government contracts and cutting deals. As such, the office was very empty as these officers were always going out instead of doing the needed political work in the office.

And the remaining civil servants felt disrespected by the minister's political appointees because they were continually bossing the civil servants around and always 'looking for ways to abuse their position'.[104] Some of these officers even tried to claim political work expenses from the ministry.

One of the reasons for this was the fact that most of these officers had no professional working experience as they were junior party members, many were unemployed and often randomly picked from among the party membership.

Although there were a lot of vacancies within the minister's office, Muhyiddin's political secretary preferred to hire people from within BERSATU, instead of looking for experienced and professional individuals outside. As a result, the office climate was very political and cold, as these BERSATU officers felt insecure and were easily agitated and downright hostile to any party outsiders who were hired, especially anyone with skills and a background for the job; the political appointees felt threatened by anyone better qualified than them.

A similar lack of experience also affected Youth and Sports Minister Syed Saddiq's political appointees in his ministry.

104 Interview with former BERSATU Supreme Council member, 10 Apr 2022, London, UK.

The problem with Syed Saddiq, according to some of his aides, was that he appeared indecisive because he was trying to appease everyone, but in the end, satisfied no one.

Syed Saddiq's office was filled with appointees mostly in their twenties and early thirties. It was also very different from other ministries in terms of hierarchy, as Saddiq had a political Secretary and a chief of staff who reported to him, and below them were ten other staffers who were all of equal rank, which meant that Syed Saddiq's office had a very flat structure.

Syed Saddiq also had no idea on how to deal with warlord civil servants within his ministry. Most of Saddiq's team were below thirty years of age and were completely green, while the other ministry officials were in their forties and fifties and had vast experience on how to deal with government issues and knew how to make life difficult for their political masters, while still being able to get whatever they wanted for their departments or agencies.

BERSATU's leadership was fully aware that unlike UMNO, there were very few professionals and experts within the party. Half of the youths in the party were in their late twenties or early thirties and out of this group, around 60 to 70 per cent had educational qualifications up to only SPM (GCSE) level. There were very few lawyers, doctors, corporate professionals, and high-ranking civil servants within BERSATU.

This was why BERSATU's Negri Sembilan Division had to be disbanded and reformed, as the previous division was constituted wrongly and many of those in the division were allegedly involved in money politics and other shady activities.

Another serious challenge was the fight for power between the old (pre-GE14) and new (post GE14) party members. The old members were strongly resisting letting better educated professionals join the party, a similar problem to what UMNO had faced when the party was in power.

The irony was that many of the old BERSATU members were actually UMNO rejects and shared much of the old and discarded mentality of trying to deter the educated and professionals from joining the party.[105]

As a result, it was impossible for the party to rely on its youth wing, ARMADA, or even the regular membership to help fill up positions within the government, as most of their members really had no idea, experience, or qualifications to hold such posts.

This was a big headache for BERSATU's leaders because if the party could not fill the posts with their members, the slots would then be taken up by PKR, DAP, and AMANAH, which meant that BERSATU would have much fewer of their people in government compared to the rest of the PH1.0 coalition.

Syed Saddiq had received a lot of good ideas and policies that needed to be implemented but there was nobody who was qualified enough or had sufficient experience to help execute these ideas and policies. Syed Saddiq openly admitted to close coalition colleagues that there was an urgent need to get smarter members as they had to guarantee that BERSATU would survive post-Mahathir.[106]

In their twenty-two months in power, they found no solution to this problem, although some ministers tried to come up with plans to run things in their ministry despite the large vacuum of talent, as the party was urged to head-hunt young professionals to join the party and the ministry. It remains a major issue for BERSATU even today.

However, one of the rare professionals that Mahathir did bring into the party and government was Maszlee Malik.

Reviews remain mixed over what Maszlee actually achieved in his term as Education Minister, as some claim he did not necessarily represent the best and the brightest of Malays.

Maybe this was because Maszlee was never Mahathir's first choice.

[105] Zoom interview with BERSATU leader 7, 10 Feb 2021.

[106] Zoom interview with BERSATU leader 5, 12 Sep 2020.

The reality was that Mahathir wanted to be Education Minister himself and had appointed himself as such. However, after a major outcry that PH1.0's manifesto pledged that its prime minister would hold no other cabinet portfolio, Mahathir, a day later, handed the Education Ministry to Maszlee, who was surprised by the appointment.[107]

Before entering politics, Maszlee was a lecturer at the International Islamic University of Malaysia. During his tenure, he held several administrative posts, including the Dean of the Kulliyyah of Islamic Revealed Knowledge and Human Sciences in 2012 and the Deputy Rector II in 2013. However, he had neither held a top leadership position in the university, nor had he any experience in managing anything more than a small faculty of staff.

And, to top it all off, he had joined BERSATU barely two months earlier.

Given his lack of experience and the dearth of skills and political acumen needed to run the education ministry, it appeared that it was to be a train wreck in the making, and no one, not even Mahathir, could stop it.

To be fair, Maszlee did implement reforms to the education system, such as introducing the Integrated Islamic Education Syllabus or KIKMAS, providing additional funds for special education, and pushing for the teaching of science and mathematics in English as well as working to decrease the overall cost of education for parents by introducing a new pricing scheme for college fees.

But his 20 July 2018 instruction that all public-school students would have to now change the colour of their shoes from white

---

[107] Adnan, Ahmad Suhael, 'Maszlee surprised by his appointment as Education Minister', *New Straits Times Online*, 18 May 2018, accessed at: https://www.nst.com.my/news/government-public-policy/2018/05/370857/maszlee-surprised-his-appointment-education-minister.

to black is what most people remember, and it was the start of some very controversial decision-making that would ultimately lead to his removal in January 2020, just weeks before Mahathir caused the implosion of the PH1.0 government.

Another major controversy was Maszlee's decision in September 2018 to accept the post of President of International Islamic University of Malaysia, despite being a politician and Education Minister, claiming that the appointment did not violate the Universities and University Colleges Act 1971.

Mahathir, who had kept quiet so far, was livid at Maszlee's actions and had called him to the Prime Minister's Office to tell him to resign the presidency.

But Maszlee chose to ignore him.

By November, Maszlee had still not resigned, and BERSATU party president Muhyiddin then ordered Maszlee in no uncertain terms to relinquish the post.

However, Maszlee held on till 6 January 2019 before stepping down.

The myriad of controversies and scandals that engulfed Maszlee and his ministry have been well covered in other books, including Maszlee's own book, so I won't delve into them except to note that the final straw came when Maszlee decided to introduce Khat or Jawi calligraphy to Year 4 pupils in all schools. Although it was only a minor change in the curriculum of ten-year-olds where Khat would be introduced to students four times a year for ten minutes each time within the Bahasa Melayu syllabus, critics, especially from the Chinese educationist group Dong Jiao Zong, expressed fears of a 'creeping Islamization' in vernacular schools. A week later, Maszlee noted that the Jawi lessons would be optional for vernacular schools but that the policy would still continue despite the massive outcry against it and the cabinet's decision to scrap it.

So, in December 2019, Mahathir sent a secret seventeen-paragraph letter to Maszlee, who was holidaying with his family in the US at the time, outlining Maszlee's failure to heed Cabinet instructions and telling him, 'it is now time for Yang Berhormat (Maszlee) to withdraw from the cabinet'.[108]

The first issue mentioned in the letter was the Jawi issue. Mahathir had taken exception to Maszlee's failure in abiding by the Cabinet's decision that the government would stop all moves on implementing Jawi, and Maszlee's continued insistence on pushing for it.

The second issue was the Free Breakfast policy. Mahathir noted that Maszlee had unilaterally made the August 2019 announcement without the Cabinet's final approval and that, there had never been any funding from the Finance Ministry made for the policy, which the government was then forced to publicly and embarrassingly backtrack on.

And despite advice from Mahathir and the Cabinet, Maszlee also did not want to split the education and higher education portfolios.

However, the most controversial part of the letter was on the 1BestariNet programme being run by telecommunications giant YTL, whose contract Maszlee refused to extend upon its expiry in June 2019.

The RM4.077 billion, seventeen-year mega project was initiated in 2011 when Muhyiddin was Education Minister and was designed to provide 4G Internet connectivity and a learning platform for teachers, students, and parents for 9,924 schools nationwide. But it was often criticized for poor internet service. This was happening amid allegations of kickbacks and corruption involving Muhyiddin's son-in-law.[109]

YTL founder and business tycoon Francis Yeoh had been closely linked to Mahathir for decades and Maszlee's decision to terminate

---

[108] 'Maszlee told to quit for failing to heed cabinet orders, PM's letter shows', The Malaysian Insight, 5 Jan 2020, accessed at: https://www.themalaysianinsight. com/s/210117.

[109] '1BestariNet: When Will Muhyiddin Be Investigated?', Seademon Says (Blog), 4 Oct 2016, accessed at: https://seademon.me/2016/10/04/1bestarinet-when-will-muhyiddin-be-investigated/.

the agreement appeared to be a slap in the face of Mahathir, especially since Mahathir had asked Maszlee to continue with the contract.

As Mahathir wrote, 'YB *tidak meneruskan kontrak 1Bestari Net YTL seperti mana yang telah saya nasihatkan*'—letting the public know that Maszlee did not proceed with the 1Bestari Net YTL contract as he had advised.[110]

In his 2022 book, *Memori Bukan Memoir*, Maszlee claimed the decision not to extend YTL's contract was purely a professional one, based on the project not meeting its objectives and performance indicators.

But that, Maszlee claimed, became one of the main reasons why Mahathir wanted him to resign, amid pressure from Muhyiddin as well. 'In my last meeting with Mahathir, I can still remember, he said, "The Bersatu president is very angry with you because of this issue."'[111]

The fact that Mahathir wrote a letter so explicitly stating that he wanted the YTL contract continued, especially since he and Muhyiddin had allegedly been enjoying numerous privileges and perks from Yeoh, was worrying.

It leads one to question whether Maszlee's dismissal was not only due to his missteps but more because a crony businessman—who was an alleged source of funding—had been hit badly?

Racial Narratives

Another issue with playing race politics is the fact that it can easily become a Frankenstein's monster and one can easily lose control of the narrative.

---

[110] Letter to Maszlee Malik, Education Minister, from Prime Minister Mahathir Mohamad, 27 Dec 2019.

[111] Ariff, Imran, 'Investigate the RM3 billion spent on 1BestariNet, says BN man', *Free Malaysia Today*, accessed at: https://www.freemalaysiatoday.com/category/nation/2021/09/06/investigate-the-rm3-billion-spent-on-1bestarinet-says-bn-man/.

For years, Mahathir had condemned the DAP as a Chinese chauvinist party and equated its actions with those of the Chinese attempting to seize greater power and control of the country at the expense of the Malays. That was the narrative Mahathir had drummed into UMNO and its BN coalition partners, so much so that there was an embedded visceral fear among heartland Malays of the DAP and it's supposed agenda to take over Malaysia.

However, Mahathir was forced to revise this narrative— although deep down he still believed it—once he had to partner and work with the DAP in order to get back into power.

After twenty-two years in power and thirteen years in retirement, during which he still continued to tout this anti-DAP narrative, it suddenly changed overnight to one where Mahathir recognized the contributions of the Chinese and their role in Malaysia's progress and endorsed the DAP as a multiracial party working towards a better Malaysia for all.

Although Mahathir could seemingly change his view of the DAP and Chinese overnight, it was a much harder proposition for Malay voters in the kampungs and towns across the country, who had been indoctrinated for decades with Mahathir's vile and bitter polemic against the DAP.

So, it came as no surprise then that UMNO and PAS, after being scolded and rebuffed by Mahathir, formed an alliance of their own in late 2018, based on Malay unity and began to portray Mahathir's new PH1.0 administration as one where the DAP was controlling the government and calling the shots in Putrajaya.

They were then able to sow worry in the minds of many Malay voters as they factually pointed out that the DAP was responsible for putting non-Malays into positions of power; the Attorney General Tommy Thomas; the Chief Justice Richard Malanjun; and the de facto Law Minister V.K. Liew. In any other country, this would be viewed as nothing unusual. But viewing it through the narrow racial lens of Mahathir's own creation meant this was now evidence of a potential takeover by non-Malays.

As PAS information chief Nasrudin Hassan Tantawi told voters, 'We are doubtful about the legal system and the judiciary which is not under the control of Muslims . . . When we raise this issue, they (DAP) say we are racist but they have grabbed these three positions and have not given anything to Muslims.'[112]

The messaging was strong and clear. PH appointments posed a direct threat to the Malay race and Islam and that the Malays were in danger of being overwhelmed by the non-Malays. This was race-baiting at its worst, but it was also a very effective way to attack Mahathir and PH1.0. And Mahathir would finally realize how dangerous a weapon this was.

International Convention for the Elimination of All Forms of Racial Discrimination (ICERD)

On 28 September 2018, when delivering his Head of State address at the United Nations General Assembly, Mahathir proudly announced to the world that 'the new Malaysia will firmly espouse the principles promoted by the UN in our international engagements. These include the principles of truth, human rights, the rule of law, justice, fairness, responsibility and accountability, as well as sustainability' and so he 'pledged to ratify all remaining core UN instruments related to the protection of human rights'. And the most notable of these was the International Convention for the Elimination of All Forms of Racial Discrimination (ICERD), which committed state parties to eliminate all forms of racial discrimination and to promote understanding among all races.

UMNO and PAS pounced on this.

---

[112] Achariam, Noel, 'PAS, Umno Youth blame DAP for putting non-Malays in positions of power', *The Malaysian Insight*, 26 Feb 2019, accessed at: https://www.themalaysianinsight.com/index.php/s/136102.

They claimed that the ratification was proof that PH1.0 was conspiring to erode the Malay's 'special position' as enshrined in Article 153 of the Federal Constitution that allowed for affirmative action and quotas for, among others, positions in the public service and permits for businesses as well as scholarships. UMNO and PAS kept stoking the issue and then capitalized on the uproar by announcing plans for a mammoth anti-ICERD demonstration on 8 December 2018.

However, in the face of such vocal opposition, Mahathir, in a statement in late November 2018, said that the government had decided not to ratify ICERD. Without giving a reason, the statement noted that 'the government will continue to uphold the Federal Constitution, which enshrines the social contract agreed to by representatives of all races'.[113]

But the statement had little impact on the anti-ICERD secretariat's plans to go ahead with the 8 December *Himpunan Aman Rakyat Tolak ICERD* at Dataran Merdeka.

The movement behind the protest was led by Gerakan Pembela Ummah (UMMAH), Sekretariat Kedaulatan Negara (DAULAT), and Malay Muslim NGOs while Pemuda UMNO and Pemuda PAS would run the anti-ICERD secretariat. It was a group filled with ultra and right-wing Malays whose racial views were directly shaped and in line with Mahathir's personal beliefs.

The reason UMNO, and to a lesser extent PAS, proceeded with the gathering was because they were confident of getting a mammoth turnout, especially from heartland Malay voters.

But for the race-based groups and NGOs organizing the rally, the demonstration had become a warning to the PH1.0 government to deliver on their promise not to ratify ICERD.

---

[113] Syed Jaafar, Syahirah, 'ICERD ratification should be revisited by new govt, say political analysts', *The Edge Malaysia*, 18 Nov 2020, accessed at: https://theedgemalaysia.com/article/icerd-ratification-should-be-revisited-new-govt-say-political-analysts.

This tied in well with conspiracy theories and rumours on the ground that non-Malay Ministers and lawmakers along with their communities were still pushing for the government to ratify the ICERD immediately.

The gathering on 8 December 2018, these groups claimed, was also to prevent the PH1.0 Government from continuing with their 'hidden agenda' behind ICERD, which included eventually removing the Malay language as the country's official language.

The demonstration, they alleged, was also to warn the non-Malays not to demand too much and not to mess with 'Tuan rumah/Tuan Tanah' who gave them citizenship and allowed them to stay in Tanah Malaya.[114]

Some of the organizing groups claimed that Malays found it galling that despite Mahathir's statement on not ratifying the ICERD, on social media and in public forums, non-Malays were still seen to be urging the government to continue with the ratification process and they were now demanding the same rights as the Malays and the Bumiputera.

They claimed that Malays believed it was unacceptable for non-Malays to claim that they deserve the same rights as the Bumiputera just because they were Malaysians, because it was the Malays/Bumiputera who gave non-Malays citizenship based on the social compact that was agreed upon back then, and which specified special rights for the Malays and independence from the British in exchange for citizenship for non-Malays.

Mahathir was now caught in a trap of his own making. His own Malay hegemonic views and attitudes were being used against him, and he needed a way to regain the narrative and Malay support. He now had to come up with a plan to shore up Malay support.

Despite decrying Najib's BR1M cash handouts to low-income Malaysians—the majority of whom are Malays—as a

---

[114] Zoom interview with ICERD leader 2, 14 Sep 2020.

bribe and corruption before GE14, Mahathir now rebranded the payments and carried on with them in the hopes of appeasing the Malay ground.

On 5 October 2019, he also launched Malaysia's Shared Prosperity Vision, a ten-year economic plan aimed at increasing Malay involvement in high-skill and technological sectors.

The following day, he took pride of place at the Malay Dignity Conference, whose objective was to build Malay unity, with the idea that all Malay political parties should unite under Mahathir's leadership.

But as the then Penang Deputy Chief Minister and DAP leader P. Ramasamy noted:

> Dr Mahathir might have missed the point that it was dignity and not a unity congress. Anyway, knowing Dr Mahathir, it really doesn't matter to him. For him, it was simply that Malays are now split into a number of political parties. This is in essence disunity for him. There is only Malay unity when Malays are behind him and the political party he heads.[115]

However, it did not matter because what Mahathir said ended up providing greater fodder for his political opponents:

> . . . although the current government is being led by the Malays, its Malay element is not as strong as the previous government . . .
>
> Previously, we could rely on the (BN) government because it was a strong Malay government but that's not the case anymore (. . .) It is us (Malays) who broke away from each

---

other. We are now in small groups and are fighting with each other and this is why we have to rely on others for victory (. . .)

Like it or not, now we have to consider the feelings of others or else, we will lose in the election and that's a fact (. . .) When we rely on others, one way or another, we will be indebted to them and we will be afraid to lose their support because it will mean losing our positions (. . .) Because of this, we have betrayed the powers given to us to the point that our dignity is being insulted and we are looked down upon in our own country.[116]

Instead of supporting his new narrative of recognizing the Chinese community's contributions and the role of the DAP as nation builders, Mahathir abandoned this in favour of claims of reliance on non-Malay support to stay in power, which only served to reinforce the UMNO and PAS narrative that PH1.0 had to be replaced by a Malay-centric government and not necessarily one led by Mahathir, who appeared to have compromised so much in order to stay in power.

So, in one fell swoop, Mahathir had effectively lost control of the narrative he was trying so hard to retain, and of the heartland Malays.

---

[116] Provera, Adib & Yunus, Arfa, 'Dr M says PH's "Malayness" not as strong as BN's', *New Straits Times*, 6 Oct 2019, accessed at: https://www.nst.com.my/news/nation/2019/10/527454/dr-m-says-phs-malayness-not-strong-bns.

Chapter 7

Batu Puteh: Who Cares About Sovereignty Anyway?

Most Malaysians and Singaporeans are fully aware of the thorny bilateral issues of water and that of the tiny rocks, known as Pedra Branca in Singapore and as Pulau Batu Puteh in Malaysia, between their two countries. These have been ongoing issues of contention, along with the railway land issue—now resolved—and the water issue—still unresolved—since, what feels like, time immemorial.

From the very outset, I must state that this chapter is based on a document I received sometime in 2023, which I believe was the final report of the government's Special Task Force reviewing the legal Case on the Sovereignty of Batu Puteh, Batuan Tengah and Tubir Selatan that had been set up by the Cabinet in 2022. I have no way of determining if the report is accurate and I urge the government to verify the authenticity of the report. However, if the report is real, and I am happy to stand corrected if it is not, then the alleged story that unfolds below would be explosive.

Batu Puteh, consists of three outcroppings, namely Batu Puteh, Batuan Tengah (Middle Rocks), and Tubir Selatan (South Ledge), located 25 nautical miles east of Singapore and 7.7 nautical miles south of Johor, where the Singapore Strait meets the South China Sea.

The dispute began in 1979 when Malaysia published a map claiming Batu Puteh was within its territorial waters. Singapore objected to this, and following much diplomatic to and fro, both countries agreed to refer the matter to the International Court of Justice (ICJ). I will not go into much detail on the case as so many academics, officials, and Cabinet ministers have written about it already except to say that in May 2008, the ICJ ruled that Singapore had sovereignty over Batu Puteh, while Batuan Tengah belonged to Malaysia.

However, in regard to Tubir Selatan, the ICJ noted that it fell within the overlapping territorial waters generated by mainland Malaysia, Batu Puteh, and Batuan Tengah, and as it was a maritime feature visible only at low tide, it belonged to the state in the territorial waters of which it is located.

So, it was quite clear who owned Batu Puteh and Batuan Tengah, but the ownership of Tubir Selatan was left to interpretation. A joint technical committee was then set up between Singapore and Malaysia to try and work out a solution to the court's decision but it ended up being suspended in 2013 because both sides could not agree on their record of discussions.

And this remained the case until sometime in late 2016, when Malaysian researchers allegedly discovered three documents that could possibly cast doubt on the ICJ's decision on the three outcroppings as a whole.

i.   A 1958 telegram from the Governor of Singapore responding to a request from the British Secretary of State for the Colonies for comments on a proposal to extend Singapore's territorial waters from 3 miles to 6 miles (in an effort to prevent the emergence of a general international entitlement to 12-mile limits). The Governor indicated that it was important to Singapore that the existing 3-mile limit be retained, as access to the channels of approach to Singapore would be inhibited if an entitlement to 6-mile limits became generally accepted in international law. For this reason, he proposed that, in the event that 6 miles became the generally accepted limit, 'special provision should be made for an international high seas corridor one mile wide through the straits between Singapore and Malayan territory on the north and Indonesian territory on the south'. He suggested that this corridor would follow the normal shipping channel from west to east, the easternmost leg of which would run 'from a point midway between the southernmost point of St John's Islands and Batu Berhanti Light to a point 1 mile north of Horsburgh Light'. This document suggests that, in 1958, the highest levels of Singaporean Government did not consider that PBP was Singaporean territory, since there would be no need to advocate the provision of an international passage near PBP if it had been subject to Singaporean sovereignty.

ii.   A map prepared by the British Commander of the Far East Fleet within the file titled 'Naval Operations in the Malacca and Singapore Straits 1964–1966' (DEFE69/359) shows the 'Restricted and Prohibited Areas in the Singapore Territorial Waters'. This map shows the limits of Singaporean territorial waters at a point south of Pulau Tekon(sic) Besar in the Johor Strait and does not extend to the vicinity of PBP. Handwritten notes on the map endorse it as an accurate depiction of the restrictions in effect in February 1966, i.e., after Singapore became independent in August 1965.

iii. A memo in one of the British files (FCO141/14808) addressed to 'GS' (presumed to be the Governor of Singapore) relates the fact that, during an incident in 1958 when a Malaysian vessel was being followed by an Indonesian gunboat near PBP, the Royal Navy was unable to act because the Malaysian ship was 'still inside Johore territorial waters'.[117]

ICJ rules allowed for a revision of its decision within ten years of its 23 May 2008 verdict, given that the new evidence was unknown to the court and the party seeking the revision and that the application had to be made within six months of the discovery of the facts.

The high-powered international legal team advising Malaysia's Attorney General, was allegedly of the view that:

> Malaysia would indeed have a plausible case, even though the hurdles would be high in the light of the provisions of the statute of the International Court, the Rules of Court and the caselaw.
>
> (However) We feel it important to point out to you specifically that our assessment of the chances of success of any such application in view of the above is that they would not be high. To put it another way, as we did in our joint opinion of 23 January, we take the view that such an application would not be likely to succeed. However, this does not take into account the wider political advantages of making such an application, something upon which we are not qualified to express an opinion.[118]

The experts were more confident of an application by Malaysia to seek an interpretation of the ICJ's 2008 conclusion on the question of sovereignty over Tubir Selatan.

> . . . a credible application can be made to the Court to clarify the meaning and scope of the 2008 judgement, and we consider

---

[117] Shaw QC, Professor Malcolm, Bethlehem QC, Sir Daniel, Plant, Dr Brendan, 'Project Phoenix: Summary Opinion', 23 Jan 2017, p. 3.

[118] Shaw QC, Professor Malcolm, Bethlehem QC, Sir Daniel, Plant, Dr Brendan, 'Letter to the Attorney General, Malaysia', 26 Jan 2017.

that there is a reasonable prospect that any such application would survive a jurisdiction or admissibility challenge, at least as it relates to South Ledge. We also believe that any such application should be broadened to include the territorial waters around PBP. If the case proceeded to the merits, we consider the most probable outcome that the Court would affirm the decision it rendered in 2008. Insofar as the waters around PBP are concerned, the Court may say something about the approach to be adopted to delimitation that may potentially be helpful to Malaysia, but could, on the other hand, say something potentially adverse to Malaysia's interests.

If the Court were inclined to interpret the Judgement to address the issue of sovereignty over South Ledge, we consider that it is more likely to favour Malaysia's position than that of Singapore.[119]

The revision application had to be made within six months of the discovery of the new evidence, which would be 3 February 2017. So, with approval from the Cabinet and then Prime Minister Najib, the Attorney General filed the application on 2 February 2017. As there was statute of limitation on applying for the interpretation, the Attorney General's Chamber, following Cabinet approval, then filed it on 30 June 2017.

The Barisan Nasional (BN) Cabinet's thinking on the issue of Batu Puteh was simple.[120] Most Ministers felt that it was a tragedy that the ICJ had handed over Batu Puteh to Singapore in 2008. So, if there was even the slightest of chances that Malaysia could get back its land, it had to proceed. And that went double for the interpretation application. But even if Malaysia didn't get a revision it didn't matter. This was because, given the possibility of

---

[119] Shaw QC, Professor Malcolm, Bethlehem QC, Sir Daniel, Plant, Dr Brendan, 'Project Phoenix: Joint Opinion on Application for Interpretation', 11 May 2017, pp. 7–8.

[120] Interview with former BN cabinet minister, 12 July 2022, Kuala Lumpur.

a long legal battle before the revision was eventually thrown out, it was more than likely that Singapore would want to work out some sort of a deal and this could be beneficial to Malaysia in terms of maritime boundaries and territorial waters.

A positive recent example was the negotiations with Singapore on the Malayan Railway land issue, which had stalled for over close to twenty years under Mahathir's first administration, but which was successfully resolved by Najib's government in 2010 with Malaysia getting six very lucrative plots of land in the centre of Singapore's financial district and the revenue from which would far outweigh any improbable joint monetization of the thin strip of railway land cutting across the republic. Of course, some of the multi-billion dollar revenue-producing land had then been sold off for short-term profits in 2019 during Mahathir's second tenure as PM, and it says plenty about what Mahathir thought about deals with Singapore.

So, following further legal exchanges between both countries, the ICJ then set 11 to 18 June 2018 to hear oral arguments from both countries in relation to the two cases, one to revise the judgement and the other to interpret the 2008 judgement's conclusion on Tubir Selatan.

Malaysia's legal team went into overdrive in preparing for the submissions, and to plead what they believed was a strong case at the Hague.

However, less than three weeks before the hearings, Malaysians voted in the fourteenth General Elections, which saw the end of the Barisan Nasional Government and Mahathir take over as PM7.

In most circumstances, this should not have changed anything as the legal applications by the Malaysian Government were not being made for the benefit of any political party and was led, not by a political appointee, but by the country's Attorney General, who was then Apandi Ali, a former Federal Court judge.

However, Mahathir's disdain for Apandi had led to Apandi being forced to take garden leave on 14 May 2018. This threw a major spanner in the works for the international legal team that was to present Malaysia's case at the Hague.

In an alleged email a day after Apandi was removed, the team's lead legal counsel, Professor Malcolm Shaw QC, emailed Azian Mohamad Aziz, the head of the International Affairs Division at the Attorney General's Chambers:

> We note that the suspension of the Attorney General has been reported in the press. If this is the case, we wish to impress upon the AGC the necessity to appoint a replacement Agent for the case as soon as possible. Clearly, the replacement would need to be an authoritative figure with the full confidence of the government, able to speak on its behalf before the Court and provide timely instructions to legal team representing Malaysia's interest. In light of the current situation and of the above, we feel it necessary to seek a reaffirmation of our instructions concerning the two applications.[121]

The day before, Mahathir, at a meeting with the government's Chief Secretary and Secretaries General of all ministries and agencies, was informed by Solicitor General Engku Nor Faziah—who was representing the AGC as Apandi had been removed—of the upcoming legal case at the ICJ and Mahathir wanted an urgent briefing by the London legal team and the international counsels on the applications.

Following a series of emails and calls between the AGC and the counsels, a rushed briefing for Mahathir was set for 17 May 2018 at the Prime Minister's Office in Putrajaya.

However, it was allegedly clear from many in attendance that Mahathir had already made up his mind. I believe Mahathir had felt slighted when the AGC had made the applications in 2017, because it was as if his administration had not done enough to

---

[121] Shaw QC, Professor Malcolm N, Email to To' Puan Azian Mohd. Aziz, AGC, 15 May 2018.

save Batu Puteh and that the new applications had to be made in order to correct the past mistakes of his administration. Moreover, he appeared to have a visceral hatred for Apandi and all that he had done.

The alleged main briefer at the meeting was Dr Brendan Plant, who represented the ICJ team, and he was accompanied by Firoz Hussein Ahmad and Abu Bakar As-Sidek, the London legal team. Also, in attendance was Ramlan Ibrahim, the then Secretary General of the Foreign Ministry, the then Director General of the Maritime Affairs Department of the Foreign Ministry Dr Azfar Mohamad Mustafar, along with the then undersecretary of the Southeast Asia Division of the Foreign Ministry. Azian Mohd Aziz, Azmir Shah Zainal Abidin, Alfian Yang Amri, and Dr Suraya Harun represented the AGC.

In a 2022 interview with a government task force set up to review the legal case of Batu Puteh, Batuan Tengah, and Tubir Selatan, Plant described the atmosphere of the meeting as 'unwelcoming'. The alleged task force report noted:

> From the tone of the meeting, Dr Plant felt that Tun Dr Mahathir had pre-judged the matter and had closed his mind to the possibility of proceeding with the applications. This was despite the fact that the applications were scheduled to be heard some 2 weeks from the date of the KL Meeting and that all submissions had been filed and duly served.
>
> Dr Plant was seated at the other end of the table from Tun Mahathir, who was flanked by senior government officers, who were 'mumbling' incomprehensively(sic) during Dr Plant's briefing.
>
> Dr Plant did not give any views as to the strength or weakness in respect of the merits of the applications. In respect of the new evidence, Dr Plant opined that no single item of evidence, on its own, is a 'silver bullet' but cumulatively the evidence may prove persuasive if put before the ICJ.

Dr Plant felt that Tun Dr. Mahathir had misconstrued his 'silver bullet' point and thought that it meant that the applications had no chance of succeeding.[122]

That was not the only thing Mahathir reportedly misconstrued. The Prime Minister also did not realize that there were two separate applications, one was the review of the judgement while the other was the interpretation of the judgement's conclusion on Tubir Selatan.

And why was this the case?

Because I believe Mahathir did not seek the opinion or advice of the senior officials from the AGC or the Foreign Ministry. All foreign ministry and AGC officials who attended the meeting and were interviewed by the task force admitted that the Prime Minister did not seek, nor was given, any advice. Azian, who had organized the meeting, and who was aware of the implications of the case, reportedly told the task force that 'she felt not incumbent for her to provide any advice to Tun Dr. Mahathir during and after the meeting'.[123]

Given that the briefing was of such importance to the nation and to bilateral relations with one of its closest neighbours, it was very worrying when the Special Task Force discovered that there were no official minutes to the meeting to verify what had transpired. As the alleged task force report noted, 'The KL Meeting was not only of importance because its outcome was determinative of whether Malaysia would or would not proceed with the applications but moreover, could have—and has since had—a significant impact upon Malaysia's sovereignty and maritime rights in the waters surrounding Pedra Branca.'[124]

---

[122] 'Final Report Sub-Committee Tort of Misfeasance', Report of the Special Task Force reviewing the legal Case on the Sovereignty of Batu Puteh, Batuan Tengah, and Tubir Selatan, 30 Aug 2022, p. 510.

[123] Ibid., p. 512.

[124] Ibid., p. 516.

However, all witnesses said that Mahathir concluded the meeting by indicating that he would decide on the matter.

Four days later, Mahathir allegedly sent a letter[125] to Solicitor General Engku Nor Faizah indicating that he wanted Malaysia to withdraw the interpretation application—as he was still unaware that there were two separate applications.

And finally, only on the 23 May 2018 did Mahathir reportedly raise the issue in the Cabinet. The Cabinet was briefed neither by the AGC nor by Foreign Ministry officials on the applications as Mahathir took it upon himself to explain the situation—which I believe even he did not fully comprehend. The cabinet then endorsed Mahathir's position, without getting the full picture.

But even more troubling was the fact that while the cabinet meeting was still ongoing, and before it had even endorsed Mahathir's decision, a *Note Verbale* had been prepared by the AGC under Mahathir's alleged instructions and sent to Singapore's Attorney General 'to convey to you the view and the wish of the **Prime Minister** and the **Government of Malaysia** (emphasis added) to discontinue the two pending International Court of Justice (ICJ) cases . . .'[126]

Ironically, the note giving up Malaysia's claim to Batu Puteh was sent exactly ten years to the day when the ICJ Judgement was delivered back in 2008.

Mahathir had, I believe, decided to junk both applications based on his personal held beliefs; without realizing that there were two separate cases each with their own merits; without

---

[125] Mohamad, Mahathir, Letter to YBhg Datuk Engku Nor Faizah Engku Atek, Solicitor General Malaysia, 'Permohonan Semakan Dan Permohonan Tafsiran Keputusan Case Concerning the Sovereignty Over Perdra Branca, Middle Rock and South Ledge Di Mahkamah Keadilan Antarabangsa (ICJ)', 21 May 2018.

[126] Engku Atek, Engku Nor Faizah, letter to Lucien Wong Attorney General of Singapore, Ref JPN9RB152/139/11A, titled 'Application for Revision and Application for Interpretation of the Judgement of 23 May 2008 in the Case Concerning the Sovereignty of Pedra Branca/pulau Batu Puteh, Middle Rocks and South Ledge 9malaysia V. Singapore), 23 May 2018.

seeking the advice of the country's top legal officer—the Attorney General who had been leading the case since 2016, or failing that, seeking the opinion of the officers in charge of the case at the Attorney General's Chambers, or even the senior diplomats from the Foreign Ministry who were involved in the two applications.

Instead, he misconstrued what he was being told, and then having made up his mind, unilaterally ordered the halt to the applications and masqueraded his decision as that of the Government of Malaysia and presented it to Singapore—even as the Cabinet was discussing the issue and before it had even made a decision—thus making it a *fait accompli*. As the task force reportedly noted, 'Tun Dr. Mahathir had knowledge that his action is unlawful or at the very least, subjectively reckless as to its unlawfulness.'[127]

And, if the report was accurate and to be believed, the task force was quite stark in its assessment of what Mahathir's 'arbitrary and reckless'[128] actions meant for Malaysia, its sovereignty, and its maritime borders:[129]

i.   Malaysia's sovereignty over Batu Puteh has been lost forever.
ii. Singapore's sovereignty over BP can never be challenged in any way whatsoever.
iii. Singapore might have now acquired a territorial sea around BP in the event that Malaysia fails to 'enclave'. The exact breadth of this territorial sea is uncertain as the seas around BP have yet to be de-limited.
iv. BP is 7.7 nautical miles from the Johor coastline and therefore lies within the 12 nautical mile territorial sea claimed by Malaysia.

---

[127] 'Final Report Sub-Committee Tort of Misfeasance,' Report of the Special Task Force reviewing the legal Case on the Sovereignty of Batu Puteh, Batuan Tengah, and Tubir Selatan, 30 Aug 2022, p. 532.
[128] Ibid., p. 534.
[129] Ibid., p. 407.

v. In the event that BP is considered to be an island capable of supporting human habitation under international law and not a mere rock, Singapore would be entitled to claim a 200 nautical mile Exclusive Economic Zone emanating from BP.

vi. Singapore is currently proposing to undertake land reclamation works which will increase the size of BP by approximately 700 per cent. This will undoubtedly encroach in what was previously Malaysia's territorial sea and will certainly have an environmental impact on the adjacent maritime areas belonging to Malaysia.

Malaysia had nothing to lose from the Application for Revision but everything to gain.

As a result of Mahathir's actions, Malaysia, today, is in a difficult position with regard to its claims on Batu Puteh, Batuan Tengah, and Tubir Selatan.

Mahathir's unilateral actions have sealed off, forever, any possibility of getting Batu Puteh back.

But the task force had also reportedly outlined a path forward for the Malaysian Government in protecting the sovereignty of Batuan Tengah and Tubir Selatan as well as the seas adjacent to the three outcroppings.

It noted that the government currently has five allegedly viable options under international law, and it is likely that the action it takes will be a combination of several of these options. It is a long-term secret strategy and has numerous moving parts. However, if the current and future administrations follow the very novel plan supposedly outlined by the international panel of experts and local counsel in the report, Malaysia will allegedly be able to:[130]

---

[130] Ibid., p. 441.

i.   Enclave BP and prevent or minimize Singapore's claim to a territorial sea emanating from BP.
ii.   Ensure that BP is ruled to be a rock and not an island so as to avoid Singapore claiming an Exclusive Economic Zone and Continental Shelf emanating from BP.
iii. Ensure that Singapore does not carry out reclamation works to increase the size of BP as this would cause environmental damage to Malaysia's marine environment and could possibly encroach into her territorial waters. Additionally, Singapore may also argue that the increase in size means that BP should be treated as an island as opposed to an uninhabitable rock.

Oh well, I suppose, as they say, something is better than nothing.

In its reportedly final recommendation to the Government, the Cabinet-appointed task force noted:

> To ensure justice for Malaysia in this regard, the Government should consider the following recommendations:
>   Appropriate action should be taken against YABhg. Tun Dr Mahathir Mohamad, Prime Minister at that time, under the 'Tort of Misfeasance in Public Office'; and
>   The need for the Attorney General's Chambers to improve work ethics in line with its function and role in providing legal advice independently and transparently covering a wide spectrum of matters to the government.[131]

When the report was submitted to the Cabinet on 7 October 2022, then PM Ismail Sabri said, 'The Cabinet meeting was told

---

[131] 'Final Report Sub-Committee Tort of Misfeasance,' Report of the Special Task Force reviewing the legal Case on the Sovereignty of Batu Puteh, Batuan Tengah, and Tubir Selatan, 30 Aug 2022, p. 532.

of possible negligence and mistakes by former seventh prime minister Tun Dr Mahathir Mohamad, when Malaysia missed the opportunity to file a review application against the ICJ judgment in 2008, and the request for interpretation of Batu Puteh, Batuan Tengah (Middle Rocks) and Tubir Selatan after Dr Mahathir decided not to proceed with the application for review and interpretation of the judgment on June 11, 2018.'[132]

Then Attorney General Idrus Harun noted that, 'based on the Cabinet decision dated 11 January 2023, the Government is of the view that the decision to withdraw both the Application for Revision of the decision of the Case Concerning the Sovereignty over Pedra Branca/Pulau Batu Puteh, Middle Rocks/Batuan Tengah and South ledge/Tubir Selatan (Malaysia/Singapura) and the Request for Interpretation of the decision in the said case was not in order and improper.'[133]

The Ismail Sabri Government, which received the report, did not act on the recommendations.

On 24 January 2024, Anwar's Unity Government announced plans to set up a Royal Commission of Inquiry (RCI) to look into matters related to the sovereignty of Batu Puteh, Middle Rocks, and South Ledge.[134]

---

[132] 'Ismail Sabri: Govt to declassify investigation report on ex-AG Thomas' claims, proceed with review bid at ICJ over Pulau Batu Puteh,' *MalayMail/Online*, 13 October 2022, Accessed at: https://www.malaymail.com/news/malaysia/2022/10/13/ismail-sabri-govt-to-declassify-investigation-report-on-ex-ag-thomas-claims-proceed-with-review-bid-at-icj-over-pulau-batu-puteh/33424

[133] 'PRESS STATEMENT: Final Repot of the special Tas Force on the sovereignty of Batu Puteh, Batuan Tengah and Tubir Selatan,' *Attorney-General's Chambers*, 27 January 2023, Accessed at: https://www.agc.gov.my/agcportal/common//uploads/publication/501/2023_01_27_Kenyataan%20Media%20Peguam%20Negara%20(BI).pdf

[134] 'Cabinet agrees to RCI on Batu Puteh', *Free Malaysia Today*, 24 Jan 2024, accessed at: https://www.freemalaysiatoday.com/category/nation/2024/01/24/cabinet-agrees-on-rci-into-batu-puteh/.

Chapter 8

New Government, Old Cronies

Mahathir's PH1.0 Government had come in on promises to put a halt to decades of crony capitalism—encouraged by Mahathir in the first place—which had culminated in the 1MDB scandal. PH1.0 was to look into how the system could be reformed and particularly the Government Linked Companies (GLCs), which enjoyed virtual monopolies in certain sectors and many of which, analysts claimed, were inefficient, drained state resources, and crowded out private investment.[135]

Under the Barisan Nasional (BN) Government, all GLCs fell under the purview of the Finance Minister—which had for long been a portfolio also held by the prime minister—and these companies had supposedly played a key role in 'Malaysia's notorious system of patronage, channelling rents to party members and well-connected businessmen in the form of contracts, permits, licenses, and financial aid'.[136] These 'cronies' were often appointed to their boards, granting them access to revenue sources.

---

[135] Shamsunahar, Imran, '"New Malaysia" under Mahathir looks much like old crony state', Nikkei Asia Online, 4 Feb 2020, accessed at: https://asia.nikkei. com/Opinion/New-Malaysia-under-Mahathir-looks-much-like-old-crony-state.
[136] Ibid.

These crony-led companies then allowed elites to consolidate power through patronage; securing the loyalty of party members through board appointments and cash; and directing government concessions to key constituencies to garner electoral support.[137]

PH1.0 was supposed to put an end to this.

But within months of the new administration taking over, civil society groups had already begun levelling accusations of practices enriching the ruling coalition and its allies in business and the fact that the new government was seemingly intent on persisting with old ways.

Sticking to PH1.0's Manifesto promise that their prime minister would not hold any other portfolio, Mahathir handed the Finance Ministry over to DAP's Lim Guan Eng.

But, as mentioned earlier, he firstly stripped the GLCs from Guan Eng's Ministry, with the two biggest and most lucrative of them—Khazanah Nasional and Permodalan Nasional Berhad (PNB)—coming under the Prime Minister's Department, with the rest coming under Azmin Ali's—Mahathir's close political ally—newly created Ministry of Economic Affairs.

Despite PH1.0's promise to halt political appointments to GLC boards, Mahathir made himself chairman of Khazanah and appointed numerous other Pakatan Harapan leaders who had lost in GE14 to various statutory boards, agencies, and organizations under the GLCs.

In so doing, Mahathir removed the Finance Ministry's control and influence over the GLCs, which now ended up being consolidated—not equally under a multiracial PH1.0 coalition but—under Mahathir and his Malay political allies within PH.

The Council of Eminent Persons (CEP)

Three years into his first premiership, Mahathir, in 1984, appointed Daim Zainuddin, a successful businessman and a close friend, as his economic adviser.

---

[137] Ibid.

Under Daim's proposed Malaysian Incorporation Policy were:

. . . significant economic policy reversals which include regressive fiscal (tax and spending) reforms, more stringent public expenditure cuts, privatization, deregulation, and financial liberalization were implemented (Jomo, 2003). This policy, and the earlier National Economic Policy (NEP), succeeded in creating a small group of super-rich bumiputra (indigenous group) class but failed to achieve its main objective of reducing economic inequalities among the indigenous group; in fact, it actually widened social inequality (. . .) The widespread poverty in Malay dominated states caused some UMNO supporters to question the policies that focused on privatisation and heavy industries run by favoured businessmen (Saw and Kesavapany, 2006), including those with family and friendship ties.[138]

During Mahathir's first tenure, Malaysia experienced twenty-five years of 'privatizing profits and profitable assets and socializing of losses and liabilities'.[139] The perpetrators were not made accountable and overly protected, which may be attributed to the personalization of power by the leadership.

Critics claimed the Cabinet was no longer used as a forum but more as a rubber-stamp that gave legitimacy to government policies.

This 'personalization of power' was achieved by ensuring that the most important posts in the cabinet and institutional infrastructure were held by loyalists, with Mahathir himself holding onto to the key home and finance portfolios.

---

[138] Amal Hayati Ahmad Khair, Roszaini Haniffa, Mohammad Hudaib, Mohamad Nazri Abd. Karim, 'Personalisation of power, neoliberalism and the production of corruption', De Montfort University, 2014, accessed at: https:// dora.dmu.ac.uk/server/api/core/bitstreams/34258e72-7ab9-4059-a795-5aa5ef93e6ab/content.

[139] Ibid.

An example of alleged corruption was oil and gas engineering company Kencana Petroleum, which was owned and controlled by Mahathir's son Mokhzani. Set up in 2001, and without any track record in the field, Kencana was awarded a major fabrication license by state petroleum company Petronas, whose management often allegedly took instructions from the prime minister.[140]

Mahathir's children were also alleged to have benefitted from a RM214.2 million fibre optic replacement contract given by Telekom Malaysia Berhad to Opcom Sdn Bhd in 2009. Telekom Malaysia was a government-linked company with the Ministry of Finance Incorporated (MoF Inc) as its special shareholder, and MoF Inc came under the direction and control of Mahathir who was both PM and Finance Minister then.

Instead of holding a tender for the best qualified and most cost-effective firm to run the project, MoF Inc issued a letter to the Finance Ministry seeking permission to engage in direct negotiations with Opcom in 2003.[141] Mahathir's family members were directors of Opcom, including eldest son Mirzan (1994–2021), second son Mokhzani (2009–2019), third son Mukhriz (1994–2019), and Mukhriz's wife Norzieta Zakaria (1995–2021).[142]

Those who opposed Mahathir were silenced or ousted like the then Finance Minister Anwar Ibrahim, who had opposed bailouts using public funds.

---

[140] Abdul Rashid, Hidir Reduan, 'Anwar vs Dr M: Bailouts and family-linked businesses', *Malaysiakini*, 15 Jun 2023, accessed at: https://www.malaysiakini.com/news/668733.

[141] 'No probe into RM214mil Opcom contract claim yet, says MACC', *Free Malaysia Today*, 27 Jun 2023, accessed at: https://www.freemalaysiatoday.com/category/nation/2023/06/27/no-probe-into-rm214mil-opcom-contract-claim-yet-says-macc/.

[142] Abdul Rashid, Hidir Reduan, 'Anwar vs Dr M: Bailouts and family-linked businesses', *Malaysiakini*, 15 Jun 2023, accessed at: https://www.malaysiakini.com/news/668733.

Mahathir and Daim had forced Anwar to suspend Malaysian stock exchange rules to allow their then leading crony, the UEM-Renong conglomerate, a bailout. That move caused Malaysia's stock market capitalization to fall by RM70 billion, or by 20 per cent, in three days in November 1997.[143]

Sometime after July 1997, Anwar said he had also rejected a request from Mahathir to bail out KPB —now known as Pos Logistics Berhad, and whose majority shareholder and director then was Mahathir's son Mirzan—which had net liabilities of RM423.94 million for the financial year ending 31 December 1997.[144] According to Anwar, Mahathir was furious, claiming that Mirzan or he would be embarrassed if the matter ended up being debated in parliament. Not to be deterred, Mahathir found a way around Anwar. The Finance Minister later found out from then Petronas president and CEO Mohamad Hasan Marican that Mahathir had allegedly ordered Petronas to bail out KPB. Anwar said he objected to the move, but Mahathir coolly told him that Petronas was not under the control of the Treasury, implying that it was none of Anwar's business.[145]

Anwar's further refusal to carry out Mahathir's bidding saw him removed as Deputy Premier and Finance Minister in 1998 and charged and jailed over allegations of corruption, abuse of power, and sodomy.

Mahathir then brought Daim back as Deputy PM and Finance Minister, which then 'allowed him (Mahathir) direct control over a

---

[143] Amal Hayati Ahmad Khair, Roszaini Haniffa, Mohammad Hudaib, Mohamad Nazri Abd. Karim, 'Personalisation of power, neoliberalism and the production of corruption'.

[144] Abdul Rashid, Hidir Reduan, 'Anwar vs Dr M: Bailouts and family-linked businesses', *Malaysiakini*, 15 Jun 2023, accessed at: https://www.malaysiakini.com/news/668733.

[145] Ibid.

variety of discretionary funds to prepare strategic bailouts for his key allies in the corporate sector'.[146]

Fast forward two decades and it is now May 2018, and Mahathir is once again ensconced in the Perdana Putra Building in Putrajaya.

In order to help the new Cabinet on policy related matters, implement PH1.0's 100-day election promises, and review the country's existing or proposed mega-projects and international business deals, Mahathir set up a five-person Council of Eminent Persons (CEP) led by Daim. His fellow council members included former Bank Negara governor Zeti Akhtar Aziz, former Petronas CEO Hassan Marican, business tycoon Robert Kuok, and economist Jomo Kwame Sundaram.

On the CEP's to-do-list was the abolishing of the Goods and Services Tax (GST) and the cull and restructuring of government institutions and state-owned enterprises. As the GST was a crucial revenue earner for the government, Jomo had wanted it to be not only reformed but retained.

'Instead of abolishing GST, I suggested an integrated tax authority, rather than a segmented one. The head of customs was very open to these suggested reforms,' Jomo said in an interview in 2023.

'Unfortunately, the (Finance) Minister at that time and perhaps the Prime Minister never considered these reforms, to my knowledge. And so, there were no discussions on this,' he said.[147]

Jomo said he had also pushed for reforms to improve health financing, but he did not see any commitment by government leaders to do so.

---

[146] Amal Hayati Ahmad Khair, Roszaini Haniffa, Mohammad Hudaib, Mohamad Nazri Abd. Karim, 'Personalisation of power, neoliberalism and the production of corruption'.

[147] Easwaran, Elill, 'CEP never produced a report, says Jomo', *Free Malaysia Today*, 27 Mar 2023, accessed at: https://www.freemalaysiatoday.com/category/nation/2023/03/27/cep-never-produced-a-report-says-jomo/.

What I believe Daim was more concerned over was the elimination of any top government leader that he felt was linked to the previous BN administration. He effectively demanded the resignation of the then Chief Justice and the President of the Court of Appeals. His council also reportedly requested the top management of Khazanah Nasional to resign. Days later, all the sovereign fund's board members handed in their resignation letters en-masse. In their place and on many other similar boards, I believe, Mahathir and Daim's cronies were then slotted in.

But all this under what authority?

The CEP was not created by statute nor was it a body of enquiry under Malaysia's Commissions of Enquiry Act 1950. And it also wasn't formed by way of a parliamentary vote, nor did it function as a select committee which was answerable to the country's lawmakers.[148] As such, was the CEP an illegal body that effectively operated as Mahathir's hatchet man in despatching all those individuals he did not like? Or was the CEP a tool for Daim to use in finding out internal information on the various GLCs and then use it for the benefit of his business interests?

Not surprisingly, there was no report on what the CEP had done or achieved at the end of its reign of terror.[149] So, not only was the council reportedly responsible for mass resignations and alleged interference in Malaysia's judiciary, but there was now no way to tell how successful they were in helping to implement PH1.0's economic pledges and manifesto.

Interestingly, on 20 December 2023, the Malaysian Anti-Corruption Commission seized the sixty-storey Ilham Tower located in one of the most expensive districts in KL and reportedly

---

[148] Gnanasagaran, Angaindrankumar, 'Malaysia's Council of Eminent Persons: A politburo?', Asean Post, 27 Jul 2018, accessed at: https://theaseanpost.com/article/malaysias-council-eminent-persons-politburo.

[149] https://www.freemalaysiatoday.com/category/nation/2023/03/27/cep-never-produced-a-report-says-jomo/

owned by Daim and his family, as part of a corruption and money laundering probe into the former minister, with other properties owned by him also facing confiscation 'following an alleged failure to explain the source of funds to purchase the properties'.[150]

But then again, as Ignatius outlined in his book, Mahathir was never committed to PH1.0's manifesto in the first place:

> Whatever else may be said about the manifesto, it had tremendous aspirational value besides serving as the common platform upon which PH cooperation was premised. It must be remembered as well that while PKR and DAP were pleased that Mahathir had joined them in the runup to GE14, they were also wary of his motives. The manifesto, which was hammered out through long negotiations, was a way of binding Mahathir to an agreed agenda for change.
>
> The real problem was not the manifesto per se but the way Mahathir and other Pakatan Harapan leaders messaged the management of their manifesto promise. Better messaging and a sharper focus might have sufficed to meet at least short-term expectations. They could have also divided their manifesto into immediate, medium, and longer-term priorities. It would have kept the manifesto front and centre of their agenda while giving themselves more time and leeway to fulfil it. Few voters after all were intimately familiar with the manifesto; to them what was important was the spirit of reform and renewal that it embodied.
>
> Voters were generally not unreasonable; they understood that 60 years of misrule and misfeasance couldn't be set right in just a few years. What they wanted were assurances that on key issues the government was moving in the right direction.

---

[150] 'MACC probing Daim for alleged corruption, money laundering, says report', *Free Malaysia Today*, 23 Dec 2023, accessed at: https://www.freemalaysiatoday.com/category/nation/2023/12/23/macc-probes-daim-for-alleged-corruption-money-laundering/.

Mahathir appeared to understand the serious dilemma he faced on the issue of promises made in the manifesto. Speaking at a closed-door Pakatan Harapan gathering a few months after the elections, he warned Pakatan had to do its best to fulfil its promises if it was to avoid a backlash from voters.

At the same time, he cavalierly remarked, 'Actually we did not expect to win, we made a thick manifesto with all kinds of promises . . .' It smacked of political hypocrisy, a lack of integrity, an indication that Mahathir was himself unenthusiastic about the manifesto. His cynicism came through very clearly when he discussed the manifesto pledge to give the leader of the opposition status equivalent to that of a minister. 'The promise,' he said, 'was made with the expectation that PH would remain as the opposition. But we won and now it feels uncomfortable to give the opposition leader an equal rank to a minister.'

So, while he wanted to secure senior status for himself in the event Pakatan Harapan lost the elections, he was unwilling to offer the same thing to UMNO-BN if they ended up in the opposition. It was this kind of cynical manipulation of promises that eroded his credibility.

He also ignored the parliamentary select committee on appointments when he appointed Latheefa Koya as MACC Commissioner in breach of yet another election promise.

Mahathir also continued the practice of appointing politicians to Government-Linked Companies (GLCs). When questioned about it, deputy rural development minister R. Sivarasa, quibbling with words, said PH never promised to get rid of political appointees in government-linked companies; the manifesto, he said, only promised that 'appointments [would be] based on merit and professionalism'. Of course, that is what they all say when they appoint politicians to such positions.[151]

---

[151] Ignatius, Dennis, *Paradise Lost*, p. 71.

Promises Undelivered

Although they were very close to their grassroots supporters prior to GE14, now PH leaders became increasingly distant and unresponsive, to the extent of berating activists and party members who criticised PH1.0's vengeful actions, even though these supporters were some of the party's most loyal members who only wanted to see it succeed.[152]

> The signs of discontent were all around them but few PH leaders were willing to take note. Mahathir himself had an almost delusional view of his own popularity. When confronted with an October 2019 Merdeka Centre survey that indicated that support for PH had dropped to 38 per cent from 80 per cent, he said, 'I do not know from where they got the number but I myself know that many people still want to shake my hands and take pictures with me. Also, others (Pakatan leaders) when they go anywhere, people want to take pictures with them (. . .) we know the support for the government is still strong (. . .) so we are not going to be ousted or pulled down (. . .)' While Mahathir and his cabinet continued to insist they remained popular, their poor management of key issues steadily eroded the support they once enjoyed.[153]

Local Elections

Another one of PH's key promises ahead of GE14, was the reinstatement of local council elections which had been abolished in 1976. Following GE14, DAP MP Lim Lip Eng said that Kuala Lumpur Pakatan Harapan lawmakers would push to revive local elections while housing and local government minister Zuraida

---

[152] Ibid., p. 198.

[153] Ignatius, Dennis, *Paradise Lost*, p. 199.

Kamaruddin said she hoped to implement local council elections within three years.[154] But Mahathir disagreed. He believed local elections 'would produce the wrong results that may end up creating divisions between urban areas and less developed parts of the nation. It would also result in conflict due to racial differences and other issues'.[155]

But many realized that his opposition to local council elections was actually based on his fear that such elections could result in having Chinese mayors in in Kuala Lumpur and major cities across the country, something that Malay supremacists could never accept.[156]

As Ignatius noted:

> At so many critical moments in our history, unprincipled and self-serving non-Malay politicians have vacillated, compromised, and acted in their own self-interest to the detriment of the nation and the people they claimed to represent. Their actions facilitated and empowered the unjust system that now plagues us all.
>
> It was a missed opportunity to seriously engage Mahathir about his commitment to Pakatan Harapan and his vision for the future. In the end, when push came to shove, the DAP and others in the coalition chose to go along to get along in the same way that the MCA, MIC, and Gerakan behaved before them.[157]

And something else that Mahathir could not accept was anyone who would interfere and disrupt this cozy crony arrangement that he and his fellow elites enjoyed with a large number of businessmen.

---

[154] Ibid., p. 200.

[155] Ibid.

[156] Ibid.

[157] Ignatius, Dennis, *Paradise Lost*, p. 95.

In his second memoir, *Capturing Hope: The Struggle Continues for a New Malaysia*, Mahathir, without naming him—but whom he later acknowledged—singled out the then Finance Minister Lim Guan Eng's political secretary Tony Pua for his unauthorized involvement in government matters, including making threats to a developer involved in the troubled Exchange106 project in the city centre. Mahathir said Pua was 'delegated a lot to' by Lim and had come to think that he could wield power over civil servants.

Exchange106, marketed as the world's most luxurious office building, is a skyscraper which forms part of the Tun Razak Exchange in Kuala Lumpur, and was developed by Mulia Property Development Sdn Bhd, a company linked to the controversial Indonesian tycoon Djoko Tjandra.

In the building agreement, which was made during Najib's administration, the government agreed to provide a loan to the developer with certain conditions, which included the entire project being handed over to the government if it fell behind schedule. In 2018, the project faced problems after the developer failed to obtain a loan for about half of the cost, and there was a likelihood that the tower could not be completed.

Mahathir became enraged when he found out that Pua had gotten involved in the government's negotiations with the developer and had 'threatened' to take over Mulia's 49 per cent stake for only RM1 after the latter had invested more than RM1.1 billion in the project already.

Mahathir said that Guan Eng felt that Najib's government was crooked and that he should do away with all the contracts entered into by the previous government.

'But when you do that, you hurt the contractors and whoever gets their jobs, including workers, suppliers and supporting companies. So, we cannot simply do away with the contracts nor reduce the contracts by force,' he said.

'As the political secretary, you (Pua) are supposed to report on the politics of the country, not go around implementing government policies.'[158]

'Now, this particular DAP adviser did in fact make this threat despite the fact that billions had already been spent, and he did so without reference to or indeed getting any authorisation from the government,' Mahathir claimed in his 2021 book. 'There were also occasions when this adviser spoke publicly on behalf of the government despite having no standing to do so.'[159]

'(While) I cited only one example (in my book), other businesspeople, (including) a Chinese person, told me that he was very arrogant. That's the word they used. He behaved as if he was the minister,' Mahathir said.[160]

Pua, acknowledging that he was the individual Mahathir was referring to, claimed that he could never have threatened the developer as he had never met or personally spoken to him. Moreover, he claimed negotiations with the company were carried out by the then Deputy Treasurer General Asri Hamidon and the Finance-Ministry-owned TRX City Sdn Bhd, the master developer of Tun Razak Exchange. Pua said that Djoko was angered by a due diligence report requested by the Finance Ministry and had met with Mahathir to complain about it.

---

[158] Adam, Ashman, 'From "arrogant" to 'socialist"', Dr M confirms Finance Ministry aide who overstepped boundaries is Tony Pua', *Malay Mail Online*, 12 Dec 2021, accessed at: https://www.malaymail.com/news/malaysia/2021/12/12/dr-m-confirms-finance-ministry-aide-who-overstepped-boundaries-is-tony-pua/2027857.

[159] Mohamad, Mahathir, *Capturing Hope: The Struggle Continues for a New Malaysia*, MPH Group Publishing: Kuala Lumpur, 2023.

[160] 'Business people complained about Pua's arrogance, says Dr M', *Free Malaysia Today*, 7 Dec 2021, accessed at: https://www.freemalaysiatoday.com/category/nation/2021/12/07/business-people-complained-about-puas-arrogance-says-dr-m/.

Pua said, following the allegation against him, Mahathir summoned Lim in November 2018 and that Lim had defended Pua's role in the dispute with the property developer, adding that the Finance Ministry's action was endorsed after several cabinet deliberations.

'It is unfortunate that he (Mahathir) prefers to believe the words of an extremely crooked foreign tycoon, previously convicted of cheating hundreds of billions of rupiah from Bank Bali in 2009, and subsequently convicted again for forgery in 2020 and bribery in 2021,'[161] Pua said.

In the end, the dispute was resolved quietly, with Mulia completing Exchange106, which was supposed to be delivered in 2018, by December 2019, and who remains a key partner in completing the development of the TRX site.

---

[161] 'Dr M prefers to believe crooked tycoon while I saved taxpayers' money, says DAP's Pua', *Malaysia Now*, 7 Dec 2021, accessed at: https://www.malaysianow. com/news/2021/12/07/dr-m-prefers-to-believe-crooked-tycoon-while-i- saved-taxpayers-money-says-daps-pua.

Chapter 9

The Attorney General: A Keen Advocate of Progress and Justice?

In a blurb on the back cover of Tommy Thomas' controversial memoir—*My Story: Justice in the Wilderness*—the editor of the Sarawak Report website Clare Rewcastle-Brown calls Thomas a 'keen advocate of progress and justice' and commends 'Malaysia's recent foremost lawyer' for his narrative of events because of his 'key insider role'.

However, many in Malaysia might take exception to Rewcastle-Brown's description.

Not only did the person who was prime minister and whom Thomas reported to as Attorney General effectively call much of his book a work of fiction, but a Special Task Force (STF) set up to investigate many of the claims in Thomas' book was of the view that Thomas had not only violated numerous laws but had also abused his position as Attorney General.[162]

If the task force's report is to be believed, Tommy Thomas's tenure as Attorney General appeared to pretty much be a case

---

[162] Laporan Pasukan Petugas Khas: Siasatan ke atas dakwaan-dakwaan dalam buku bertajuk *My Story: Justice in the wilderness* Tulisan YBHG, Tan Sri Tommy Thomas bekas Peguam Negara, 2022, p. VIII, accessed at: https://www.bheuu.gov.my/pdf/Penerbitan/LAPORAN%20PPK%20TT_kelas%20semula_terbuka%201.pdf.

study of what not to do when appointed as the country's top legal officer.

There is no need to dig hard to find out about his alleged transgressions and interference in the country's judiciary because he admitted as much in his book—although they are touted as achievements—published just months after his resignation and when the facts and events were still very much fresh in his mind and thus cannot be later excused as mis-remembered or forgotten due to the fog of time. As Thomas refused to take part, rebut, or clarify his position in the STF's investigations, what he said in his book was taken as fact, and I have also done similarly in quoting from the now declassified report, which has been in public circulation since October 2022 and is easily accessible online.[163]

After the report was released, Thomas filed a lawsuit against the STF and the government, alleging that the report was a 'breach of law and his constitutional rights'. He asked for a declaration that the task force was an unlawful body and had no legal authority to perform the function assigned to it by the Cabinet. He also asked for compensation from the government and for 'aggravated and exemplary damages from the task force members to be paid by each of them personally'.[164]

However, it is interesting that Thomas has not challenged any of the allegations in the report concerning his violation of the Constitution, the Official Secrets Act, or the Penal Code.

---

[163] Laporan Pasukan Petugas Khas: Siasatan ke atas dakwaan-dakwaan dalam buku bertajuk *My Story: Justice in the wilderness* Tulisan YBHG, Tan Sri Tommy Thomas bekas Peguam Negara, 2022, accessed at: https://www.bheuu. gov.my/pdf/Penerbitan/LAPORAN%20PPK%20TT_kelas%20semula_ terbuka%201.pdf.

[164] 'Tommy Thomas sues task force, govt for publishing report on his memoir', *Free Malaysia Today*, 27 Oct 2022, accessed at: https://www.freemalaysiatoday. com/category/nation/2022/10/27/tommy-thomas-sues-task-force-govt-for-publishing-report-on-his-memoir/.

The legal strategy was possibly to attempt to discredit the task force and, in so doing, discredit the report instead of dealing with the allegations within the report—which are based on evidence and fact and would thus be almost impossible to disprove.

This was not surprising given that a few days after the damning report was made public, the Prime Minister's Office said that Thomas would be investigated for sedition and various other offences as recommended in the report. The government has now also sought to quash Thomas' lawsuit which it says is 'scandalous, frivolous, vexatious, and an abuse of the court's process'.[165]

Using the STF's report as the basis, if one wrote *A Dummy's Guide to being Malaysia's Attorney General,* these would likely be the key 'dont's':

- Do not openly condemn the professionalism and capability of your own chambers.
- Do not interfere in the judiciary and trash the Constitution by involving yourself in the appointments of the country's top judges (see Chapter 4 of this book and Appendix 2).
- Don't appoint large numbers of private lawyers and consultants to do the job of your own legal officers, and
- Don't appoint your close friends, who are also your former law firm partners, to key legal positions representing the government.

The problem, I believe, was Thomas was just not experienced enough and was seriously out of his depth in the post of Attorney General. I believe his prejudices and baggage of being in the opposition for years appears to have coloured his actions against

---

[165] 'Court grants Tommy Thomas time to appoint new counsel in suit against task force following Sri Ram's demise', *The Edge Markets*, 30 Jan 2023, accessed at: https://www.theedgemarkets.com/node/653489.

individuals and organizations as well as his views on his fellow governmental legal officers.

As noted in the STF's report that was submitted to the Cabinet in 2022:

> Tan Sri Tommy Thomas was appointed as the Attorney General from the Bar. Though he is legally qualified to be appointed as the Attorney General, he lacked the experience and management skills to head or be in charge of a large Government Department like the Attorney General Chambers with over 2,000 legal officers and many supporting staffs.
>
> Although Tan Sri Tommy Thomas was critical of what he perceived as lack of experience of legal officers in certain areas of the law and their lack of commitment in their work, he did not take or initiate any measures to remedy these shortcomings, the only measure he took was to appoint external lawyers of his choice at the Federal Government's expense.[166]

So, how did Thomas become AG, despite his lack of experience and skills?

Admitted to the Malaysian bar in 1976, Thomas, appears to have had an average career, dealing mainly in company law, where one of his biggest claims to fame was being a lawyer for Chin Peng, the notorious long-time leader of the Malayan Communist Party and the Malayan National Liberation Army.[167]

---

[166] Laporan Pasukan Petugas Khas: Siasatan ke atas dakwaan-dakwaan dalam buku bertajuk *My Story: Justice in the wilderness* Tulisan YBHG, Tan Sri Tommy Thomas bekas Peguam Negara, 2022, p.X, accessed at: https://www.bheuu. gov.my/pdf/Penerbitan/LAPORAN%20PPK%20TT_kelas%20semula_ terbuka%201.pdf.

[167] Between 1948 and 1960, 1,345 Malayan troops and police were killed in addition to 519 Commonwealth personnel. 2,478 civilians were killed, with another 810 recorded as missing. 'The Malayan Emergency', Wikipedia, accessed at: https://en.wikipedia.org/wiki/Malayan_Emergency.

But more importantly, Thomas was a lawyer for Democratic Action Party (DAP) supremo Lim Guan Eng and was a close friend and confidante of Lim and his father, the veteran opposition politician Lim Kit Siang. And as with most politicians, a lot of Thomas' work for the Lims and for other DAP leaders was done pro-bono, or for free.

Many lawyers working for the various political parties in Malaysia have become inured to the situation where their political clients do not or rather rarely pay in full for legal services provided, promising that they will either pay later or make it up when they are in some position of power. However, many of these lawyers appear not to mind it because they are likely ideological supporters of their clients, and they also have the cache and status of being identified as a certain leader's lawyer or legal representative.

Thomas was one of Lim's counsel when he was charged with using his position as then Penang Chief Minister to allegedly gain gratification for himself and his wife, Betty Chew Gek Cheng, by approving an application in 2015 by Magnificent Emblem Sdn Bhd, a company owned by businesswoman Phang Li Koon, for the conversion of agricultural land in the town of Balik Pulau to a public housing zone.

In 2016, Lim had then allegedly used his position to obtain a plot of land and a bungalow from Phang for RM2.8 million, at below market value. The market price for the land and bungalow at that time was allegedly RM4.27 million. Lim allegedly knew Phang had a formal relationship with the Penang state government.

Even before GE13 in 2013, Thomas had been lobbying the Lims and the then Pakatan Harapan leadership for the post of Attorney General, should the coalition have won the elections, but Barisan Nasional (BN) managed to retain their hold onto power and Thomas' hopes were dashed.[168]

---

[168] Thomas, Tommy, *My Story: Justice in the Wilderness*, Strategic Information and Research Development Centre, 2021, p. 226.

However, Thomas' chances improved dramatically when Mahathir was appointed as leader of PH1.0 ahead of GE14 and which, Thomas admitted, had 'a profound effect on my chances of becoming Attorney General'.[169]

Within the opposition leadership, it was well known that Guan Eng and Kit Siang were strongly lobbying for Thomas as the PH1.0 Government's Attorney General despite his serious lack of experience.

The majority of Malaysia's former Attorney Generals were not only very senior in the legal field , but also had the breadth of experience and expertise in managing or running large legal organizations. However, Thomas did not rise through the ranks within the chambers nor had he been appointed a chief judge, who would have had such attendant experience.

Mahathir had met Thomas in 2015 on the issue of 1MDB, and according to Thomas' account, Mahathir appreciated Thomas' contributions and had about ten meetings with him 'discussing the administration of the state of justice and the ways and means of improving it'. It's a shame that very few—if any—of these 'ways and means' were implemented when Thomas held the post of the Attorney General.

However, Thomas was fearful that he would be pipped to this position:

> On election night, Zainur, Ambiga, and I were invited to the Sheraton Hotel, Petaling Jaya, which was the base for the leaders of the Pakatan coalition. We were shocked to see Gopal Sri Ram. As was his wont, he immediately surrounded himself with Tun Dr Mahathir, and the other leaders of Pakatan. We were aware that Haniff Khatri was vying for the post of Attorney General.[170]

---

[169] Ibid., p. 227.

[170] Ibid., p. 230.

However, it was obvious that the strong lobbying by the Lims had worked when Kit Siang , in a cryptic phone conversation on the Saturday following GE14, told Thomas that 'all legal reforms are in your hands'.[171] A few days later, Thomas claimed that Mahathir told him he would be AG despite resistance from the King.[172]

Within days of taking over as Attorney General, Thomas's disdain for his officers became obvious:

> I realized that lawyers from the AG's Chambers acting for the government did not have the same commitment, passion and drive to succeed as their counterparts in the Bar.[173]

Instead of leading the legal officers and service by helping to build this commitment and passion among his officers as well as improving their skills and abilities, Thomas effectively side lined a large number of his officers, claiming they were incompetent and inexperienced, and in so doing, appointed a plethora of external lawyers whom he considered top notch, to advise or represent the government in several high-profile cases. Is it then a wonder that the officers at the Attorney General's Chambers became demoralized and demotivated?

> This situation has not happened in the history of the Civil Service, where so many external lawyers were appointed as the AG to advise on legal matters and/or to represent the government in cases.[174]

Twenty-two lawyers and law firms were appointed, including foreign lawyers, and this did not sit well with government

---

[171] Ibid., p. 231.

[172] Ibid.

[173] Ibid., p. 236.

[174] Laporan Pasukan Petugas Khas, p. 193.

procedures as these external lawyers, who were appointed to advise or represent the government, had access to highly confidential documents and information. During his short tenure, Thomas spent over RM3.5 million[175] on these external and foreign lawyers.

What was even more galling was the fact that many of these supposedly top-notch lawyers were actually close friends and/or former partners in his legal firm. There appeared to be a serious lack of transparency and integrity in the manner in which these external lawyers were selected or appointed.

One of Thomas' first challenges as Attorney General, and which showed just how out of his depth he was, was the case of the *Equanimity*.

As was widely reported, the superyacht was believed to have been purchased by fugitive businessman Jho Low using funds embezzled from 1MDB and the ship had been detained by Indonesian authorities. With permission from the Indonesian authorities and the US Department of Justice, the vessel was handed over to Malaysia and docked at Port Klang on 7 August 2018.

In his book, Thomas claimed the whole *Equanimity* case was very complex:

> I discovered that no one in the AGC had any experience in shipping and maritime matters. They had neither arrested ships nor opposed arrests. AGC lawyers had never had an opportunity to appear before the Admiralty Courts. I turned to Malaysia's leading shipping law barrister, Sitpah Selvaratnam. She was my partner in Skrine & Co., where both of us began our legal careers, and in our small firm which we established in 2000. She was excited by the good news from Indonesia, and happy to lead the team.[176]

---

[175] Ibid., p. 112.

[176] Thomas, Tommy, *My Story*, p. 290.

Because of the complexity of the matter, I had appointed Joseph & Partners, a leading shipping firm, as Malaysia's solicitors. As counsel, I also appointed Ong Chee Kwan and Jeremy Joseph, both stars in the shipping fraternity. From the AGC, Alice Loke, Senior Federal Counsel, attended court from time to time or sent a colleague. (Thomas's special assistant) Rahayu, who had much shipping experience in the Bar, was also a member of our legal team. Counsel, led by Sitpah Selvaratnam, appeared before Justice Khadijah Idris, the Admiralty judge. The court issued the Warrant of Arrest.[177]

Again, the Special Task Force was confounded by Thomas' explanations and justification in appointing his former partner and other external lawyers for the case.

This is because regardless of whether AGC officers had any experience in arresting ships etc, Order 70 of the Rules of Court 2012 laid out very clearly all that needed to be done in order to commence an admiralty action and secure a warrant of arrest against a vessel, something that any competent lawyer could do. Given that no one had entered a caveat against the Malaysian Government's arrest in the caveat book at the High Court, and that the ship was in the physical possession of the Malaysian Government and being guarded by the Malaysian Navy, this also meant that it would be a straightforward and simple case of Malaysia's admiralty court allowing the government's arrest and disposal of the ship. Instead, Thomas made the process look like some massively complex and gargantuan task that required several specialists.

As the task force concluded:

This gives rise to a reasonable inference that he was more keen to engage private lawyers, including a former partner in

---

[177] Ibid., p. 292.

private practice, to handle this matter for 1MDB Group and the Government of Malaysia rather than to let himself or the officers from his Chambers, under his guidance, to carry out the conduct of the legal proceedings relating to the arrest and sale of the Equanimity in accordance with the procedures so clearly set out in Order 70 Rules of Court, 2012 and armed with the facts obtained from DOJ, MACC and 'specialist officers in AGC on money laundering' in support of the cause of action.[178]

The open tender for the judicial sale of the *Equanimity* closed on 28 November 2018. Sealed offers received were opened by the sheriff the next day. Unfortunately, none of the bids were above the expedited sale value of the *Equanimity*. So, the sale was aborted.

According to the task force's finding, Thomas then decided that he would become the salesman for the vessel and negotiate a deal directly.

On 13 December 2018, on our application, the Admiralty Court ordered the *Equanimity* to be sold by way of private treaty or private direct sale at a price higher or equal to the appraised value. This marked the beginning of the Second Phase Judicial Sale of the Equanimity. The cut-off date for the second phase was 31st March 2019.[179]

With the dateline of 31st March 2019, I had to take some action. I thought a direct approach to Genting Bhd, who are experienced in the cruise business, would be fruitful. Through an intermediary, I asked to see Tan Sri Lim Kok Thay, the principal director and shareholder of Genting, and son of the founder. I had never met Tan Sri Lim; our path had never crossed. Tan Sri visited my residence on 20th March 2019. The intermediary was present. Over tea, the three of us

---

[178] Laporan Pasukan Petugas Khas, p. 96.

[179] Thomas, Tommy, *My Story*, p. 296.

chatted. After about twenty minutes, I brought up the subject. Tan Sri Lim immediately agreed to purchase the yacht. I told him the guide price fixed by the Court was US$130 million, which fact he knew, hence, an offer from Genting must be sufficiently close to that guide price or even higher. Tan Sri Lim said that the highest he could go was US$126 million. I immediately accepted.

On the 3 April 2019, the Admiralty Court approved the acceptance of Genting's offer to purchase the *Equanimity* on the Sheriff's terms and conditions. I issued a media release on the same day. The US$126 million purchase price was paid by Genting by the end of April 2019.[180]

Note that the Admiralty Court, in Thomas' words, had instructed that the vessel be sold at a price 'higher or equal to the appraised value' of US$130 Million. Yet, Thomas had 'immediately accepted' to sell it for US$126 Million, which was below the appraised value. And Thomas was alleged to have unilaterally accepted the lower offer without consulting or making reference to 1MDB, the Minister of Finance Incorporated—that owns 1MDB—nor the National Anti-Financial Crime centre—which handles seized financial crimes properties.

Was Thomas so desperate to sell the vessel to Genting that he was willing to unilaterally accept a lower offer and do anything to sweeten the deal for Genting?

The task force thought so:

The STF's investigation reveals that at about the same time, there was a judicial review application by Genting Berhad against the Minister of Finance (Permohonan Bagi Semakan Kehakiman No. WA-25-397-12/2018) seeking an order of the Court to quash a decision of the Minister of Finance to cancel

---

[180] Ibid., pp. 297–298.

the tax incentive approved by the Minister vide letter dated 17 December 2014 and a declaration that the terms of the tax incentive approved for the applicant through the said letter, including Genting Berhad's income from its various business activities as derived from one business source for the purpose of claiming the tax incentive granted in 2014, be reinstated. The Minister of Finance through the AGC had resisted Genting Berhad's application and had prepared an affidavit in the opposition.

However, when the sale of the *Equanimity* to Genting Berhad was approved by the MOT Court, the application by Genting was withdrawn and the Minister of Finance by letter dated 4th July 2019 agreed to restore the original decision of the Minister, whereby the investment incentive can be claimed against all income of Genting which is stated to be derived from one source.[181]

So, was this a quid pro quo for Genting's acceptance of the *Equanimity* sale deal?

His alleged lack of probity could also be seen in the case of the Malaysian Government's bid to challenge the European Union over its discriminatory laws on palm oil, when Thomas summarily discharged—without consultation or any authority to do so—the veteran foreign lawyers appointed by the Ministry of Primary Industry for Malaysia's challenge against the EU, on the pretext that foreign lawyers were more expensive than local lawyers who would 'loyally serve the national interest'[182] but then subsequently appointed Toby Landau QC and another junior foreign barrister, to the case.

In early 2019, the then Plantations Minister Teresa Kok told Thomas that the Cabinet wanted to challenge the EU's

---

[181] Laporan Pasukan Petugas Khas, p. 100.

[182] Thomas, Tommy, *My Story*, p. 370.

discriminatory laws against Malaysian palm oil, which Malaysia claimed was a violation of the EU's obligations under World Trade Organization rules. Since 2017, the Ministry and various other bodies, including the Malaysian Palm Oil Board and the Palm Oil Research Institute of Malaysia had been preparing a challenge, having set up a Palm Oil War Room to monitor and assess the EU's RED II and DR regulations—which effectively identified palm oil as the only feedstock to be excluded from the EU's renewable energy market. The War Room consisted of senior officials from the Malaysian Palm Oil Board, the Malaysian Palm Oil Council, the foreign ministry and the international and trade ministry. The group was advised by a European lawyer, Paolo R. Vergano, who had vast experience in the EU and World Trade Organization legal arena.

However, instead of taking advantage of the significant intelligence and experience these teams had in preparing earlier representations to the EU, Thomas decided to reinvent the wheel.

His first act was to appoint—as was now his modus operandi—a group of five lawyers from the Bar, namely Sitpah Selvaratnam—Thomas' former law firm partner, Yeo Yang Poh, Dhinesh Baskaran, Cheng Mai, and Fahri Azzat. This in and of itself was not an issue. What was, was the fact that none of them had any significant experience in handling trade disputes before the WTO.

Thomas admits as much, when he says in his book that 'influencing my choices were their familiarity with business and scientific issues',[183] not international trade law or anything else more relevant.

He then asked Kok to get her ministry to hold a meeting to brief the five lawyers on the case. The ministry officials, who had worked for years on the case, were unhappy with the sudden

---

[183] Ibid., p. 369.

attempt to hand over the case to these five lawyers who had no experience in trade disputes.

Ten lawyers—the five above and another five from the Attorney General's Chambers—accompanied Thomas to the meeting, which was attended by dozens of stakeholders and senior officials from the various ministries. After a lengthy briefing by a ministry official, Thomas gave his view on the legal issues involved and invited his team to give their views.

As the STF noted:

> To (Thomas') perception, the civil servants and their 'guests' from various governmental bodies were not happy with his approach and his appointment of the five lawyers from the Bar. He learnt that the Ministry has appointed a European firm which had a presence in Belgium who were apparently specialists on WTO law. (Thomas) responded by saying that 'since this was a Malaysian case involving Malaysians working in the oil palm industry it was critical that our lawyers be involved. Not only would they be cheaper, they would loyally serve the nation's interests.[184]

Thomas was unhappy with the way he felt that his legal team was treated.

> What is obvious is that TSTT (Thomas) was unhappy with the Ministry which did not like his appointment of the five lawyers from the Bar and bringing them to the meeting chaired by the Ministry.
>
> On account of this, he retaliated by preparing the case for the challenge to the EU, without or little input from the Ministry which has jurisdiction of palm oil and the issues surrounding the discrimination of this commodity by the EU.

---

[184] Ibid., p. 370.

TSTT arbitrarily took over the function of the Ministry and made his own decision as to how he wanted the EU challenge to be handled essential through the five lawyers he appointed and an (foreign) arbitration specialist, Toby Landau who has no track record of handling trade dispute settlement at the WTO.[185]

Given that Thomas himself was also no expert on trade law and neither were his legal team, the sum total of all work done on the EU challenge amounted to very little.

The first step in the WTO challenge process was that of consultation between Malaysia and the EU at the WTO. In fact, a draft request for such a consultation had already been prepared in December 2019 and could have jointly been submitted with a similar consultation request that Indonesia had submitted that same month.

However, the inexperience of the new legal team and the fact that they were still not up to speed meant that when Indonesia held consultations with the EU in February 2020, all Malaysia could do was attend as an observer. Not surprisingly, once Thomas stepped down as Attorney General, all these external lawyers that Thomas appointed ceased to act for Malaysia.

So, all the taxpayer funds expended on the expenses and fees of these local and foreign lawyers appeared to be a total waste. And all the work and opinions produced by Thomas' team did not appear to be useful in Malaysia's eventual WTO submissions.[186]

The only ones to benefit from the case were most of the external lawyers who not only got their fees but who could also now claim on their resumes or publicity materials that they had WTO trade dispute experience and had also represented the Malaysian Government.

---

[185] Laporan Pasukan Petugas Khas, p. 125.
[186] Laporan Pasukan Petugas Khas, p. 120.

The task force's investigations also found that Thomas had attempted to have three members of the Bar, selected by himself, directly appointed to the Court of Appeal, on the pretext that the court's 'weakness' was the lack of judges with 'commercial experience'[187], a view that was not shared by the Bar Council or his replacement for the post of the Attorney General.

As if that was not enough, Thomas' involvement in the dismissal, arrest, detention, and prosecution of Sundra Rajoo, the then Director of the Asia International Arbitration Centre, was also very worrying. Sundra Rajoo, as head of an international organization, enjoyed diplomatic immunity under Malaysia's AIAC Regulation Act.

However, after Thomas received an anonymous letter alleging Sundra Rajoo's involvement in corrupt practices, the Director was arrested upon his return to KL in November 2018 and charged in court. While Sundra Rajoo was being charged in court, and following assurances from a Malaysian Anti-Corruption Commission officer of a solid case against Sundra Rajoo, Thomas told his assistant to call Sundra Rajoo's lawyer and 'to demand his client's resignation to be texted to her within half an hour, failing which I would dismiss him as Director'. Sundra Rajoo sent a handwritten note of his resignation as the AIAC director within the specified time.[188]

Thomas forced Sundra Rajoo to resign—not take leave or be suspended—within hours of being charged and long before a court could determine whether Sundra Rajoo was guilty or not.[189]

How could Thomas do this given that the Director of the AIAC was *not* appointed, nor could be fired, by the Attorney

---

[187] Thomas, Tommy, *My Story*, p. 344.

[188] Ibid., pp. 392–393.

[189] The forced resignation was a finding of fact made by the High Court in 2019.

General as the AIAC came under the purview of the minister in the Prime Minister's Office in charge of Law, V.K. Liew?

Thomas said that he told Liew, 'I would act on my own on behalf of the government to take all necessary steps with regards to the next appointment of the AIAC's director, because the minister had been named in the poison letter. I advised the minister that he would therefore have a conflict of interest.'[190]

Allegations had been made in a poison-pen letter and none of the claims had been proven in court yet. As such, there was, at the material time, no ministerial conflict of interest. And the Attorney General was in no position to dismiss or make appointments, unless it was gazetted in law, which it was not. This is because the AIAC was the minister's responsibility, not Thomas'.

Yet, Thomas took it—illegally?—upon himself, not only to demand Sundra Rajoo's resignation, but 'within eight hours' found a replacement in the form of Vinayak Pradhan, who was one of Thomas' mentors, whom he studied with in school, who was a senior partner who brought him into his first legal practice, and who was also one of his former legal firm partners.

It is interesting to note that Sundra Rajoo was only charged on the morning of 21 November 2018 but by the afternoon of the same day, Thomas—not the minister or the minister's office—had issued a press release announcing Pradhan as replacing Sundra Rajoo as Director.

The press release is also controversial because Thomas claimed in it that his actions were supported by Dr Kennedy Gastorn, the Secretary General of the Asian African Legal Consultative Organization (AALCO), of which the AIAC was a part. However, Gastorn denied ever agreeing to Thomas' actions and later even wrote to the High Court judge hearing Sundra Rajoo's judicial review application.

---

190   Thomas, Tommy, *My Story*, p. 393.

The MACC officers attempted to remand Sundra Rajoo despite the fact that he notified them that he was immune from arrest and detention as he was a High Officer under the AIAC Regulation Act 485 and Act 636. The Court rightly threw out the MACC's application.

On 5 March 2019, Sundra Rajoo sought leave to commence judicial review proceedings against the Attorney General, the government, and others, seeking a declaration that he was immune from criminal proceedings as he was a former High Officer and the claimed 'offence' occurred when he was carrying out his duties as Director.

Thomas was unhappy with this situation. At his urging, the government had written to the AALCO to waive Sundra Rajoo's immunity, and Thomas had also worked with Pradhan in getting Pradhan to withdraw his predecessor's immunity, which failed as only AALCO could do this. On 22 March 2019, the AALCO sent a letter to the Foreign Ministry rejecting Thomas' request.

On the same day as the request for the waiving of immunity had been rejected, Thomas proceeded to approve three charges against Sundra Rajoo for criminal breach of trust for the alleged wrongful use of AIAC monies to purchase copies of *Law, Practice, and Procedure of Arbitration* that had been authored by Sundra Rajoo.

The fact that the AALCO had formally approved the AIAC's purchase of Sundra Rajoo's book and that all royalties were previously given to the organization, appeared irrelevant to Thomas.

The High Court initially dismissed Sundra Rajoo's judicial review application. Thomas then ensured that Sundra Rajoo was charged in the Sessions Court with the three trumped-up charges. Again, Sundra Rajoo rightly claimed immunity.

Things looked bleak for Sundra Rajoo, who appeared to be railroaded.

But the Court of Appeal eventually overturned the dismissal and sent it back to the High Court to be heard on its merits.

This time, the High Court allowed the application, issued an order to quash all three charges and made a finding of fact that Sundra Rajoo was 'forced to resign as Director of AIAC'.[191]

But, in violation of the High Court's ruling, the Deputy Public Prosecutor, on the instructions of Thomas, insisted at the Sessions Court that proceedings and charges continue. Wisely, the Sessions Court judge dismissed the charges.

Later, not only did the Federal Court affirm the High Court's decision, but it noted:

> (Thomas) was aware that (Sundra Rajoo) had the necessary immunity; that the charges were baseless as the purchase of the book was done officially for the purposes of promoting arbitration in Malaysia and having the sanction from AALCO; and that (Sundra Rajoo) did not enjoy any form of gratification as a result of AIAC's purchase of the Book.
>
> <u>In short, Thomas had persecuted Sundra Rajoo by using his prosecutorial powers as the then Public Prosecutor.</u>[192]
>
> The Federal Court also ruled that '(Thomas) had acted in concert with (Pradhan) to appoint (Pradhan) as the then Acting Director of AIAC. In appointing (Pradhan) as the then acting Director, (Thomas) had usurped the powers of the Minister of Law, Liew Vui Keong, in contravention of the Ministerial Functions Act 1969'.

The task force also noted how Thomas had 'manipulated' the tabling of the Cabinet paper on the appointment of Pradhan as

---

[191] Laporan Pasukan Petugas Khas, p. 143.
[192] Ibid., p. 144.

the Director of the AIAC by using the Foreign Ministry instead
of going through the minister in the Prime Minister's Office for
Parliament and Law.

Claiming that the appointment of the Director of the AIAC
came under the duties of the Foreign Minister—when it legally
and constitutionally did not—Thomas was able to usurp Minister
Liew's power and pushed through his Cabinet Paper appointing
Pradhan, through the Foreign Minister—although the funding and
salaries for Pradhan and the AIAC still came from Liew's office.[193]

And what is even more damning is the fact that nowhere in
the Cabinet Paper or in Thomas' letter to the Cabinet is his close
relationship with Pradhan listed or mentioned. This was despite
the fact that the Cabinet Meeting memorandum noted that the
procedures and processes in selecting the AIAC Director was free
of any bias or conflict of interest.[194]

One wonders how the selection could be free of bias and
conflict of interest if Thomas didn't even declare his close and
personal relationship with Pradhan to the Cabinet?

More   importantly,   under   the   Malaysian   Anti-
Corruption Act 2009:

> An officer of a public body shall be presumed, until the contrary
> is proved, to use his office or position for any gratification,
> whether for himself, his relative or associate, when he makes
> any decision, or takes any action, in relation to any matter in
> which such officer, or any relative or associate of his, has an
> interest, whether directly or indirectly.[195]

---

[193] Ibid., p. 157.
[194] Ibid., p. 158.
[195] Ibid., p. 163.

And why did Thomas have it in for Sundra Rajoo?

> Sundra Rajoo had an excellent personal relationship with my
> predecessors and the Law Ministers. Sundra Rajoo shunned
> the desk officers, and would always go above their heads,
> directly to the Minister or the AG. Sundra Rajoo was seeking
> a third extension, which would have entitled him to serve for
> twelve years in total. The Law Minister, V.K. Liew, mentioned
> this to my surprise shortly after I took office.[196]

Could it be that Thomas was disgusted with Sundra Rajoo's close
relationship with his political foes, the former Barisan Nasional
Attorney General and ministers and felt Sundra Rajoo had to be
gotten rid of as he was a BN stooge in Thomas' eyes?

And that even the then Minister responsible for the AIAC
Liew Vui Keong—who had also been part of BN previously—
held a positive view of Sundra Rajoo, which was why Thomas
couldn't get the Minister to fire Sundra Rajoo and hire Pradhan,
and so Thomas hatched a plan to get his way by sidestepping
Liew and using the Foreign Minister to propose Pradhan in order
to get Cabinet approval, but failing to mention his very close
relationship with the appointee?

Yet another alleged instance of Thomas wasting government
funds and time came when he decided to set up a government
tribunal to remove six Election Commission (EC) Commissioners
even though five had already resigned and would leave office
before the tribunal could even get started.

Thomas' strong support and belief in the BERSIH
movement—ostensibly fighting for free and fair elections—
appears to have coloured and shaped his views of the EC.

---

[196] Thomas, Tommy, *My Story*, pp. 397–398.

Following a letter from BERSIH alleging electoral misconduct and irregularities, Thomas decided to pursue what appeared to be a personal grievance against the EC and its commissioners in support of BERSIH's allegations.

After all, in his book, Thomas claimed:

> Mishandling general elections for decades by successive Election Commissions had been the norm . . . Free and fair elections have not been held in Malaysia for decades. Gerrymandering and voter manipulation have been the order of the day. Hence, Bersih's rallying cry that the GE13 and GE 14 should be conducted freely and fairly received the support of millions of Malaysians, noting that, 'Bersih organized rallies questioning the freeness and fairness of our electoral process. Thousands attended peacefully. I went to all the rallies.'

EC Chairman Azhar Azizan Harun had informed Thomas that the five would be leaving office by 1 January 2019 and he didn't think any action ought to be taken. More importantly, the minister in the Prime Minister's Office, Liew Vui Keong, whose portfolio covers the EC—yes, the same Minister whose powers Thomas had usurped in the Sundra Rajoo case—had told parliament that as the commissioners were resigning, no tribunal would be set up.

Yet, in direct contradiction of what the minister told parliament, Thomas went to see Mahathir to push through the setting up of the tribunal with the body beginning work on 28 January 2019. Was Thomas looking for revenge for the decades of supposedly unfair elections?

But what Thomas didn't expect was the fact that his own chosen legal counsel disagreed with what amounted to a personal vendetta against the commissioners.

Lead counsel M Puravalen had more than thirty-five years of experience as a trial lawyer and was touted by Thomas as an 'election expert'. He was fully aware of the facts in regard to the EC commissioners and was clearly uncomfortable with what appeared to be yet another railroading exercise by the Attorney General.

So, on the first day of the tribunal's hearings, when asked by the members whether its work was academic, given that the Commissioners had left office, Puravalen replied that it was.

This shocked and enraged Thomas, who immediately fired Puravalen and appeared in person before the tribunal to argue on what was ostensibly a waste of the tribunal's time.

In the end, the tribunal by a majority of three to two decided that its proceedings were academic and an 'exercise in futility'.[197]

In its findings on Thomas' actions, the government's Special Task Force noted:[198]

> All the above facts are a clear manifestation of abuse of powers in the pursuit of TSTT's personal grievances against the EC and its commissioners and in support of Bersih's allegations of misconduct and lack of fairness in the conduct of elections in Malaysia.
>
> (...) Although he has resigned from office and disciplinary action may not be taken against him by the Government, but the Government may be exposed to being sued by the affected Commissioners on the grounds that there was misfeasance in public office committed by TSTT as in the Datuk Sundra Rajoo case.

Thus, it was not surprising that the Cabinet-appointed Task Force's conclusion on Thomas' book and on his actions was damning:[199]

---

[197] Laporan Pasukan Petugas Khas, p. 175.

[198] Ibid., p. 180.

[199] Ibid., p. 217.

That TSTT had involved himself in the appointment of senior members of the superior courts whereas under the Federal Constitution and the Judicial Appointments Act, 2019 (JAC 2019), there is no role for an Attorney General (who appears in Court like his other legal officers and members of the Bar) to play in the appointment of Judges to the superior courts. In the circumstances, the active involvement of the Attorney General in the judicial appointments could create a perception of the close affinity between the AG and his officers with the Judiciary, a situation which he himself expressed concern over in his book.

That he attempted to have three members of the Bar, selected by himself, for direct appointment to the Court of Appeal, on the pretext that Court's 'weakness' was the lack of Judges with 'commercial experience' (Thomas, *My Story*, p. 344)—a view not shared by the Bar Council and the present Attorney General.

TSTT revived stale allegations of 'forum shopping' to tarnish the image of the Judiciary, which could erode public confidence in our judicial system, even though he must have known from his experience in the Bar before his appointment, that the current electronic filing system, as explained by the Chief Registrar of the Federal Court (who came to assist the STF in its deliberations), the assignment of Judges and Courts to hear cases would be done under this electronic filing system. No mention was made in his Book about the current electronic filing system, thus giving an impression to a reader of his Book that the unhealthy practice of so-called 'judge shopping' is still prevalent.

There had been unauthorized disclosures of government information and official secrets including the publication in his Book of such information obtained whilst holding office as Attorney General, without the requisite authorization, and an investigation ought to be carried into the infringement of various laws and Government regulations by TSTT in the publication of such information and official secrets.

There had been instances of abuse of authority, as highlighted in this report, particularly in the exercise of statutory powers to appoint external lawyers (many of those appointed were close friends or former partners of his such as Sitpah Selvaratnam and her husband) to represent the government in cases or disputes with third parties or to prosecute offences. His purported justification was that there was lack of experience amongst his officers in the Attorney General's Chambers to handle certain matters which he deemed complicated. But there was also lack of transparency and integrity in the manner in which the external lawyers were selected or appointed and his discharge of the lawyers (in Brussels) appointed by the Ministry of Primary Industry for Malaysia's challenge against the EU's discriminatory laws on Palm Oil, was arbitrary and upon the untenable pretext that foreign lawyers are more expensive than local lawyers who would 'loyally serve the national interest'—he himself subsequently appointed a foreign lawyer, Toby Landau QC and another junior barrister, for this Malaysian EU Palm Oil dispute to be taken up to the WTO.

Additionally, there had been non-compliance with government regulations and circulars governing the procurement of services of external lawyers and in the settlement of cases relating to the sale of the Equanimity and the claim by the estate of Boonsom Boonyanit under the ASEAN Agreement for promotion and protection of investment 1987.

Since TSTT, a senior practicing lawyer, was appointed from the Malaysian Bar, the legitimate expectations of the Government and public was that the standard of ethics and professional conduct of the Malaysian Bar as prescribed in the

Legal Profession (Practice and Etiquette) Rules 1978 [PU(A) 369/1978] would be duly observed and maintained by him. Thomas' revelation in his book of conversations between him and the-then Prime Minister, regarding his appointment, but intended to be confidential, before he took office as Attorney General, and his revelations of his conversation with the Chief Justice during a courtesy call on her, must be viewed as breach of confidence and unethical behaviour.[200]

So, the Task Force recommended, among other things, that Thomas be investigated under the following sections for the 'possibility of . . . offences being committed':[201]

Sections 124I and 203A of the Penal Code.
Section 4 of the Sedition Act 1948.
Section 8 of the Official Secrets Act 1972.
Section 23 Malaysian Anti-Corruption Commission (MACC) Act 2009.

The Special Task Force (also) recommends that the Auditor General's Office and related government agencies conduct an audit and appropriate investigation on the Attorney General's Chambers to determine if there were any misconduct by TSTT when he was the Attorney General. This investigation should focus on among others but not limited to the prosecution of high-profile cases, appointment of external lawyers and the setting up of the Election Commission Tribunal. This is to also determine if there are any circulars and/or instructions that were not adhered to in his position as a Public Officer.

---

[200] Ibid., p. 217.
[201] Ibid., p. 220.

Following the Task Force's recommendations, the government in January 2023 agreed to set up a Royal Comission of Inquiry to further investigate Thomas' book and the allegations of misconduct.[202] So, is Thomas really 'a keen advocate of progress and justice'?

---

[202] Khairulrijal, Rahmat, 'RCI to be set up to investigate Tommy Thomas' controversial memoir', *New Straits Times*, 11 Jan 2023, accessed at: https://www.nst.com.my/news/nation/2023/01/869404/updated-rci-be-set-investigate-tommy-thomas-controversial-memoir.

Chapter 10

Asal Bukan Anwar!

Mahathir's claimed that he had no problems with Anwar prior to GE14. He said he had no issue with Anwar during his twenty-two months in power and even after PH1.0 imploded in February 2020. However, I believe these claims can be summed up in one word:

Rubbish.

Mahathir had never wanted to hand over power to Anwar and even though he had agreed to Anwar taking over—as part of the deal with DAP and PKR in becoming the leader of PH1.0—he plotted and schemed to ensure that this would never happen.

When asked in Doha in December 2019 about his plans to hand over power to Anwar, Mahathir claimed that he could not guarantee that his successor would be up to the task as Mahathir had 'bad experiences' with his successors as 'when they took over, they did different things'.[203]

And the biggest slur he could use against Anwar, just weeks after the collapse of the PH1.0 Government, was to publicly call him a 'liberal'.[204] It was the ultimate insult against a Malay Muslim leader, as the term is local code for those who support Western values and LGBTQ+ rights, which a majority of Malay Muslims shun. It was also a veiled reference to Anwar being tried and

---

[203] Ignatius, Dennis, *Paradise Lost*, p. 41.
[204] Ibid.

found guilty of sodomy. So, calling Anwar liberal meant that he was morally unfit to be prime minister.

'When Anwar left (UMNO) he formed a liberal party. He wanted the support of Democratic Action Party, so he invited DAP in, invited Parti Islam Se-Malaysia (PAS) in. His philosophy is liberal,' Mahathir told a news portal in March 2020.[205]

But then, by this same logic, didn't Mahathir's deal with DAP in forming PH1.0 mean that Mahathir was head of and encouraged a 'liberal' government?

Even before GE14, Mahathir was already plotting how he would be able to bypass Anwar and still secure the leadership of PH. And the solution came to him in the form of Azmin Ali.

Azmin had known Mahathir for decades and, funnily enough, had started working for Anwar in 1987 as his personal secretary after Mahathir had advised Azmin to do so.

Over the years, Azmin became a close Anwar loyalist and remained as Anwar's aide until his sacking in 1998, and he along with Zahid Hamidi led protests against Anwar's dismissal, following which Azmin was arrested. Out in the political wilderness while Anwar was incarcerated, he and Anwar both became founders of Parti Keadilan Nasional, which eventually became today's Parti Keadilan Rakyat (PKR).

Azmin won the parliamentary seat of Gombak and a state seat in 2008, became PKR Vice President in 2010, and eventually Menteri Besar (MB) of the Pakatan Rakyat (PR)-held state of Selangor.

And this is where the clash between Azmin and Anwar and his family began.

The 'Kajang Move' was a 2014 plan to replace incumbent PKR MB Khalid Ibrahim with Anwar. It was to be achieved with Anwar contesting the state seat of Kajang in a by-election and winning it before the PR-dominated legislature appointed

---

[205] ibid.

him as the new MB. However, after Anwar's conviction over the
Sodomy II case just weeks before the by-election, his wife Wan
Azizah contested the seat and won. PKR, with DAP's support,
then nominated Wan Azizah as the new MB, but both the Sultan
of Selangor and coalition partner PAS wanted other options.
PKR and the DAP submitted only Wan Azizah's name, while
PAS submitted others. But on 22 September 2014, the Sultan
announced the appointment of Azmin as MB, which he held
until GE14.

Following his appointment, relations between Anwar and his
family and Azmin became cool as two factions began emerging
within the party. Regardless, Azmin was still close to Anwar and
a key ally. Now, with Anwar in jail, Azmin's supporters were keen
to see him take over as party president. So, although both leaders
appeared united in public, their factions within the party began
warring, with Azmin now eyeing the presidency for himself.

And as serendipity would have it, this was when Mahathir
reappeared on the scene, holding secret meetings with Azmin
and fellow conspirator Zuraida Kamaruddin, in a bid to secure
Anwar and PKR's support for Mahathir's bid to lead PH1.0 into
the general elections.

Azmin knew that he did not stand a chance at winning the
party's top post by himself, but if Mahathir was able to win GE14,
Azmin's star would be ascending.

Witnesses at the series of meetings said Azmin and Zuraida
were 'confident in having the numbers within the party, to go
against the Anwar family if needed, to secure the party's support
for Mahathir'.[206]

'It was clear that Mahathir did not want to hand over power
to Anwar and the feud between Azmin/Zuraida and the Anwar
family was very obvious,' according to the witness.

---

[206] Interview with PKR Source 2, Kuala Lumpur, 20 Jan 2023.

'This was why,' the source said, 'following GE14, when the Cabinet list was discussed, PKR did not include Azmin in the party's list of Cabinet candidates.'

But Mahathir didn't care. To sidestep PKR, he unilaterally created the new and very powerful Ministry of Economic Affairs that would oversee the trade and industry ministry, Government Linked Companies, the Economic Planning Unit, Petronas, Majlis Amanah Rakyat, FELDA, and FELCRA Berhad.

And Mahathir made Azmin its minister.

This was a clear indication to the PH1.0 coalition parties that Mahathir wanted only to deal with Azmin rather than Anwar and would prefer to hand over power to Azmin. But most chose to ignore the signs.

This was also when Anwar should have acted decisively against Azmin. But he didn't. But groups within PKR that were allied to Anwar saw it for the threat that it was, and unbeknownst to him, began planning operations to topple Azmin. And this would prove to be a major blunder.

Privately, Mahathir had told his party leaders that if Anwar ended up sidelining Azmin, then Azmin might join BERSATU and that was something that Mahathir wanted to encourage. Mahathir felt that Azmin could take the Malaysian United Indigenous Party (BERSATU) and the country to new heights.

Prior to GE14, relations between Mahathir and Azmin had cooled following the initial meetings in 2016 and 2017. Sensing the need for closer cooperation between the two, aides said that Syed Saddiq stepped in to try and rekindle the relationship, engineering a meet between the two at the premiere of the movie *Lee Chong Wei* on 14 March 2018 at Bukit Jalil stadium.

According to an aide of his, Syed Saddiq used Siti Hasmah's office to send an invitation to Azmin, in Mahathir's name, to watch the movie. As a result, Azmin turned up, and the two sat next to each other. They spoke on and off during the entire movie and that appeared to have 'fixed' their relationship. It then began to flourish to a point where Mahathir really saw Azmin as his likely successor in the party and coalition, and once PH1.0 won the elections, as prime minister.

By December 2018, it became abundantly clear to Mahathir's staffers that the prime minister viewed PKR, rather than DAP, as the biggest threat to his leadership and future political plans.

Officials said Mahathir started directing Special Branch to follow Anwar and PKR's top leaders as they appeared, according to Mahathir, to be plotting 'all kinds of actions' against him.

Former Special Branch (SB) Chief and then Police Chief Hamid Bador turned up at Mahathir's office frequently to update him on what Anwar and PKR were up to. Hamid's orders were to track and determine what plots Anwar was involving himself in, and what their plans were to remove Mahathir from power. Hamid allegedly briefed Mahathir on several PKR plots aimed at toppling him and claimed that Anwar was behind several of these.

Hamid showed Mahathir a chart that the SB had worked out, showing the various people Anwar and his party had appointed to positions within the government and those in important posts who remained loyal to Anwar. The number of posts and positions appeared quite extensive.

Although Hamid had made Mahathir aware of what was supposedly a significant threat, surprisingly, Mahathir did not try and counter Anwar by appointing Mahathir loyalists to other government posts to checkmate Anwar at his game.

This was because Mahathir just didn't have any people he could appoint to these posts. Most people that he would have appointed would have normally come from United Malays National Organization (UMNO) in the first place. But with BERSATU, there was no such talent pool as the majority of BERSATU members were either not qualified or would end up creating even more headaches for Mahathir.

Mahathir had also instructed the SB to continue monitoring DAP leaders—as they had done under Barisan Nasional's rule—including Lim Kit Siang, who had been 'quiet' recently. The reason, SB noted, was that Lim had been making numerous trips overseas to meet with Chinese Malaysian communities and the Chinese diaspora around the world, in order to urge them to come to Malaysia and help rebuild the Chinese population and government.

Hamid allegedly reported that Kit Siang had been quite successful so far and the fear now was that he would try and bring in an influx of Malaysian diasporic Chinese to try and increase the community's political dominance in the country and government.

On the other hand, the DAP appeared to be much more 'loyal' than PKR, and Mahathir told aides that Guan Eng was giving him less headaches and was more willing to go along with what Mahathir wanted to do.

An example of this was the often-thorny bilateral relations with neighbouring Singapore. Mahathir told staff that in the cabinet, it was the DAP ministers who backed his position on Singapore in terms of taking a hardline stance on Singapore's access to Malaysian airspace and in the water renegotiations.

He allegedly said the DAP ministers not only voiced their support in the Cabinet but were also publicly singing off the same page, while PKR remained silent on the issue, and it was clear that they were unhappy with Mahathir's posturing against Singapore.

To Cabinet officials, the only PKR minister that appeared 'solidly behind' Mahathir was Azmin. But it was clear to all of them that once Anwar took over, Azmin would likely be out of power.

Mahathir had also become so paranoid that his officers were rumoured to have set up a spy-cam system in his Perdana Putra and Perdana Leadership Foundation offices so that the meetings he had with people could be recorded, and this could later be used as proof or blackmail.

And it had become clear to all and sundry in Perdana Putra that the then ninety-three-year-old politician appeared to suffer from the 'grumpy old man' syndrome in that he 'complained about everything' and 'is unhappy unless things are done in his exact way and his style'.[207] They noted that Mahathir was also slowing down and didn't appear to have the energy for political fights and challenges that he had during his first tenure as prime minister. And he would lose his cool very easily.

This was evident in May 2019 when the crown prince of Johor state or Tengku Mahkota Johor Tunku Ismail Sultan Ibrahim, also known as TMJ, criticized the federal government over a dispute over the ownership of a plot of land that belonged to his father, the Sultan of Johor.

In a heated response, Mahathir, whose relations with Malaysia's royalty had been very cool since he reined in their powers during his first tenure as PM, said:

> I don't want to comment on the Sultan, because if I say anything that is not good, it is not nice because he is the Sultan. But this TMJ, he is a little boy. He is stupid because he does not know what is happening. So, don't talk. When you do not know anything, don't talk.[208]

It was stunning that a head of government would openly attack what many interpreted as a broadside against the country's hereditary rulers. But those working close to him were not surprised, noting that Mahathir had become 'really very emotionally unstable in the office, unlike when he was PM before'.[209]

Privately, some of his aides admitted that Mahathir was 'mentally unstable at times and was not really mentally fit to be PM'. They said that 'he loses his cool very easily and is very

---

[207] Zoom interview with BERSATU leader 3, 15 Mar 2020.

[208] Othman, Ahmad Fairuz, Ariff, Syed Umar, 'Dr M labels TMJ "stupid" and a "little boy"', *New Straits Times*, 6 May 2019, accessed at: https://www.nst.com.my/news/nation/2019/05/486134/dr-m-labels-tmj-stupid-and-little-boy.

[209] Zoom interview with BERSATU leader 5, 12 Sep 2020.

grumpy all the time, scolding his staff and people for no real reason'. They also added that 'he also looks annoyed most of the time'.[210]

> I have lost count how many times Tun has threatened that he will resign. When TMJ made his latest comments, Tun again got enraged and told his staff that he didn't have to put up with all this and that he would resign. But again, he cooled down later. This does not make for a very calm working environment in PMO because it's hard to tell when Mahathir is stable or when he is emotional. It's like working for your grandfather who is not senile but very grumpy and not in control of emotions and words.[211]

Previously, Mahathir had allegedly called the Crown Prince 'a stupid moron' in an interview with a local news outlet and one of Mahathir's very senior aides had to use all his persuasive skills to convince the outlet not to report it.

But the outbursts did not mean that Mahathir didn't have a plan of attack with which to further rein in the royals.

Although he publicly appeared to pay deference to the country's royals, in private he allegedly told his staff during his weekly meetings with them that they should use the instruments of state and the law 'to bog them down'. He urged them to continue to 'find more scandals' and to use the courts and government agencies to take action against them. Mahathir allegedly said that these official actions would bring the royalty to their knees, and they would eventually want to settle and he would be able to rein them in.

An example of the use of the law against the royals, Mahathir reportedly told his staff, was a Facebook post by Mahathir's special media adviser Abdul Kadir Jasin, urging the police chief

---

[210] Zoom interview with BERSATU leader 7, 10 Feb 2021.

[211] Ibid.

and income tax authorities to investigate a company owned by the Johor Royal family.[212]

> Kadir Jasin was effectively Mahathir's private mouthpiece and could say the things that Mahathir cannot say publicly as prime minister. As such, almost everything that Kadir says and does is at the behest of Mahathir and is what Mahathir wants to be said.[213]

Staffers were told that while Mahathir was 'officially' taking the legal route to deal with the Johor royalty, Kadir had been tasked with carrying out an unofficial propaganda and political war against them. Mahathir, they believed, was relying on Kadir to try and destabilize the Johor royalty but not to the point of toppling it.

But again, the problem Mahathir faced in implementing all these plans to 'get things done' was that he just didn't have enough officers or 'hatchet-men' like he did when he was prime minister before.

Mahathir now had to rely on very inexperienced ministers, many of whom were not loyal to him and who ran their 'own kingdoms' and who would have to minute and sign off on any actions being taken by their ministries or agencies, rather than just implementing them blindly.

> This made it hard for Mahathir to carry out 'black operations' like he did when he was PM before, as he just didn't have the machinery and yes-men that he had as President of UMNO.[214]

---

[212] 'Mahathir's adviser urges authorities to probe company linked to Johor royalty', *The Straits Times*, 7 May 2019, accessed at: https://www.straitstimes.com/asia/se-asia/mahathirs-adviser-urges-authorities-to-probe-company-linked-to-johor-royalty.

[213] Zoom interview with BERSATU leader 5, 12 Sep 2020.

[214] Zoom interview with BERSATU leader 5, 12 Sep 2020.

And just when it seemed like the PH1.0 Government would finally get down to the job of governing the country, the battle among factions within PKR pulled the coalition down.

It was obvious that the political alliances within PKR had changed dramatically while Anwar had been incarcerated from 2015 to 2018. While Anwar was detained the first time, the party that Anwar had co-founded with Azmin, had been rebuilt and led by Azmin to a very large extent, and this was also the case during Anwar's second incarceration. As a result, the deputy president now had very significant control and support within the party and this was a threat to many of Anwar's supporters, who felt that Azmin, who was still Menteri Besar of Selangor state, was vying for the party's top post.

It didn't help matters that four months after Anwar's release, the party held a leadership election in November 2018. Although Azmin didn't challenge the post of president and contested his incumbent deputy president's post, Rafizi Ramli—then seen as a very staunch ally of Anwar—decided to take Azmin on in what became a very tight race, with Azmin winning just 51 per cent of the votes.

However, Anwar's supporters were unable to accept Azmin's win, given that Azmin was also a cabinet minister holding the powerful economic affairs portfolio and had the ears of Mahathir. They had been watching Azmin's moves closely and were aware of the talks their deputy president was having with Muhyiddin in trying to form a coalition that would exclude Anwar.

So, they began plotting how to ensure that Azmin would be eliminated as a potential leader within the party and more importantly deep-six his ambition to be a future PM. And it began, yet again, with another 'black operation', which inevitably in the Malaysian political context meant a sex scandal.

So, in the early morning of Tuesday 11 June 2019, the WhatsApp messaging app on the phones of many local and some foreign journalists in Malaysia began pinging. The message was a videoclip that showed someone allegedly resembling Azmin having sex with another man in what appeared to be a hotel room. Some of the clips also included images of alleged funds transfers to Azmin. The clip spread like wildfire with online portals and news sites reporting on it.

By the afternoon, Mahathir had denied knowledge of the video, and the mainstream media had begun publishing stories about it. In the wee hours of the following morning, a young man, Haziq Aziz—who was the principal private secretary to the then Deputy Primary Industries Minister and current senior political secretary to Anwar, Shamsul Iskandar—confessed in a video posted on his Facebook page that he was the man in the video with the minister.

'I urge MACC to investigate Azmin for corruption. He is not an individual who is qualified to be a leader,' Mr Haziq said in the video.[215]

Azmin, of course, denied he was the man in the clip, calling it a 'vicious libel' aimed at destroying his political career. The PKR political bureau also issued a statement rejecting gutter politics and calling for a stop to the distribution of the video. Within days, Haziq was suspended from his post and then fired and expelled from the party. He was detained but later released, while the Malaysian Anti-Corruption Commission cleared Azmin of any wrongdoing. Haziq was eventually arrested, along with eight others including Anwar's political secretary Farhash Wafa Salvador Rizal Mubarak.

Mahathir called for an urgent meeting with Anwar to discuss the situation.

---

[215] Teoh, Shannon, 'Pakatan Harapan's internal feud boils over with gay sex video clip', *The Straits Times*, 12 Jun 2019, accessed at: https://www.straitstimes. com/asia/se-asia/pakatan-harapans-internal-feud-boils-over-with-gay-sex-video-clip.

He strongly believed that Anwar's people were responsible for the tape and were trying to destroy Azmin's reputation and told Anwar he was very unhappy about this.

He then asked Anwar point-blank whether Anwar's people were responsible for the tape, and Anwar vehemently denied that he had anything to do with it.

However, Anwar couldn't say that his people were not involved as it could have been done by some of his more 'extreme' followers.

Anwar told Mahathir that upon finding out about the video on the news, he had ordered his people to stop any such activity if they were involved in any way.

Then, on 18 July 2019, police chief Hamid Bador told the media that the sex tape, which had been forensically examined by Cybersecurity Malaysia, was authentic. But in a strange twist, Hamid said the police were unable to determine the identity of the two men on the tape.

This sent the political rumour mill into overdrive. Many suspected if both or even one man was 'identified', the authorities would have to take legal action against that individual and the individual charged would then be able to bring his allegations to court and would also have the right to forensically examine the video. So, being unable to identify the two meant that the whole issue would be nipped in the bud, even though the accuser, i.e., Haziq, would get away scot free.

But this did not explain why Azmin had not taken separate legal action against Haziq for making slanderous allegations and criminally defaming him.

By 20 July 2019, PKR said it accepted the police chief's statement that Azmin was not the person in the video, and the following day, Anwar, at a PKR retreat, said he was willing to work with Azmin.

However, Azmin, refused to attend the retreat and then openly pledged his loyalty to Mahathir. Mahathir then said the sex video was circulated for political purposes and he would not take any action against Azmin.

Mahathir was livid with Anwar for allowing this internal PKR power struggle to continue and for attempting to destroy Azmin's credibility and career. It was ironic, that Mahathir was fully behind Azmin despite the issue of morality, given Mahathir's obvious 'moral amnesia of what he did to Anwar'.[216]

The fact that Mahathir continued to back Azmin instead of cutting him loose indicated that Mahathir still wanted to hand over power to Azmin rather than Anwar despite any and all of Azmin's failings. Mahathir then ordered his people to carry out a robust defence of Azmin.

The sex-tape plotters were hoping that the video would lead to criminal charges against one of, if not both, the individuals shown in the video and so would end up taking Azmin out of any leadership contest for the party presidency or the country's premiership. But they did not expect to be outmanoeuvred in this manner. Instead of destroying Azmin's reputation and career, all the plotters ended up doing was destroying any last hope of rapprochement between Azmin and Anwar.

Although Azmin felt under attack, he rounded up the party's senior leadership and members of both factions, who met a day before the PKR National Convention on 7 December 2018. At the tense meeting, a ceasefire had been brokered.

However, a day later, Anwar, in his policy speech, warned against individuals behaving like 'Si Kitol',[217] which Azmin

---

[216] Zoom interview with BERSATU leader 7, 10 Feb 2021.

[217] According to the *Malay Annals*, Si Kitol and Raja Mendeliar were treacherous and divisive individuals in 16th century Malacca, who created a situation where Malacca was left vulnerable to the invading Portuguese and which then led to the collapse of the Melaka Sultanate.

claimed served as an opening salvo for several delegates to lash out at him, with one referring to Azmin as an 'ushering minister', given his frequent appearances at the side of Mahathir.[218] That was the final straw for Azmin. He and several delegates walked out of the hall.

Now, it was war.

---

[218] Othman, Ahmad Fairuz, 'Anwar denies policy speech aimed at Azmin', *New Strait Times*, 7 Dec 2019, accessed at: https://www.nst.com.my/news/politics/2019/12/545717/anwar-denies-policy-speech-aimed-azmin.

Chapter 11

The Sheraton Move

I believe that Mahathir was determined to stop Anwar from succeeding him as prime minister at all costs. He put on a good front about respecting PH1.0's succession plan, but it was all a show. I believe his hatred for Anwar was visceral.

Mahathir, as shown in earlier chapters, resented having to rely on the Democratic Action Party (DAP) and Parti Keadilan Rakyat (PKR) to keep him in power. His entire political career had been built around strengthening Malay hegemony and staving off perceived threats from non-Malay parties. So, the current dependence on non-Malay parties was only a means to buy time in order to build an alternative structure.

Mahathir believed his policies and ideas were always right, and it was either his way or the highway. He wanted to rule as he had always ruled, with absolute and unchallenged authority.

Having failed to grow his party sufficiently through early defections, he masterminded a grand scheme to extricate himself from Pakatan Harapan by forging an alliance of Malay parties. This new coalition of Malay parties would immediately block Anwar's ambitions and remove DAP from the government. The only problem was that he could not, and would not, accept both Najib and Zahid as part of this new coalition.

By February 2019, Mahathir had his people working full-time on the top-secret Project Hijrah, in a bid to get more

United Malays National Organization (UMNO) members to defect to the Malaysian United Indigenous Party (BERSATU). He was hoping he could prevail upon Malay leaders to form a new power-sharing arrangement without Najib and Zahid.

The biggest Malay party around was Parti Islam Se-Malaysia (PAS), and its president Hadi Awang had already made entreaties to Mahathir the year before. So, more meetings were now arranged to build that relationship. Following one such meeting in February, Mahathir told his staffers that Hadi was fundamentally looking at ways in order to withdraw their support from UMNO although remain on friendly terms.

Mahathir said that Hadi's meetings with him were really aimed at building bridges with him and BERSATU as Hadi wanted Mahathir to ensure the federal government looked favourably on Kelantan and Terengganu and that the PH1.0 government would be supportive of the PAS-led states rather than be obstructionists.

He said that was most likely why Hadi had also mentioned that if there was a vote of no confidence against Mahathir in the parliament, which Hadi claimed could happen due to strong rumours that Anwar and Kit Siang were trying to topple Mahathir early, that the PAS MPs would throw their support behind Mahathir and not allow the no-confidence motion to succeed.[219]

Mahathir believed Hadi was really upset with DAP, and Hadi admitted as much at the meeting, saying that it was important for the Malays and the Gerakan Pembela Ummah (UMMAH) to be united against the non-Malays, i.e., DAP.[220]

Mahathir was keenly aware that Hadi had supported Zahid and UMNO in the Cameron Highlands by-election because they were opposing a DAP candidate. And Hadi told Mahathir that PAS would not go all out in supporting the opposition—Barisan

---

[219] Interview with former BERSATU Supreme Council member 3, London, 15 Jan 2023.
[220] Ibid.

Nasional—in the Semenyih by-election as BERSATU was viewed as a real Malay party, and so PAS could be more friendly towards them.

Mahathir told his officers that he was well aware that Hadi's 'support' was contingent on the kind of help and funding that the federal government provided to Terengganu and Kelantan but that despite that, Mahathir was happy to have the 'support' of PAS.[221]

Mahathir was also focused on getting the Sabah UMNO MPs to defect and join BERSATU as he also needed these parliamentarians in order to see off any no-confidence motion or plan to try and oust him.

In the ensuing weeks, Inspector General of Police Hamid Bador briefed Mahathir several times on the various plots that elements within Parti Keadilan Rakyat (PKR) and DAP were planning in a bid to oust Mahathir and that one of the more frequently discussed ones was the plan for a no-confidence motion against Mahathir.

But by then, senior BERSATU party officials were already taking about 'Mahathir's Grand Plan', which the prime minister had only revealed to his core confidantes and on which Mahathir was spending a lot of his time.

The plan was to firstly engineer the deregistration of UMNO as Mahathir believed that once UMNO was deregistered, the majority of UMNO's rank and file membership would 'jump to BERSATU'.[222] And Mahathir was planning to get UMNO deregistered in such a way that all of UMNO's assets and funds would also be transferred to BERSATU. So, the 'grand plan' was really 'to make BERSATU effectively turn into UMNO Baru 2.0'.[223]

---

[221] Ibid.

[222] Interview with PMO Source 2, Putrajaya, 11 Sep 2022.

[223] Zoom interview with BERSATU leader 7, 10 Feb 2021.

Mahathir told his staffers that he was aware that UMNO knew his intentions and that was why so many UMNO leaders like Hishammuddin and his followers had come to see him in recent months and weeks, some to pledge loyalty and support and others to plead with him not to deregister the party.

However, Mahathir said that the problem with UMNO was that they were no longer unified and half of the party wanted the status quo while the other half were happy for the party to dissolve and be merged into BERSATU.[224]

But even as Mahathir made plans to destabilize and destroy UMNO, his relations with Azmin and his faction began to cool, following missteps by his prospective protégé.

The East Coast Rail Link (ECRL) was a US$20 Billion, 688-km double-track railway project to link Port Klang on the West Coast to Kota Bharu in northeastern Kelantan state and, in the process, providing a direct communication and commercial link between the East Coast Economic Region or ECER states—Pahang, Terengganu and Kelantan—and the country's main shipping hub.

The ECRL was also the centrepiece of China's infrastructure push in Malaysia and was the Malaysian component of China's massive One Belt, One Road international infrastructure expansion program.

Although construction began in 2017, it was suspended two months after the PH1.0 victory, with the new Government attempting to renegotiate the deal signed with the China Communications Construction Company (CCCC). By then, Malaysia had already paid US$4.8 Billion to CCCC.

While negotiations between the CCCC and the government's team—helmed by Finance Minister Lim Guan Eng—continued, Mahathir in a January 2019 Cabinet meeting, told ministers that

---

[224] Interview with former BERSATU Supreme Council member 3, London, 15 Jan 2023.

he wanted to exit the East Coast Rail Link deal but that there was no exit clause in the contract. Mahathir expressed concerns about the exorbitant amount of compensation that Malaysia would shell out to Beijing if the contract was terminated prior to completion. 'Tun said that Najib was coerced not to put an exit clause and that had effectively chained the country under China and Tun wanted to break this,'[225] said one of the premier's close aides.[226] However, Mahathir's position on the issue was for the internal consumption of cabinet colleagues, as Guan Eng was still in the midst of discussions with the Chinese.

But two days later, Economic Affairs Minister Azmin told the media that the government had decided to cancel the ECRL project because the country could not afford to pay the annual interest on the project.

'This is the final decision,' he said. 'It was decided that the cost to develop ECRL is too high, and we don't have the financial capability to see it through at this moment. If this project is not cancelled, the interest that the government would have to pay reaches nearly half a billion ringgit.'[227]

The announcement came as a shock to the market and to Guan Eng, who initially claimed that Azmin was not at the cabinet meeting but then retracted it, saying, 'Sorry, I wouldn't say that Azmin wasn't in the cabinet meeting. What I meant is that he wasn't privy to the decision made by Tun. Anyway, a statement will be issued subject to the instruction by Tun.'[228]

---

[225] Interview with PMO Source 2, Putrajaya, 11 Sep 2022.

[226] Interview with former BERSATU Supreme Council member 3, London, 15 Jan 2023.

[227] '(Updated) Malaysia cancelling ECRL project with CCCC: Azmin', *New Strait Times*, 26 Jan 2019, accessed at: https://www.nst.com.my/news/nation/2019/01/454624/updated-malaysia-cancelling-ecrl-project-cccc-azmin.

[228] 'Lim Guan Eng shocked by Azmin's announcement on status of ECRL', *New Strait Times*, 26 Jan 2019, accessed at: https://www.nst.com.my/news/nation/2019/01/454662/lim-guan-eng-shocked-azmins-announcement-status-ecrl.

'Guan Eng had been tasked with trying to find a way to negotiate an exit,' said officials. 'So, what Azmin said only complicated matters because the government was still negotiating some kind of exit deal and so saying that the ECRL deal was dead meant that the Chinese would dig in their heels harder,' they added.

So, Mahathir was then forced to step into the issue but to also somewhat support the position Azmin had taken. 'It is not that we don't want to honor our contracts, but we just cannot pay,' he said.

'As such, we seek the understanding of the parties concerned. We don't want to frustrate or throw out a contract, but we are really tight in terms of finance.'

'No final decision has been made. Not off yet. No call off, no final decision yet,'[229] he added.

Following a heated discussion[230] between Azmin and Guan Eng in Cabinet the following week, Lim told the media that Malaysia would continue negotiating terms of the project, but the talks would be held away from the public spotlight and the only individual who would comment on the negotiations moving forward would be the prime minister.

As an aide noted, 'Azmin was right because it was Mahathir's view that they needed to end the deal now, but the problem was that without an exit clause, Malaysia would be open to paying huge damages. So Azmin should not have opened his mouth to make the announcement.'

Following Azmin's comments on the ECRL project and the continuing slow progress of the PH1.0 government's economic

[229] 'Malaysia, China to Carry on With Talks on $20 Billion Rail Project', *Radio Free Asia*, 30 Jan 2019, accessed at: https://www.rfa.org/english/news/china/malaysia-project-01302019160918.html.

[230] Interview with PMO Source 2, Putrajaya, 11 Sep 2022.

reforms, Mahathir was no longer as impressed with Azmin as he
had been the previous year.

'Mahathir felt slightly disillusioned with Azmin's leadership
abilities and his economic acuity,' announcing a few weeks later
the setting up of a sixteen-member Economic Action Council to
'help' Azmin to come up with policies on stimulating economic
growth, equitable distribution of wealth, and improving the
wellbeing of the people.

'It was clear to many of us that Azmin was unwilling to listen
to much of what Guan Eng had to say. He didn't respect Guan
Eng because he didn't agree with the DAP's policies or the fact
that the DAP had so much control over the economy,' according
to a Cabinet colleague.[231] 'So, the economic council, which was
then chaired by Mahathir, aimed to ensure greater coordination
between Azmin and Guan Eng on the economy.' Interestingly,
Anwar was kept out of the Council.

Mahathir also told his officers at their weekly meeting that
Azmin was out of his depth when it came to economic matters
and that Azmin had not been delivering on the kinds of economic
policies and actions that really needed to be taken in order to
shore up the economy.

Mahathir said that a key example was the land scandal and the
critical cash flow situation faced by the Federal Land Development
Authority (FELDA), which meant the body was unable to cover
its operating expenses, replantation costs, and aid as well as
provide loans for settlers, who form a very significant chunk of
the Malay voter base. Mahathir said Azmin had been tasked with
resolving the situation, and Mahathir had wanted Azmin to drive
the whole thing.

However, Mahathir told his officers that Azmin was 'unreliable'
as he promised to resolve it quickly and yet there was no solution

---

[231] Zoom interview with BERSATU leader 7, 10 Feb 2021.

in sight, with Mahathir complaining the whole FELDA issue had made his administration look 'dysfunctional'.[232]

Mahathir then went on a 'rant about Azmin, saying that this is the reason why the PH government is so slow to do things in the eyes of the people'.[233]

An aide noted that 'Tun told us he had high hopes for Azmin and so gave him a lot of power so that he could prove himself. Tun said he was "too tired already" and needed a "new generation of Malays" to make the necessary changes and reforms needed'.

According to the aide, 'Tun said it was a pity that Azmin was doing jackshit with all that power.'[234]

According to a then BERSATU Supreme Council member, 'Mahathir's inner circle was aware of the situation but there was not much that these "old men" could do, if the younger generation of leaders like Azmin were so incapable.'[235]

It also didn't help that Azmin's advisers on economic policy had a poor understanding of the subject. At one discussion with senior party officials, it was obvious that they did not have much of a clue as to why the economy was so slow, even suggesting 'silly ideas like greater investment was needed in the military because unemployment could be solved immediately by sending hundreds of thousands into the army, failing to grasp the fundamental point that the government didn't have any funds to expand the army in the first place'.[236]

> You have to find a catalyst first, make money, then think about
> spending (i.e., on the army). It's basic maths. And this explains
> why Azmin was so clueless. He had lousy advisers. Other than

---

[232] Zoom interview with BERSATU leader 5, 12 Sep 2020.

[233] Zoom interview with BERSATU leader 5, 12 Sep 2020.

[234] Ibid.

[235] Zoom interview with BERSATU leader 3, 15 Mar 2020.

[236] Zoom interview with BERSATU leader 6, 10 Nov 2020.

the DAP ministers, no one seemed to be smart enough to do their jobs in the Cabinet.[237]

Even as the botched sex scandal attack on Azmin was unfolding, in September 2019, Anwar did a routine interview with Bloomberg TV in which he said that he would 'take power around May 2020'. 'There's an understanding that it should be around that time, but I don't think I should be too petty about the exact month,' Anwar said. 'But there is this understanding that he will resign at the appropriate time.'

But the interview incensed Mahathir and his followers. Again, ranting at his officers, Mahathir said he was convinced Anwar was dead serious in trying to unseat him before their agreed handover in 2021 and he told his staff that handing over power to Anwar would be the very last option to be considered.

Mahathir began considering four options.[238] Option A would be to groom a leader from within BERSATU to start taking over responsibilities and to succeed him as prime minister. But, according to a close aide, 'Mahathir was unwilling to consider Muhyiddin for the spot as he was too old, and Mahathir wanted someone from the next generation to take over the reins of power. So, Option A was a pipedream as there was no one then who had the clout, charisma, and intelligence to take over.'

Mahathir's Plan B was to—allegedly—soon announce Hishammuddin as a new BERSATU member and to get Hishammuddin to follow through with Project Hijrah to get more UMNO MPs to defect and join BERSATU. This would happen as Mahathir moved to get the Registrar of Societies to deregister UMNO, or UMNO would simply collapse as a result of the defections. The senior aide said Hishammuddin would then be the next in line to be prime minister, with Mahathir's son Mukhriz as

---

[237] Ibid.

[238] Zoom interview with BERSATU leader 5.

possibly one of two deputy premiers. He said Mahathir believed that Hishammuddin's reputation was sufficiently clean and that he was a 'likeable' politician who would be acceptable to the other Pakatan Harapan component parties.

Mahathir's less preferred Option C was to allow UMNO to be strengthened but to ensure that they first got rid of Najib, Zahid, and former UMNO Secretary General Tengku Adnan. Once this happened, the aide said Mahathir would want to install Mohamad Hasan as UMNO president and call for a unification or merger of Malay parties under Mahathir's leadership.

And Mahathir's least preferred option would be Plan D, which would be to allow Anwar to take over, but to then engineer a compromise that allowed the deputy prime minister post to be held by a BERSATU leader like Mukhriz.

The hope that Mahathir had placed on Azmin had been dashed as it was unclear if Azmin would be able to survive the July 2019 sex tape scandal, and even if he did, whether he would be in any position, after being weakened so badly, to be able to get PH to agree to his appointment as PM. As such, Mahathir was, for now, leaving Azmin out of the succession strategy.

By October 2019, Mahathir was getting party reports indicating that while Anwar was pretending to toe the official line on succession in front of Mahathir, privately Anwar had been going round the country to get enough lawmakers' support so as to have the numbers to force through a vote of no confidence in Mahathir and have the King appoint Anwar as PM, ahead of the agreed transition, which was supposed to be in 2021. This fed into Mahathir's darkest fears that Anwar was 'once again' attempting to topple him.

As Mahathir told journalists in 2021:

I tested Anwar (in the 1990s), by giving him—for two months he was, I think, prime minister. We have never had an acting prime minister before. I gave him two months, and he couldn't do anything. He couldn't administer. All he could do was politicking. It was all for himself. He joined UMNO not because he likes UMNO, but because if he joins PAS, he will never become prime minister. He saw the chance to become prime minister by joining UMNO, although he was initially fighting against UMNO.

I supported him (Anwar). It was all part of the plan to become prime minister. He programmed himself, after ten years he should become the prime minister. Yet, after ten years, I was still there. He had to get rid of me, and he stabbed me in the back. And, of course, his behaviour is something I could not accept. If you stab me in the back, try to fight against me, I will fight you. Tengku Razaleigh Hamzah also tried, but I was open about it. When Tengku Razaleigh attacked me, we conducted a proper election and he lost. I won only by forty-two votes.

If Anwar wants to be the prime minister, he could have done it in a proper way. But he used his people to stab my back, calling me dictator, cronyism, and all that. When all the time, it was him doing all that. See, that is Anwar. Anwar, I think should never become the prime minister, because he has no interest about other people. His only interest is himself. He wants to be the prime minister.[239]

Sensing Mahathir's unhappiness, Muhyiddin volunteered to build a strong enough support base of MPs so as to prevent Anwar from being able to launch a no-confidence vote against Mahathir and to ensure that Anwar would never become PM.

It was an event reminiscent of the quote attributed to Henry II of England, when he said, 'Will no one rid me of this meddlesome priest?' in reference to Thomas Becket, the Archbishop of Canterbury, in 1170. Reportedly, upon hearing the King's words, four knights travelled to Canterbury to confront

---

[239] Transcript of Mahathir interview with Journalists, Putrajaya, 13 Jan 2021.

Becket and eventually killed him. The King did not order the Knights to kill Becket, but they interpreted the King's displeasure as instruction enough.

His close aides said Mahathir was fully aware and had been briefed on what Muhyiddin was doing but 'closed both eyes' as he did not want his fingers seen in the attempt to block Anwar, if Muhyiddin's move backfired.

To Muhyiddin, it appeared as if the stars were beginning to align in his favour.

Firstly, within BERSATU, he could already count on the loyalty of the majority of leaders and and lawmakers. Secondly, because of the cooling of relations with Mahathir, Azmin and his band of Parti Keadilan Rakyat (PKR) defectors were now getting closer to Muhyiddin and were supportive of his move as Azmin believed that Muhyiddin was supportive of his bid for power. Thirdly, within UMNO, Hishammuddin's group was already willing to work with Muhyiddin and, barring a few conditions, Zahid and Najib's faction would also back Muhyiddin's efforts in opposing Anwar in a no-confidence vote against Mahathir. And fourthly, conversations and cooperation with PAS had also gotten stronger as the Islamist party viewed Muhyiddin's ultra-credentials positively, and they were also keen to get into power. As such, by preaching the need to unite the Malays against PKR and DAP's suspected no-confidence vote, Muhyiddin had begun to create what would eventually become the basis for his Perikatan Nasional (PN) coalition.

Although Mahathir was still telling the media in December 2019 that he planned to hand over power to Anwar despite what people were saying, I believe his key supporters like Syed Saddiq knew full well that handing over power to Anwar would be the old man's very last and final course of action.

According to another key party leader, it was not a coincidence that Haniff Khatri, the lawyer representing former Anwar aide Yusoff Rawther, who in December 2019 had accused Anwar of sexually assaulting him, was Mahathir's personal lawyer. 'Do you think Haniff would take Yusoff on as a client if Tun did not give his approval? That would be suicidal for Haniff, wouldn't it?'[240]

In the meantime, realizing for the first time that he actually held quite a few cards in his pocket, Muhyiddin, with Daim's help and backing, spoke to Mahathir about the possibility of becoming the next prime minister, given that the Azmin option appeared to be off the table.

After the meeting, Mahathir told his close aides that at that point, he was willing to consider any option, even Muhyiddin. But ever the shrewd politician, Mahathir said he would support the parallel moves by Azmin and Muhyiddin to become PM until a clear victor emerged, at which point, Mahathir would throw his open support behind that person.

Within days, Muhyiddin began his jockeying for power, telling Mahathir's senior staff that he wanted to be next in line to be prime minister.[241] Muhyiddin said that his cancer had gone into remission, and he now wished to put up a fight against Anwar. Muhyiddin asked for support from Mahathir's staff, telling them that Mahathir had given his blessing that Muhyiddin pose a challenge to Anwar.

Muhyiddin now began trying to also build public support around the idea that he should be the next prime minister, and his people started lobbying the media and influencers. Muhyiddin then personally asked several people in Syed Saddiq's camp to help rally BERSATU youths along with UMNO and PAS youths to support his potential candidacy as PM.

Muhyiddin set up his own kitchen cabinet to help him with building this Grand Malay Alliance.

It was headed by former UMNO Domestic Trade Minister Hamzah Zainuddin, who had defected to BERSATU after GE14.

---

240 Zoom interview with BERSATU leader 7.

241 Zoom interview with BERSATU leader 6, 10 Nov 2020.

Also on the team were Faizal Azumu—who became Perak MB after GE14, Zahid Mohamad Arip—a former political Secretary to Mahathir and who had defected to Muhyiddin's camp, Wan Saiful Wan Jan—deputy head of BERSATU's policy bureau, and Datuk Latif Ahmad—who became Rural Development Minister in the PN Government.

Hamzah's office in Publika became the focal point of Muhyiddin's operations, and a War Room was set up, with charts and pictures of MPs, including those in Azmin's bloc, Mahathir's bloc, Syed Saddiq's camp, and the GPS bloc.

At the height of their operations to secure enough support to keep Mahathir as prime minister and later to make Muhyiddin PM, the room was filled with calculations on the whiteboards, constituency maps, and post-it notes stuck on all these surfaces. This was to become the Sheraton Move War Room.

Hamzah led backroom negotiations with UMNO while Muhyiddin did so with PAS for their support for Mahathir in case Anwar or his DAP supporters moved for a vote of no confidence in parliament.

More importantly, UMNO/PAS indicated that they would also support Muhyiddin if he wished to contest against Anwar for the prime minister's post, but this was conditional on working out an eventual power sharing deal between BERSATU, UMNO, and PAS.

By December 2019, the fear among BERSATU's leadership of an Anwar and DAP led no-confidence vote was palpable, and plans to deregister UMNO and implement Project Hijrah shifted into high-gear.

Mahathir's closest aides like Syed Saddiq told their staff to get ready for a rough few months as Mahathir was to allegedly ensure Najib was found guilty by mid-2020, and by which time, UMNO was also likely to be found guilty of accepting laundered money and be deregistered.

This, the thinking went, would then cleanse the party of Najib, Zahid, Annuar Musa, and Tengku Adnan and UMNO would then eventually merge with BERSATU 'without these traitors'. But even before that, Mahathir would engineer the defection to BERSATU of at least twenty-two UMNO MPs. Hishammuddin had allegedly been tasked with engineering this move.

Mahathir's team also began working on a plan to manage the fallout and impact on Mahathir, BERSATU, and PH1.0 when it happened, as there was likely to be tremendous backlash given how popular UMNO was becoming once again because of Najib's *Malu Apa Bossku*[242] re-branding that had brought the former UMNO leader and his party a new lease on life and a sudden increase in support among the Malay grassroots.

According to the deal negotiated by Muhyiddin's team, Azmin would be bringing in at least sixteen MPs—with another ten still unconfirmed—from PKR.

BERSATU Supreme Council leaders believed that if their Grand Malay Alliance plan succeeded, they would likely have twenty-five BERSATU MPs—following previous defections—twenty-two UMNO MPs, and sixteen PKR MPs. That would bring the current tally of MPs who supported Mahathir as PM to sixty-three BERSATU, including UMNO/PKR defecting MPs, ten GPS MPs, nine Warisan MPs, and eighteen PAS MPs, which would give Mahathir 100 seats.[243]

The leadership believed that if Mahathir got these 100 seats, then DAP and the National Trust Party (AMANAH) would

---

[242] Najib's 'Malu Apa Bossku' ('What are you ashamed of, my boss?') branding was born in January 2019, when he made trips to rural areas to profess his innocence. A videoclip of Najib replying with the phrase as he rode on the back of a motorbike became viral and the branding stuck, with Najib regaining his popularity among large swathes of the Malay heartland and the phrase entering popular culture.

[243] Zoom interview with BERSATU leader 7.

automatically support Mahathir. This was how Mahathir was planning to block Anwar from becoming PM in mid-2020 if their plan succeeded. By having sixty-three seats in BERSATU, Anwar would be checkmated as Anwar would have been left with only twenty seats in PKR.

But by late December 2019, it was still not clear who Mahathir was supporting as a challenger to prevent Anwar from becoming prime minister.

Mahathir was still disappointed with Azmin over the sex video and his lack of focus in managing the economy and had stopped vouching for Azmin's abilities and credibility as a minister and future leader. He was now looking at UMNO's Tok Mat and Hishammuddin to carry the Malay-agenda torch. Mahathir also did not fully trust Muhyiddin because he felt Muhyiddin had become very ambitious of late. If only he had known the extent of Muhyiddin's planning.

The uncertainty became very stressful for party members, with leaders like Syed Saddiq telling close friends that BERSATU needed the 'uncertainty' to be 'over and done with'. He told them, 'Tun not giving a clear indication even among his inner circle whether he would install someone else or give up and give it to Anwar makes the situation worse as no one knows how to ally themselves or with whom.'[244]

Although Mahathir continued his secret talks with PAS in January 2020, his PH1.0 coalition was beginning to unravel, with several PKR and BERSATU MPs urging Mahathir to leave the PH block and form a new alliance that would isolate DAP and Anwar.

Syed Saddiq allegedly told his staff that Mahathir wanted BERSATU to form a Grand Malay Alliance with the remnants of UMNO and PAS but minus Anwar. But the problem was that it

---

had begun to take a life of its own and was currently moving at a pace Mahathir couldn't control.[245]

He reportedly said that as chairman of PH, Mahathir couldn't be seen to champion it and he couldn't be officially known to 'own' the movement. So, when Mahathir didn't take ownership, a few factions came up to own the movement, and they were now trying to get the crossovers and defections using their own ways and tactics, insisting that Mahathir must stay on as PM for as long as possible.

This was when things began to get out of hand. This was because Muhyiddin was now driving the main faction with individuals like Azmin strongly incentivized to do whatever it took to keep Anwar out of power. So, while Azmin and his supporters were attempting to get as many PKR MPs to cross over to support BERSATU, PAS was supportive of a Malay unity government while the various factions in UMNO were united over the idea of getting back into power without having to deal with DAP, something that Mahathir's own party was also clamouring for.

This grouping viewed Anwar and the DAP as enemies of the state and would do whatever it took, whether it was ensuring that Mahathir stayed in power or a new PM was chosen, as long as it wasn't Anwar.

Anwar's supporters and the DAP had also gotten wind of some of the moves being made by Muhyiddin's faction and so began calling for Mahathir to announce a handover date to Anwar. Unlike Anwar, his supporters did not believe that Mahathir would hand over power, and so they wanted to pile pressure on the PM to announce an explicit date for the handover.

Syed Saddiq told party members that Mahathir was 'trying to keep PH together'. But unlike Syed Saddiq, Mahathir's idea of keeping PH together excluded DAP.

---

[245] Zoom interview with BERSATU leader 6, 10 Nov 2020.

Syed Saddiq knew that Mahathir wanted to step down but the people around him and in the Grand Malay Alliance movement were taking matters into their own hands by trying to keep Mahathir in power for their own selfish agendas.

This move, he admitted to members, had now resulted in 'causing PH to go haywire'.

Both Anwar and Mahathir had their respective supporters who began overstepping their boundaries, by pitting Mahathir against Anwar on a daily basis, and these groups formed factions aimed at trying to split PH1.0.

Syed Saddiq said that, as a result, 'Believe it or not, they now have Tun and Anwar at ransom! These supporters want to prop up their leaders to remain (or get) the PM's post, otherwise they have threatened to pull support from them. It's mind boggling.'[246]

Syed Saddiq had a hard time explaining the situation even to his DAP colleagues, because it was the players around Mahathir and Anwar who were jockeying for each of their respective leaders to either remain in or take power.

Syed Saddiq said his public war of words was not with Anwar but trying to put the people surrounding these two leaders, who are trying to manipulate the situation, back in their places. 'What's messed up to me is the fact that Tun and Anwar have hardcore supporters who are too hardcore to the extent that whatever they are doing in support of their leaders have now ended up sabotaging their own leaders,' he told close friends.[247]

The end was nigh.

---

[246] Zoom interview with BERSATU leader 6, 10 Nov 2020.

[247] Interview with BERSATU leader 9, Kuala Lumpur, 10 Jul 2022.

Chapter 12

'Backdoor' Rule

On 1 March 2020, Muhyiddin Yassin was sworn in as Malaysia's eighth prime minister.

Although he had outmanoeuvred Mahathir and the Pakatan Harapan coalition in forming what has come to be known as the 'backdoor government', Muhyiddin initially believed that he could achieve some sort of rapprochement with Mahathir.

Muhyiddin had told his team that he was willing not to run for BERSATU chairman, allowing Mahathir to win uncontested. He would run for his current post as president of the party. He then reportedly asked Yahya Jalil—an UMNO member and director of Gerbang Perdana—to act as key mediator between his and Mahathir's camp. However, Muhyiddin said that if Mahathir wanted to fight, he was prepared for this as well.[248]

Mahathir, however, was in no mood for compromise. The night after the King's announcement of Muhyiddin's premiership, Mahathir published a list of 115 lawmakers whom he claimed would still support him as prime minister.

However, none of this made any difference as the only way Muhyiddin could be challenged now would be in the holding of a vote of no confidence in parliament. And this was what Mahathir was agitating for.

---

[248] Zoom interview with BERSATU leader 3, 15 Mar 2020.

Muhyiddin also realized this, as holding a session of parliament would clearly show whether his new Perikatan Nasional (PN) government had the numbers to remain in power. But the reality was that this was shaky at best. Given the need for a stable government and the fear of major protests if a perceived non-Malay government was to take power, it was not surprising that Muhyiddin's assurances of having the majority was accepted by the Palace.

But as they say, the proof is in the pudding, and Muhyiddin could not produce that pudding. Of course, this was not his only preoccupation.

By March 2020, the Covid-19 pandemic had paralysed the world. Politics had to be put aside in the mad dash to save as many lives as possible and to try and keep the then untreatable virus at bay. Of course, the pandemic also provided a good excuse not to convene parliament, with the country going into lockdown on 18 March 2020 and parliament postponed till May 2020.

Although reports by the security services to Muhyiddin's cabinet indicated that Malay sentiments were generally accepting of PN due to the fact that it was a 'Malay-centric Government',[249] Muhyiddin's challenge within his new coalition was that UMNO with thirty-nine seats, as compared to BERSATU's roughly twenty seats, was, in reality, the majority partner. This meant that Muhyiddin would be forced to give in to many of UMNO's demands, which he did not want to.

UMNO as a bigger partner in the coalition demanded the deputy premier's post, along with key ministries, but Muhyiddin had to also balance this with demands by the east Malaysian parties, the PKR defectors, and his party's demands for the deputy's post. So, instead of appointing a deputy prime minister, Muhyiddin appointed four senior ministers, thus temporarily satisfying the demands of the various parties.

---

249 Zoom interview with PN leader 2, 6 Nov 2021.

BERSATU was also in chaos as the pro-Mahathir faction within the party led by Syed Saddiq, Mukhriz, and Maszlee were attempting to regain control of the party. In a last-ditch attempt to bridge differences, Syed Saddiq met with Muhyiddin to try and find common ground between Mahathir and him.

According to aides who attended the meeting, the discussion centred around Mahathir's desire to bring BERSATU back into PH.

Syed Saddiq presented his case to Muhyiddin—that there were indications that UMNO was planning to betray BERSATU. Syed Saddiq said that according to intelligence gathered by PH, it would appear that after the Movement Control Order—Malaysia's version of lockdown declared on 18 March 2020—was lifted, UMNO would slowly demand Muhyiddin step down to make way for a UMNO leader to take over as PM. Syed Saddiq said that UMNO would exert the power of their bloc along with PAS—through Muafakat Nasional—to pressure Muhyiddin to step aside.[250]

UMNO was also ensuring that they had enough BERSATU MPs on UMNO's side, so that they could then expel Muhyiddin if he refused to do UMNO's bidding.

Syed Saddiq said UMNO, at the moment, was split into three camps: Zahid, who controlled the warlords; Hishammuddin, who was leading a faction that wanted reforms, and a third faction led by Mat Hasan, who appeared to have a strong relationship with Najib.[251]

UMNO, Syed Saddiq said, remained divided on who their PM candidate should be, but once they firmed it up, they would pressure Muhyiddin to step down. If he then refused to step down or UMNO somehow failed to get enough BERSATU MPs on their side, UMNO would push for fresh General Elections to be held.

Syed Saddiq told Muhyiddin that there were only two things keeping him as PM: UMNO's disunity and Covid-19.

---

[250] Zoom interview with PN leader 5, 3 Mar 2021.

[251] Ibid.

But despite Syed Saddiq's arguments, Muhyiddin flatly turned him down. As far as Muhyiddin was concerned, there was no way he would consider cooperating or working with Anwar or the DAP, because he felt the DAP was only interested in getting Anwar in as PM, and Muhyiddin would never accept that.

But none of this mattered to Mahathir, who was now a man on a mission to overthrow Muhyiddin and had Warisan's Shafie Apdal seek a parliamentary motion of confidence in Mahathir to show that Mahathir commanded a majority of support in the house. Although this was rejected by the Speaker, Mahathir was not be deterred. He then sought a motion of no confidence against Muhyiddin, which the Speaker accepted for debate when the parliament resumed on 18 May 2020.

However, Muhyiddin could not allow this to happen. So, just days before the opening of parliament, the Speaker announced that, at the direction of the government, the parliament would only sit to hear the King's opening address, and there would be no debate following it, thus styming Mahathir's plan.[252] Holding a press conference following the King's speech, Mahathir, accompanied by Shafie, Mukhriz, Guan Eng, and Mat Sabu, alleged that BERSATU remained a member of Pakatan Harapan (PH) as the BERSATU Supreme Council had not made the decision to leave PH but had given Mahathir a week to decide and that Muhyiddin's action in announcing BERSATU's pull-out was made unilaterally and without the Council's approval. Anwar, who had by now been named as Leader of the Opposition in Parliament, and other PKR leaders were conspicuous by their absence from the press conference.[253]

---

[252] 'Malaysia's parliament debate ban reflects ruling alliance's anger: AMANAH president', *The Straits Times*, 14 May 2020, accessed at: https://www.straitstimes.com/asia/se-asia/malaysias-parliament-debate-ban-reflects-ruling-alliances-anger-amanah-president.

[253] Annuar, Azril, 'Anwar goes from PM-in-waiting to new Opposition leader', *The Malay Mail*, 7 May 2020, accessed at: https://www.malaymail.com/news/

Not surprisingly, within a week, Mahathir, Mukhriz, Syed Saddiq, Maszlee, and Amiruddin Hamzah were expelled from BERSATU.

It was obvious now that Mahathir had lost all support from PKR, and the remaining PH leaders were also slowly distancing themselves from him. As Mahathir mulled the setting up of yet another Malay-centric political party, individuals like Syed Saddiq began moving in other directions.

Syed Saddiq told his friends that he wanted to set up a new coalition of youths, targeting the 3.8 million new Undi18 voters, and 7.8 million youth voters across the country. He believed that PH would return to power with the help of these youth voters who were less racial and who had new aspirations and ideals.

His new movement would aim to obtain at least ten to fifteen parliamentary seats and be kingmakers come GE15 and form the government with PH. This new party would champion new ideals that promoted centrist policies and one that was geared towards enhancing Malaysia's global competitiveness.

Moreover, Syed Saddiq had to come to the realization that following Mahathir was likely to lead him nowhere politically and that he had to start fending for himself.

So, his team began planning to get young MPs from BERSATU, DAP, and other PH parties to form a loose alliance or bloc that would eventually transform into a political party.

The last serious meeting to rebuild PH1.0 took place in June 2020, when Mahathir went to PKR Headquarters at Merchant Square in Petaling Jaya to meet with Anwar. There was much hope on both sides that this meeting to try and patch differences would mean that Mahathir and PH would join forces to remove Muhyiddin from power.[254]

---

malaysia/2020/05/07/anwar-goes-from-pm-in-waiting-to-new-opposition-leader/1863929.

[254] Zoom interview with PKR leader 7, 8 Jan 2022.

However, the situation for PH had changed. Most of their leadership had finally awoken to the realization that they had been taken in by Mahathir's promises, over and over, and that nothing had been delivered. Instead, they had sold their souls and tied everything to Mahathir, only for him to have destroyed all that they had worked so hard for. Now, they were wiser and made it very clear from the beginning that PH's prime ministerial candidate would be Anwar Ibrahim.

Sources in the meeting said Shafie Apdal and the pro-Mahathir BERSATU members wanted Mahathir as the PM candidate while DAP and PKR were in favour of Anwar as the PM candidate, and both sides could not reach an agreement on it.[255]

They did agree that PH would try to retake the government by seeking an audience with the King and showing him the statutory declarations they'd acquired from a majority of MPs.

However, the leadership felt this was unlikely to succeed because the King appeared to be 'much more supportive of the PN government and would not want to destabilize the situation'.[256]

In terms of seats, PH would in reality likely fall short of a majority but could still cause a hung parliament, so Muhyiddin and PN would still have the edge in holding onto power. Therefore, PH would have to take a calibrated approach as they wanted to re-take power but avoid an immediate General Election at all costs because of the Covid situation.

Moreover, none of the PH parties, especially Mahathir's team, were prepared for a GE, as they had neither the machinery in place nor did they have an election war chest ready. So, the strategy was to try and get a change of power through parliamentary votes by convincing the King to let PH form the government, rather than

[255] Zoom interview with PN leader 2, 6 Nov 2021.
Zoom interview with PKR leader 7, 8 Jan 2022.
[256] Zoom interview with PKR leader 7, 8 Jan 2022.

push for elections. This was why PH had not been supportive of calls by UMNO and BN for fresh polls.

As for UMNO, the leadership had become seriously unhappy with Muhyiddin who had promised during negotiations for the party's support that he would stop the political persecution of its leaders and ensure that Najib and Zahid faced fair trials on their charges. However, this did not appear to have happened as the various individuals that Mahathir and Thomas had appointed, many with alleged conflicts of interest, were still involved.

As such, UMNO's leadership ended up willing to support a move by Anwar in October 2020 to form a government. Anwar only had letters of support from party leaders but would present the King with the statutory declarations shortly, according to an aide at the meeting.[257]

Anwar wanted the King to ask Muhyiddin to step aside gracefully because it was apparent from the statutory declarations that the upcoming tabling of Muhyiddin's budget would fail. To prevent chaos, Anwar asked the King to appoint him to form a new government so that it could pass the budget quickly.

He told the monarch that Najib and Zahid were in full support and had brought over around twenty-four to twenty-six UMNO MPs who would support Anwar. The idea, said the aide, was for PKR to form the government with BN and PAS, and the East Malaysian parties would automatically join up with whoever was in power, once the King agreed to the change of government.

If he was unwilling to replace Muhyiddin, Anwar urged the King to insist Muhyiddin immediately announce a date for GE15 in exchange for—what would become—PH2.0's support to pass the budget.

In any other circumstances, this would have likely seen a change of Government.

---

[257] Interview with Palace aide 2, 12 Sep 2022.

But in October 2020, with the Covid-19 pandemic at its peak, skyrocketing death rates, chaos spreading throughout the country, and the government paralysed due to the ongoing political crisis faced by its leadership, it was highly risky to change the government.

Muhyiddin asked the King to declare a state of emergency in October 2020, but after consulting his fellow rulers, it was refused. This was likely because the rulers believed that the move to declare a state of emergency was not only to handle the Covid situation but so that Muhyiddin could get the country's budget passed without calling for parliament to sit—where the budget vote would likely fail because Muhyiddin did not have enough support—thus allowing Muhyiddin to kill two birds with one stone. The budget was eventually tabled and passed in December 2020 because of a call by the King to lawmakers to pass the bill, but with the session allowing debate on no other matter.

Malaysia finally declared a state of emergency in January 2021, and following more political manoeuvring and backroom deals, UMNO in August 2021 announced that it was pulling its support from Muhyiddin as prime minister, and Muhyiddin stepped down on 16 August 2021.

UMNO's Ismail Sabri then became Malaysia's ninth prime minister and, following discussions with Anwar as Leader of the Opposition, signed a memorandum of understanding on bipartisan cooperation, which saw PH2.0 support the government in the interest of the country. This remained the state of affairs until GE15 in November 2022, which saw Anwar's PH2.0 Coalition winning the largest number of seats but not enough to form a government.

Following the King's call for the creation of a Unity Government and UMNO/BN's decision, and that of several other East Malaysian parties, to support Anwar's PH2.0 coalition, Anwar was sworn in as Malaysia's tenth prime minister on 24 November 2022.

Chapter 13

Epilogue - A Guide to Save 'New Malaysia'

> Malaysia can only have a stable government, prosperity, and progress if both the Malays and the Chinese work together as partners in forming a government and in sharing political and economic power.[258]

I think the quote above summed up my view on how Malaysia's future could be saved, when I wrote *Final Reckoning* in late 2021.

And this view hasn't changed.

But since then, Malaysia has gone through much change.

The political rollercoaster of Ismail Sabri's patched-together eighteen-month administration at the tail-end of the Covid pandemic and its lack of any significant improvement to the country's economy and development was symptomatic of the fact that despite having an UMNO/BN prime minister, the majority of his government was effectively a recycling of the previous ultra-Malay PN ministers and officials.

---

[258] Bose, Romen, *Final Reckoning: An Insider's View of the Fall of Malaysia's Barisan Nasional Government*, Penguin Random House SEA, 2021, p. 296.

PKR and DAP—which has represented a majority of the country's Chinese for over a decade now—were, only by association through an MOU, helping to prop up the government. There was no real cooperation between the government and opposition, and so the administration stumbled all the way to GE15.

UMNO and BN, in the form of Najib and Zahid, fully understood that a government like that, which did not have the mandate of the people, would never be able to deliver anything of consequence.

And this was a view shared by Anwar and the DAP's Anthony Loke, who, in March 2022, replaced Guan Eng as the DAP's Secretary General and brought in a new era for his party, sans the historical baggage of vengeance and retribution that had blinded earlier leaders.

Even before his elevation, Loke and his team had already been holding secret talks with UMNO in mid-2021 in a bid to find some common political ground between them. Discussions had also taken place between Anwar and Zahid's teams following the renewal of their relationship during Anwar's October 2020 bid to form the government.

However, PN was unwilling to hold polls because they rightly feared that the hustings would mean an end to their grip on power, and they were at pains to pressure Ismail Sabri to delay the elections for as long as possible.

But GE15 proved to be a very rude awakening for UMNO, which, for months before, had refused to contemplate working with any element of PH because they believed they would win a landslide victory.

In their worst ever showing, UMNO won only 30 out of 222 parliamentary seats, ending up third after PH with 81 seats and PN with 74 seats. And the reason for the large loss was the fact that a large proportion of Malay voters believed that the party was still badly tainted by corruption and abuse of power allegations, preferring to give their support to PN's main coalition partners BERSATU and PAS, whom they viewed as relatively 'cleaner'.[259]

This, of course, resulted in a hung parliament.

So, when the King urged the formation of a Unity Government, it was no surprise that PKR, UMNO/BN, DAP, and the east Malaysian parties were able to come up with a proper power-sharing partnership that would now make both the Chinese and the Malays significant stakeholders in the country's future once again.

I do not know if Zahid, Anwar, and Loke read the last chapter of *Final Reckoning,* but I am very glad they used a similar political calculation in figuring out a solution that will hopefully see the end of the continual politicking and governmental paralysis and the beginning of one where Cabinet ministers and government officials are actually moving to deliver on their promises.

This does not mean that everything is hunky-dory and that the Unity Government is the best one ever. But what it does mean is that for the first time since 2004, Malaysia has a relatively politically stable government that is not in fear of being toppled every other month. So, they should be able to get on with the business of governing and prospering the country.

This also does not mean that race politics, corruption, patronage, and abuse of power have all disappeared overnight.

These remain crucial problems facing the government and the people. There has been a very significant loss of trust between Malays and non-Malays, and this spiralling of race relations, I believe, began with UMNO's push—under Mahathir's leadership—to out-Islamize PAS in the 1980s and has continued ever since.

---

[259] The same effect was seen in the December 2023 Kemaman by-election. In GE13 in 2013, UMNO had won the seat with more than a 10,000 vote majority, but in the 2 Dec 2023 by-election, PN's PAS won the seat with more than a 37,000 vote majority. In the space of a decade, an UMNO stronghold had become a PAS bastion.

It is not an easy task to halt this slide in perception and relations, much less to start building new bridges among the races.

The various ministers holding the Unity portfolio over the years have all tried but failed because of a serious lack of political commitment and drive to really bring the various races together under a system that is equitable and beneficial to all. And this is because it is so easy for politicians on all sides to use the race card and the fear of each other to win the support of their communities.

I believe the narrative of race politics must change if Malaysia is to survive as a multiracial and multicultural nation that it touts itself to be.

Although the vast majority of Malays are well-educated and are fully aware that their rights, special privileges, and status are fundamentally enshrined in the federal constitution and are very hard to change, if at all, it takes very little when Malay extremist groups claim that Malay rights and power are under attack—without any real evidence—for many in the community to get their hackles up and vote on racial lines rather than for the best candidate for the job.

Meritocracy is not a bad word, and it does not equate to an erosion or attack on Malay Muslim culture, religion, rights, values, customs, or traditions. The concept can coexist with the special status, aid, and position of the Malays.

And non-Malay Malaysians are not the enemy.

They are not stealing anyone's *hak*, or rights, nor are they guests in this land.

And they do not have to be grateful to any race for being a Malaysian citizen.

Many are unaware that one of the more important aspects of Malaysian independence was the backroom deals among the Alliance coalition parties and the British colonial government in 1957 that led to articles 14–18 of the federal constitution—which provided citizenship for Chinese, Indians, and other minorities—

being introduced 'in exchange for' Article 153, which largely ensures the quotas and rights of the Bumiputeras.

And much of Malaysia's growth and development in the 1960s and 70s was also due to Malaysia's first Finance Minister Tun HS Lee and the country's second Finance Minister Tan Siew Sin, both of whom were non-Malays and helped to build the nation.

So, not only do non-Malays have the right to be called Malaysians, they have also worked hand in hand to build the country that we see today. They have not stolen anyone's rights, and they are not guests, visitors, or immigrants.

They are Malaysian.

Only the most racist, historically ignorant, and uneducated (*kurang ajar*) would call non-Malay Malaysians *Pendatang*.

Of course, one of the biggest fears that non-Malays have and which has been fed by many of their politicians is the continual 'Greening' or Islamization of Malaysia. If we are to believe the various statements issued over the years warning that Malaysia was on the verge of becoming an Islamic state, Malaysia today should already be an Islamic Caliphate.

Instead, it is a nation that continues to have a plurality of voices and religions, underpinned by the various protections afforded by the federal constitution and government policies.

Yes, it is not perfect in any sense of the word, and there are many areas where rights have been eroded and groups marginalized. And racism is seen being practised very openly and without shame.

But it is also not the Taliban.

And why is it that a Malay voter is racist and 'is only interested in supporting his own kind' when voting for UMNO or PAS or BERSATU but when a Chinese voter votes for the predominantly Chinese-led DAP—where the top three posts are held by Chinese—this is not seen as just as racist?

I believe some rely on these racial and religious tropes to inform their analysis on the Malay voter block, which is not as homogeneous as one would like to think. Many Malay voters today are economically more prosperous, better educated, and exposed to a much more globalized world and media, and many understand the impact of their votes.

So, a significant proportion of Malays today don't necessarily vote solely on racial lines but rather for candidates—of course, preferably of their race, which is similar to that of the Malaysian Chinese—who are clean and can perform as well as deliver on the needs of the people.

Yes, racism, corruption, patronage, conflict of interest, and abuse of power remain systemic ills facing any government that comes into power, and it is something that almost all politicians and political parties have to grapple with in Malaysia.

It would be trite to say that these issues can be resolved and eradicated by any one political party, coalition, or government given that even countries like Singapore, which prides itself on its squeaky-clean reputation, has had to deal with the alleged corruption of some of its leaders.

However, that does not mean that Malaysians have to accept the increasing levels of racism, graft, and nepotism. But it is something that only a strong, stable government can attempt at minimizing in the long run. And for that to happen, the levels of fear among the races have to be dramatically reduced, and levels of trust have to be significantly ramped up.

Malaysians must move on beyond the polemics of the three Rs—Race, Religion and Royalty—that they had been indoctrinated in since the early 1980s. They must move away from a culture of patronage and of fear of each other's race, which had been nurtured and fostered by individuals who should have known better, but who were more interested in applying the divide and rule mentality—which they learned from their colonial masters—to control and rule the country.

So, if Malaysia, as a whole, is to succeed, it is only through the various races and religions working as partners, rather than rivals, that the country can even hope to survive, much less compete with its neighbours.

Funnily enough, this racial divide was something that Najib was trying to overcome, when I helped him draft the National Reconciliation Plan or NRP back in 2013. It was a plan to help reunite the various races in the country and build a shared vision for all Malaysians. The plan and strategy were based on four key areas, namely, social, political, government, and international relations. These were underpinned by the principles of respect, working, and playing together, and the spirit of give and take. These were concepts that were easy to understand and, according to our online analysis then, was broadly acceptable and something that all races were already calling for.

But the problem in 2013 was that there was absolutely no buy-in from the Chinese community because they believed in the race-baiting propaganda that had been spread by many leaders in their community, and the same went for the Malays.

In addition, the non-Malays had totally rejected the BN government as they did not feel they were partners in the then ruling coalition.

Today, however, we have a Unity Government whose parties represent a significant majority of the Malays and, similarly, a vast majority of non-Malays as well.

So, in a situation where there is now goodwill from all sides to work together and rebuild the nation, there is no more opportune time to introduce a National Reconciliation Plan 2.0, which is guaranteed to now get the buy-in of the various communities because everyone—with the exception of the extremists, of course—feels they have a stake in the current power structure.

This goodwill should not be squandered away through inaction.

To paraphrase Charles E. Weller's famous typing drill that many of us punched away on typewriters back in ancient times (1985): 'Now is the time for all good men (and women) of all races to come to the aid of their country.'

The current government must also move away from PH1.0's politics of retribution and vengeance and stop acting like a party in opposition.

In order to really govern Malaysia, it must come up with a real vision for Malaysia.

Whether it be Wawasan 2020, a National Transformation Plan, or Malaysia Madani, it needs to be concrete, comprehensive, and detailed in outlining not only how to revive and boost the economy but to also ensure that the people are brought beyond the status of a developed nation, and into an era of unparalleled progress and prosperity for all Malaysians.

It is not a simple task, and the plan will take years to achieve. But it is doable if we are serious about building a new, brighter future and country that all Malaysians would be proud to call home.

Appendix 1

Eliminating Anwar

His (Mahathir's) treatment of Anwar Ibrahim – the ruthlessness in which he set about destroying the man – was a turning point for me. I was never enthusiastic about Anwar (who was one year my senior in school and in university), but I found the way he was treated completely unacceptable. Anwar's treatment brought a great deal of shame and disgrace to our nation. It damaged our credibility and diminished our image in the eyes of the world. It was all downhill after that.[260]

An often-quoted phrase ascribed to Mahathir over the years is that of, 'Melayu Mudah Lupa' or 'Malays easily forget'. It comes from a poem he wrote and delivered at the United Malays National Organization (UMNO) Annual General Assembly in 2001.[261]

The poem refers to how the Malays had forgotten their history and urges them to remember their bitter past because their struggle still continues. But today, the phrase is often used to describe how Malaysians in general do not remember their recent past, and it is a shame because as the famous philosopher George

---

[260] Ignatius, Dennis, *Paradise Lost*, p. ix.

[261] *Bernama*, 'Dr mahathir sebak sampaikan sajak 'melayu mudah lupa', 23 Jun 2001, accessed at: http://lib.perdana.org.my/PLF/Digital_Content/ Prominent_Leaders/Mahathir/News_1968-2004/2001-2005/2001aj/dr%20 mahalupa.PDF.

Santayana once noted, 'Those who cannot remember the past are condemned to repeat it.'

I suppose this could explain why the Malaysian electorate, despite living through Mahathir's initial twenty-two years as the prime minister, had forgotten the *Maha Firaun* or Mighty Pharaoh's—a term coined in reference to his ruthlessness in the dispatch of his political enemies—excesses, during the intervening fifteen years when he was in supposed 'retirement'.

Due to this 'amnesia', they were happy to have him again as prime minister in 2018 to replace a leader and system that he was responsible for anointing and creating in the first place.

It also explains why many Malaysians today don't remember the harassment, nor can they recall the kind of continued persecution Anwar Ibrahim faced at the hand of, or by individuals closely associated with, Mahathir, for more than two decades.

Most are roughly familiar with the first corruption, abuse of power, and sodomy cases that Anwar faced after he was unceremoniously removed as deputy premier, UMNO deputy president, and party member in 1998.

I am not going to rehash history that is already well documented. But I think many need to be reminded that even following Anwar's first release in 2004 and in the decade that followed, Anwar remained in Mahathir's crosshairs. I use the following two instances that I witnessed first-hand—out of numerous other similar moves against Anwar in that time—as examples.

I was very lucky when working in Kuala Lumpur in the late 2000s as a correspondent for the French newswire agency *Agence-France Presse* (AFP) to have very dedicated veteran colleagues who knew how to navigate the ins and outs of Malaysian politics and who could easily measure the pulse and heartbeat of the nation.

One such individual was M. Jegathesan, who had already served with AFP for more than a decade when 1 had joined. Educated in Malaysia and Japan, and after having worked in local media, Jega, known fondly to many of us as 'Uncle', joined AFP in the 1990s.

Many politicians and colleagues from other agencies often underestimated Jega, who appeared very mild and self-effacing, often giving the impression that he was a newbie to the field. But behind that exterior stood a very bright, intelligent, and analytical journalist, whose frequent jokes meant that newsmakers would let down their guard, at which point he would pounce and secure news exclusives and scoops that would be spoken about, across the media fraternity, for years!

I had joined AFP for a few months, when I was sent on the ground to cover the political drama surrounding Anwar, when one of his former aides had accused the politician of sodomizing him.

On 15 July 2008, I was there at Anwar's newly built house—he had recently moved from his old home in Bukit Damansara—in Segambut, along with a huge number of journalists, photographers, and cameramen, on an empty plot of land opposite his house awaiting his return from the parliament. There had been rumours circulating over a few days that Anwar would be arrested, and the media wanted to be there to get the pictures, remembering the video footage and photographs of police commandos raiding Anwar's house in 1998 to arrest him.

None of us wanted to miss the dramatic moment, so we had colleagues waiting along Anwar's route from the parliament to his home, and given that there was, at that time, only one main road leading into the area where Anwar's house was located, we felt safe in the knowledge that we would not miss the arrest.

However, when being driven back home after an interview at the Malaysian Anti-Corruption Commission (MACC) headquarters in Putrajaya, his convoy was waylaid by a team of police special forces in the middle of the road, about two kilometres away from his home. All of us were caught by surprise and tried to rush over to the location of his arrest. But by the time we got there, it was all over. Anwar had already been arrested and taken away, then detained, interrogated, and charged over what became known as Sodomy II.

It was a very dramatic day; fuelled by adrenaline, I dictated my story over the phone to Jega, who was in the office and who then proceeded to file my copy to AFP's news desk in Hong Kong, which would then edit and process the story before it was released to all its subscriber news organizations around the world. Anwar's arrest was big news, and I was very excited to be the one covering the event.

Returning to our bunker-like offices, located in the belly of the old Equatorial Hotel on Jalan Sultan Ismail, I was vitriolic in my view of how Machiavellian the then PM Pak Lah and his deputy Najib had been in allowing another travesty of justice to take place, just to prevent Anwar from contesting in the Permatang Pauh by-election and getting a seat in parliament. Jega, to his credit, remained silent. I would only understand it much later, but to this day, Jega will not confirm or deny my interpretation.

More shenanigans took place in the intervening nineteen months before the trial began in February 2010.

During that period, we learnt that Anwar's arrest and rough treatment during detention had been overseen by Police Chief Musa Hassan, who had been upset when, two weeks prior, Anwar had lodged a report with the MACC, claiming that the Police Chief had fabricated evidence against him in the investigation into his beating while in police custody ten years earlier.

Anwar's claim of political persecution was buttressed in 2011, when former city criminal investigation chief Mat Zain Ibrahim, who had led the investigation into the 'black eye' inflicted on Anwar by police chief Rahim Noor in 1998, claimed in an open letter to then police chief Bakri Omar that Musa—who was at the time Assistant Criminal Investigation Chief and under the direction of the then Prosecuting Officer and Attorney General from 2002 to 2015 Gani Patail—had in 1998 fabricated evidence against Anwar by stealing his DNA to ensure he would be convicted of sodomy.[262]

And during the trial, we learnt that the aide and alleged victim Mohd Saiful Bukhari Azlan had met with another senior police officer, Senior Assistant Commissioner Mohd Rodwan Mohd Yusof, at a hotel room in Kuala Lumpur just a day before the alleged incident with Anwar. We also learnt Rodwan had played a key role in the police team in Anwar's earlier trials in 1998 and was particularly remembered for allegations of illegally using Anwar's blood sample for DNA testing and planting fabricated DNA samples on the mattress brought to court.[263] And we learnt that Rodwan had brought Saiful to meet with Najib following the incident. It transpired that Rodwan, though intermediaries, had allegedly urged Najib to meet Saiful, who had something 'explosive' to reveal. Putting the pieces together, it was hard not to conclude that there could possibly have been some form of planned entrapment.

After covering the day's hearing, I stormed into the AFP offices, after cursing and swearing at Najib and his officials for attempting to railroad Anwar yet again.

I could not understand why so many senior journalists like Jega did not appear angered by the situation. But another senior journalist and close friend—who does not wish to be named—who had overheard my outburst outside court earlier explained why, when he called and told me, 'Don't get so worked up.'

---

[262] Trowell KC, Mark, *Anwar Returns: The Final Twist: The Prosecution and Release of Anwar Ibrahim*, Marshall Cavendish, 2018, p. 77.

[263] Ibid., p. 79.

I said, 'How am I not supposed to get worked up, especially when you see these links and connections?'

He said, 'Macha, you must understand that what you are seeing is only a very small part of the big picture, and the connections and links you are making in your head, may not necessarily be as accurate as you think.'

'And if you think the current leaders are the ones in charge, then you do not understand Malaysian politics nor the power of the Old man,' this senior hack said, referring to Mahathir.

'I'm not saying that Pak Lah and Najib are not partly responsible for what is happening, but it is not as simple as it seems,' he added.

'Ask yourself these questions. Who is the one person who appointed or was responsible for a vast majority of the current top officials in the police force, including the PM, in getting their current position? Who was the one who pushed the original prosecution of Anwar in 1998 and got him convicted? Who appointed the current Attorney General, and who, despite, being out of office for more than seven years, still commands a strong loyalty within the security services and apparatus in this country? And who is the one person who had, and still holds, a personal vendetta against Anwar?'

'In answering these questions, you will better understand, like the senior journalists in your office and news organizations in Malaysia, who really controls the politics of this country, without even having to occupy the Prime Minister's Office. Instructions do not have to be given. These officials know who they owe their jobs to, what is required of them, and what they need to do.'

Wise words indeed, but I did not believe it at first.

But as the trial dragged on, and more and more sordid details began filtering out, like the slipshod police investigations, the discrepancies in the chain of custody, and the lack of professionalism in carrying out the trial, I began to realize that there was much more at play.

In March 2011, hearings had again begun on Anwar's case, and I covered it for several days, noticing that there had been an increase in the number of police personnel at the court on a daily basis.

Following the enormous public interest in the case, the police had begun following a standard operating procedure of issuing courtroom passes to the media and setting up crowd control points throughout the building.

As part of this plan, they had a daily deployment list that was handed out to the officer in charge on the ground floor of the building, which identified where each police officer was to be deployed and the mobile phone numbers of the key officers involved in the operation.

The list was issued on a daily basis, and one day, the officer in charge left his copy on a chair in the public area of the courthouse, which the cleaner threw into the wastepaper basket next to where the media lined up for access to the court room.

OPS PADAM DSAI
DI MAHKAMAH TINGGI JENAYAH 3,ARAS 5
& BICARA KES KEMATIAN TEOH BENG HOCK
MAHKAMAH N-C-V-C ARAS 3
MAHKAMAH JALAN DUTA
PADA 04/03/2011 (JUMAAT)
* TAKLIMAT DI LOBI MAHKAMAH 0700 HRS *

PEG. PEMERINTAH	: ACP. ZAKARIA BIN PAGAN	(KPD STL)	H/P = 019-
PEG. MEDAN	: DSP MOHD FADZIL BIN A. RAHMAN	(KBSJND)	H/ P = 013- (SIERRA 1)
	1 X APR = PENCATAT L/KPL MOHD NAZARI	(GRKN)	H/P = 016 (STL 25)
	1 X APR = RT	(KOM)	H/P =
PEG. PENYELARAS	: C/INSP SHANKER A/L SHANMUGAM	(KBKA)	H/P = 019-

I saw the document in the bin and picked it up out of curiosity.

And there I saw, the headline title of the document. It was titled 'OPS PADAM DSAI', which translated to 'OPERATION ERADICATE DATUK SERI ANWAR IBRAHIM'.

I was stunned.

The name of the operation clearly suggested the attitude and perception of the police towards Anwar and the sodomy trial. Over the next few days, I observed the police officers with that day's deployment sheet, and every single one had 'OPS PADAM DSAI' listed at the top of it.

It was clear that the overriding plan was to eradicate Anwar, and in my mind, it was now clear who was behind it.

And if that was not enough, what happened at the end of that month proved my suspicions.

It was the morning of 21 March 2011, and the Sarawak state assembly had just been dissolved, paving the way for elections in the East Malaysian state. Although it was only a state election, its large number seats in parliament meant that they would be kingmakers in any General Election. Both BN and the opposition were fighting for the hearts and minds of the people whose votes would play a key part in determining which coalition led the country in GE13.

I had just finished covering Anwar's trial in the morning and was at the police headquarters at Bukit Aman to cover a press conference by Hishammuddin Hussein and the Saudi Arabian home minister when I received a call from my friend Shah at *The Malaysian Insider* news portal. He told me that an anti-Anwar group was calling for a press conference at the Carcosa Seri Negara at 11.45 a.m. This was strange because the Carcosa was a historic building in the middle of Kuala Lumpur, occupying several hectares of green scape. Once the residence of the

British High Commissioner, it was returned to Malaysia in the early 1980s and part of it had been used as a guest house to host the late Queen Elizabeth II when she visited Malaysia, while the other half had been turned into a boutique five-star hotel.

I decided to go for the anti-Anwar presser as the Hishammuddin press conference had been delayed to 1 p.m., and so I headed for the Carcosa.

On arrival at the hotel, I saw several online media reporters from *Free Malaysia Today* (FMT) and one of *Bernama*'s very senior editors Datuk Y waiting downstairs.

Y said that several groups had been brought upstairs in pairs of three or four to one of the hotel rooms to view a video of Anwar, but he did not know any more.

He said that he was attending a meeting at *Bernama* when one of *The Star* newspaper's senior editors called him and told him, 'No matter what you are doing, drop it as this is very, very important, you must come immediately to the Carcosa and see this. Cancel everything, this is too important.'

Y said that the first group had included *The Star*'s editor and three others, and they had already left the hotel. He said the group currently upstairs consisted of then *New Straits Times'* (NST) managing editor Nuraina Samad, NST crime-reporter-turned-political-reporter Alang Bendahara, a reporter from the Chinese-language *Oriental Daily*, and two others.

When Nuraina came down, she said, 'I have a heavy burden on my shoulders,' and left without saying anything else. I then cornered the *Oriental Daily* reporter, who showed me a copy of the press statement given to him by someone identifying themselves as 'Datuk T', claiming that Anwar had sex with a Chinese prostitute and the reporter said he was shown the entire seventeen to twenty minute CCTV footage of the encounter.

DATO' SERI ANWAR IBRAHIM

On 21 Feb 2011, Dato Seri Anwar Ibrahim went to a hotel in Kuala Lumpur that offered sex services and spa facilities.

After Anwar left the hotel, he realised he had left behind his Omega watch in a room that he had occupied earlier.

I was asked to search for the watch in the room. As I could not find the watch on the table, I searched for it behind the dresser. I was shocked to find many strands of wire behind the dresser.

Upon close inspection, I found four well-hidden CCTV cameras. I tried to open the two dresser drawers, and found one was locked. I pry open the locked drawer using a sharp object. I found an active CCTV recorder. I disconnected the wiring and took the recorder out of the hotel.

The recorder contained footages of Dato Seri Anwar Ibrahim in sexual acts.

No one else has this recording, and I will not hand over copies to any quarters for fear of reproduction and distribution.

I want the media to watch the footages showing Dato Seri Anwar in compromising positions with a hooker from China before sending a copy to Dato Seri Anwar and his wife Datin Seri Wan Azizah to identify the person on the video.

Many people know that Datin Seri Wan Azizah is well aware of the truth and Dato Seri Anwar's alleged involvement in Sodomy I (Azizan-Sukma) and Sodomy II (Saiful).

But evidence presented in court is not strong enough, and this has left many members of the public confused and unsure as they do not know Anwar personally. But, Datin Seri Wan Azizah and those close to Dato Seri Anwar know the truth.

One week from today, I will give a copy of the recording to Dato Seri Anwar and Datin Seri Wan Azizah for them to ascertain if the individual in the footage is Anwar.

If it is true that the individual in the footage is Datuk Seri Anwar, Dato Seri Anwar and Datin Seri Wan Azizah must step down from politics. Anwar is not a pious person with high moral value and integrity as portrayed, and therefore he is not fit to be a leader.

If Dato Seri Anwar and Datin Seri Wan Azizah do not quit politics within seven days after receiving a copy of the footages, I will call on several NGOs to set up an independent panel to investigate and seek professional forensic services to study the authenticity of the recordings. The whole world will know, and it is up to Datuk Seri Wan Azizah and Dato Seri Anwar to decide.

Why am I doing this? There is a limit to lies - "Enough is Enough" and it is high time the public know .....THE TRUTH

THE INSIDER

Following this, Shah turned up at the hotel and we all waited for the organizers of this event to come down.

As we were waiting, two Special Branch officers of the police, who monitor the media, turned up. They said that they had heard of the press conference, and their boss had asked them to turn up, but that they were at a loss as to what was going on.

When the journalists explained what they knew to the two Chinese officers and showed them the press release, they appeared very surprised. The officers said they wanted to know who the individuals were who were organizing the event as they had not been briefed about such a thing, with the two calling their bosses in Bukit Aman.

I then took the opportunity to message NN, a good friend of mine from when I did my master's degree in London in 2005, and who was now a close aide of Anwar, telling him of the unfolding events at Carcosa and sending him a copy of the statement. NN was stunned, saying this appeared to be yet another attack on Anwar and that he would inform Anwar and the party's top leadership of what was happening. He said that he could not comment on it at the moment, but once he had more details, he was sure Anwar would respond.

While this was going on, I was at the hotel lobby when a short Malay man wearing dark sunglasses, followed by a person who was clearly his bodyguard, descended from the second floor.

To my surprise, I recognized him as AK, a very senior military official. He was dressed in a suit and wore dark glasses, but his trademark smile was obvious.

I approached him and said, 'Long time no see, Datuk. How are you?' at which point he smiled and said 'Hello', and then he suddenly asked, 'Who are you, when have we met?'

I decided it would not be wise to blurt out that I had met him at the last Five Powers Defence Arrangements Exercise Opening Ceremony in Butterworth the previous year, when he had given me his business card and had chatted with me for about ten minutes on inconsequential matters.

So, I told him, 'We met at Kementah—the Defence Ministry—once, a while ago' at which point he said, 'Oh I have already left,' and then selected four of us, including me, Datuk Y, Shah, and the FMT reporter, to head up into the room.

He took our name cards and brought them into the room on the second floor and made us wait outside the room for about five minutes.

He then came out and told Datuk Y, Shah, and the FMT reporter to go in, but told me that I would have to wait until 2 p.m. before I saw the video as that was when the foreign media would be allowed in.

I then went downstairs and waited as a reporter from *Harakah* took my place and went into the room upstairs.

I then called up one of the media liaison officers at the Defence Ministry, Lieutenant Colonel S, and she did not answer the call but texted me saying that she was in a meeting and to text her what I needed.

I then texted her to ask if AK was still holding his naval position as I was interested in doing a piracy story and wanted to get his comments. She texted me a few minutes later stating, 'u mean . . . in Lumut . . . yes masih (still) AK . . . by mid of April maybe there are some changes', alluding to the fact that AK would be leaving that position soon.

I then got into talking with the Carcosa's receptionist Hadi, who was surprised to see so many media personnel turn up at the hotel, and he was curious as to what was going on. When I asked, he said that AK had checked into the room under his own name yesterday and had taken the room key but that he did not spend the night there at all and that he came early this morning with about five to six people, who were still in the room, and more people started to arrive at about 10 a.m. and that there were now so many (about six) people in the lobby when it was normally deserted. I then showed Hadi the part of Lieutenant Colonel S' text message showing AK's name, and he confirmed AK's name as the one on the guest register.

The *Malaysiakini* reporter had arrived at the hotel by this time and was upset that *The Malaysian Insider* had gotten into the hotel room before him and so wrote a quick story on what was happening and filed it.

AK then came down a few minutes later to say that they were going to stop showing the video and that they had all our cards, and they would call us to show us the video at a later date that was yet to be assigned.

AK was clearly getting instructions from someone else to say these things as he was on the phone and relaying what was being said to him to us and it was obvious that they were halting the screening because the news had gotten out beyond the pro-government and online media and had reached the opposition as well as Special Branch and that *Malaysiakini* had now run a story on it, with more and more people turning up at the hotel, including opposition activists.

When Shah came out of the room, he quickly dragged me aside and then described how they were brought into the room, told to remove their equipment, were 'wanded', and then made to wear a white robe before they sat on chairs in front of a table where a laptop was placed, and the video was played from the laptop.

He said the image was that from a CCTV camera with the screen split in four, with one allegedly showing Anwar in the toilet and another screen showing a girl with Chinese features, coming into the room with another man who was unidentified.

Shah said that it was clear that the person having sex with the girl was supposedly Anwar as there did not appear to be any editing from what he could see.

He said there also appeared to be a camera behind one of the mirrors and that there was a scene where the individual identified as Anwar allegedly pulled up his trousers in front of the camera and it was clear that it was someone who could possibly be Anwar in the footage with his stomach seen very clearly.

Shah said the footage also showed Anwar allegedly entering the toilet and the girl stealing Anwar's gold Omega watch, which he had left on the table.

He said that Datuk T then showed them an Omega watch, saying it was the one in the video, and thus implying that they also had the girl in the video, who could testify to the event. Shah said that they then left the room.

The *Malaysiakini* reporter, H, had taken my picture sitting with other journalists and used it in his article, and, as a result, I received numerous calls asking if I had seen the video after *Malaysiakini*'s story appeared online.

I left the Carcosa at about 1 p.m. and returned to the office where we were trying to get comments from Anwar but to no avail.

I called H, who was still at the Carcosa at 3 p.m., and he said that close to thirty reporters and cameramen were at the hotel lobby following the article in *Malaysiakini*, in the hopes of seeing the video.

I called Hadi, the receptionist, who said that he was quite busy with guests but was sure that AK had left as their cars were gone when he checked at about 2 p.m., but that the Datuk had yet to check out as the keys to the room had yet to be returned.

At 3.45 p.m., NN called me to say that Anwar was going to have a press conference at Parti Keadilan Rakyat (PKR) headquarters at 5 p.m. to deny the allegations. I attended the press conference along with huge numbers of media and met Alang there and had a quick chat with him.

Alang told me that from the people who talked to him and Nuraina in the room, it appeared to him that these were present and former MIO (the intelligence arm of the Malaysian Armed Forces) and Special Branch officers, and one of them was the individual that had been 'asked to retrieve the watch', and who had supposedly spilled the beans to his friends, who were now using the tape to pressure Anwar.

Alang said that he was trying to find the source of the tape and would let me know if he found out any further details but that he did suspect the involvement of the security and intelligence services, because of the way the individuals in the hotel room did things, especially the removal of the various recording devices and phones, and the insistence of wearing white robes before watching the video, which would prevent anyone who wore a concealed camera on their body from recording the video. He said that they also used a wand to check each person before they allowed them into the room.

Friends from the government's communications team called me up after reading the story online, and from the questions they were asking, it was clear that they were also trying to find the source of the video and whether it was authentic or not.

One of Najib's very efficient media officers and a former veteran journalist, HD, also called me to find out what Anwar had said at the press conference. When I asked her how Najib reacted, she said that, 'I told Datuk Seri about the reports of the video, and he is polished enough that I couldn't tell whether this was the first time he was hearing about it, or if it was old news, but he told me to keep monitoring it and asked me what I thought Anwar's reaction would be.'

She said that she thought Anwar would deny the allegations, which Anwar did, and she then passed the phone to her boss DJ, who asked me to tell him what I had seen. I gave him a summarized version, and he said that he was trying to figure out if the video was real and who had leaked the video and if this was some sort of attack by pro-Mahathir groups that would end up backfiring on Najib, should the organizers be exposed. He said that he suspected that some 'former military intelligence boys' could be involved but he was not sure how far up this went.

The next afternoon, I received a call from Alang, telling me that he had gotten another statement from 'Datuk T'. He said that he received the statement from a senior reporter who was with *The Star* newspaper, SH, and that she forwarded the statement to him after asking him to distribute it to the alternative online media as she had already emailed copies to the mainstream media, including *Berita Harian* and *Utusan Malaysia*.

Alang said he felt that SH was close to Datuk T's group as she was the one who had called journalists to tell them about the press conference on Monday and was now emailing statements on behalf of Datuk T.

This appeared to make sense as when I had spoken with *Xinhua*'s Malaysian correspondent JN the day before, she said that she had gotten hold of one of the people in touch with Datuk T and it was someone called 'S' and who told her that Datuk T was not going to show the video again after news of the screening was leaked.

It also explains why one of *The Star*'s top editors was the one who called all the other chief editors and asked them to attend the screening as SH was one of his trusted political journalists who was very pro-government and who took any opportunity to take potshots at Anwar and the opposition.

I had met SH before at one of Mukhriz Mahathir's Buka Puasa functions, and she was extremely critical of Anwar and the opposition and defended the government's every move.

Alang said that he still felt that the mastermind behind the whole tape were former 'ultra-Malay politicians from the Mahathir era'. He said the fact that they had now chosen, in their new statement, not to give Anwar a copy of the video and instead wanted to give it to an independent commission set up by media and NGOs, indicated that the group was unable to proceed with its initial plan for whatever reason and now had moved to a contingency plan.

He said that by doing this, Datuk T and his group had lost credibility as the public would have no confidence in the tape, especially when there was no one to stand up for the tape and that the group was not even willing to give the person they accused a copy of the tape showing his crime. Thus, the feeling now was that the tape was an elaborate forgery and another psychological war tool being used in the run-up to the Sarawak elections and to try and further destroy Anwar's reputation.

On 23 March 2011, the Judge in Anwar's ongoing Sodomy II case reversed his earlier ruling to bar DNA evidence taken from items used by Anwar in a police cell, saying that it could be used as Anwar's arrest and detention was lawful.

Although the prosecution now had Anwar's DNA sample with which to compare DNA samples taken from Saiful, the greater issue was the fact that under cross-examination by Anwar's lawyer Sankara Nair, the investigating officer Judy Blacious admitted that DNA samples taken from Saiful had been done fifty-six hours after the alleged incident occurred. So, clearly, it was not safe to rely on the DNA tests conducted on those samples.[264] And that meant there was only the uncorroborated evidence of the complainant that the act took place.[265]

After the verdict was delivered, I was packing up my things in the Jalan Duta courtroom when I was approached by *Malaysiakini*'s veteran legal reporter, HY, who had been covering the Carcosa case as well.

HY showed me a picture of Shazryl Eskay Abdullah and asked me if I recognized him. I told him that I did. After all, Eskay was a good contact when I was a senior news producer with the English service of *Al Jazeera International*.

Eskay was a former honorary consul at the Royal Thai Consulate in Langkawi and was a key facilitator in talks convened by Mahathir between the Thai Government and Southern Thai separatist groups in Malaysia, in a bid to open dialogue on the

---

[264] *Malaysian Law Review* (High Court), 'PP v Dato' Seri Anwar Ibrahim', 9 Jan 2012, accessed at: https://www.flipsnack.com/B6BDF7EC5A8/pp-v-dato-seri-anwar-ibrahim.html.

[265] The High Court acquitted Anwar on 9 Jan 2012 based on the lack of DNA evidence, but the prosecution appealed the case, and the Court of Appeal overturned the acquittal on 7 Mar 2014. The Federal Court reaffirmed the conviction and five-year sentence on 10 Feb 2015. On 16 May 2018, King Muhammad V formally pardoned Anwar.

violence in Southern Thai border provinces. After meeting Eskay at an event hosted by Mahathir and Mukhriz, he helped arranged interviews for me with the top leadership of the separatist movement, which led to several big stories on *Al Jazeera*, but we had lost touch over the years.

HY then asked me whether I recognized Eskay's picture as that of Datuk T and I said that I didn't as I had not seen Datuk T, who was inside the room, and I had only seen his flunkies who had escorted the reporters in.

Hafiz then turned to the FMT reporter EL next to me, who had seen the sex tape, and EL said that Datuk T did look like Eskay.

HY then said that the reason he was asking was because he was covering a court case on the abandoned Crooked Bridge that was supposed to be built between Malaysia and Singapore, to replace the Causeway, but was shelved by the government in 2006.

HY said that Shazryl was suing Merong Mahawangsa Sdn Bhd and Datuk Yahya A. Jalil for RM20 million for not compensating him for using his influence to secure a RM640 million government project to construct the bridge, despite the government compensating Merong Mahawangsa RM155 million for cancelling the project.

Eskay claimed that Yahya had sought his help in 1998 to procure the project and foreign funding. Shazryl claimed he had secured the funding and allegedly met with the then Finance Minister Anwar, following which Merong Mahawangsa got the deal.

HY said that earlier in the day, Eskay's lawyers on the Crooked Bridge case had spoken to him to ask him if he knew of Eskay's whereabouts as they had lost contact with him over the last three days and were very concerned, hinting that Eskay was somehow involved in the Datuk T Anwar sex tape episode.

HY said that as he was trying to locate Eskay, he received an email pointing him to a website[266] which outlined how Eskay and disgraced former UMNO politician Rahim Thamby Chik were involved in the whole sex tape episode.

HY said that he believed Eskay' was involved in the whole sex tape issue because Eskay felt he had been double-crossed by Yahya and Anwar and wanted to seek revenge.

As we were discussing this, PKR announced that they would be having a press conference with one of its senior lawmakers Johari Abdul on the Datuk T issue, and we all rushed to PKR headquarters at the Tropicana to report on the revelations.

Alang, who was already there when I arrived, told me that the police had already interviewed *The Star*'s editor and SH over their involvement in the sex tape conspiracy. He said that the police were trying to narrow down where the tape came from as his contacts in Special Branch were caught completely unawares over the whole tape and were trying to get to the bottom of it.

Alang also showed me that he had a mobile phone number for Datuk T and that he had been corresponding with Datuk T over the last evening, but he did not know Datuk T's identity although, after reading the blogs, he was now sure Datuk T was Eskay as that was the man he had seen at Carcosa.

In the press conference, Johari outlined how he was approached on 21 March by Eskay and Rahim and how they had not only shown him the video but had also urged him to leave PKR and bring along others so they could view the video and also abandon the party. Johari claimed that Rahim had also offered him and other PKR MPs money to switch sides.

---

[266] 'Update: Who is Datuk T and the People Behind the Screening of the Sex Tape?', Malaysians Unplugged Uncensored, 23 Mar 2011, accessed at: http://malaysianunplug.blogspot.com/2011/03/who-is-datuk-t-and-people-behind.html.

Following the conclusion of the press conference, I spoke with PKR's Saifuddin Nasution, and he said that they had been on the verge of finding out who the conspirators were on Monday night when Johari had come to them with details of his meeting with Eskay and Rahim.

Saifuddin said that they had found out from their contacts that *The Star*'s SH was involved and as she was very close to one of Saifuddin's staffers, they called her, but she initially denied any involvement.

However, she finally admitted that she was the one who had drafted the second Datuk T statement on Tuesday, and she had also been the one to call reporters to check that they had seen the videos and were going to write on it.

Saifuddin said that SH had refused to divulge the name of the conspirators, but it did not matter as Johari had told them the names, and when she was confronted with this, she confessed to Saifuddin's staff that she was one of the conspirators in that she was shown the tape last week, and she was responsible for coordinating the media coverage at Carcosa.

Saifudddin said that the cat was now out of the bag but that he didn't believe that there were only these three conspirators and that there must have been others who were also involved but who are keeping low.

He said that not only did Datuk T show the video to Johari, but that it was also screened for a few Barisan Nasional (BN) MPs in parliament and that on Monday evening, the tape was also screened for some royalty.

Following the press conference, I called HD to brief her on what had transpired, and she called me back half an hour later to say that when she broke the news of the identity of Datuk T to Najib, he appeared really surprised and said that although he knew Rahim Thamby Chik, this was all really news to him and that he definitely did not know Eskay at all but was aware that Eskay was a close aide to Mahathir.

Once it became clear that Eskay was involved, I realized that this was most probably why I was not allowed to view the video at the Carcosa on Monday, as he must have seen my business card, which had been collected from us before we were allowed into the room, and felt that if I were allowed in, I would have immediately recognized him, and the whole game would be up.

At about 2 p.m., we were told that Rahim Thamby Chik and Eskay would be holding a press conference at the Impiana Hotel at 4 p.m., and I made my way there with a colleague from *Agence-France Presse*.

As we arrived at the hotel, Rahim and Eskay also arrived and they were being escorted by AK and two or three others, all of whom were keeping in the background.

Once the press conference started, Eskay saw me and nodded to me as Rahim began to speak, and when Eskay spoke, he tried to justify what he was saying and even went so far as to say that he really trusted the media and had good friends in the media and mentioned me by name.

A little later, he also mentioned Alang as a person in the media who knew him and who could vouch for his attempt to try and tell the truth.

I was furious that he would mention me as his friend given that he did not even let me watch the video in the first place and was now trying to use me to bolster his credibility.

I then asked him openly why it was that he did not allow me to view the video to which he said, 'I'm sorry but I was afraid that there were too many media who were arriving and so I had to cancel the rest of the screening.'

Following the press conference, I approached Eskay to ask him for his mobile number and he said, 'Give me your card and I will call you.' He called me half an hour later to half-heartedly apologize for not showing me the video, and I then asked him if he would show me the tape.

Eskay said that if I wrote a glowing piece about what he was trying to do and about his good reputation, then I would definitely get to see the video, and I said thanks but no thanks and hung up. That was the last time I spoke or had any dealings with Eskay.

Later in the evening, HD called and commiserated with me, saying that as Rahim was involved in the whole affair, it was clear to anyone in the know that this was a move directed by someone else, as Najib would never use Rahim at all. She said if Najib ever did something like this, which she didn't think he ever would, it would not be done in such a bungling and unprofessional manner.

I then spoke to Mukhriz's then press secretary, my good friend the late Azrin Zizal, and reminded him of how I was introduced to Eskay by Mukhriz and Mahathir and what a mess he had gotten himself into with the tape.

Azrin said that since 2008, Eskay had gone to the dark side and had become very dodgy in what he was doing. He said that the police were sure to arrest Eskay for his involvement in the sex tape incident.

Azrin said it appeared that Eskay and Rahim were seeking publicity for their video and that even after being exposed, they were still trying to justify their scheme in the eyes of the media, hoping that the media would take their side against Anwar but that this did not appear to have happened.

In the end, Datuk T, which we later found out stood for 'Datuk Trio', and consisted of Eskay, Rahim, and Perkasa Treasurer Shuib Lazim, pleaded guilty to the screening of a pornographic video at the Carcosa Hotel in violation of section 292 of the Penal Code[267].

---

[267] Kow, Gah Chie, 'Sex video: Datuk T trio pleads guilty, fined RM5,500', *Malaysiakini*, 25 Jun 2011, accessed at: https://www.malaysiakini.com/news/167883.

Once the three were identified, their links to Mahathir and Anwar became clear.

Rahim was one of Mahathir's staunchest supporters but was forced to resign from UMNO Youth and as Malacca Chief Minister in 1994 after being charged with statutory rape of an underaged girl. However, he was unhappy when Anwar in 1999 filed a police report alleging that Mahathir, the then Attorney General, and the then Senior Deputy Public Prosecutor Gani Patail—the current Attorney General in 2011—were involved in abusing their power by covering up a corruption case involving Rahim.

Shuib was treasurer of Perkasa, a right-wing Malay-rights group which had Mahathir as its chief supporter and patron, who felt that Anwar had let down the Malay cause.

But Eskay's relationship was a little more complex. From Kedah and of Thai descent, Eskay worked as a sports therapist in the United States, including for the US Olympics gymnastics team as well as the Dallas Cowboys, a professional American football team. He was one of only a handful of people to have stayed close to both Mahathir and Anwar. In the 1990s, Mahathir, always on the lookout for successful Malaysians abroad, brought Eskay back to Malaysia to help Anwar with his back problems caused by the latter's riding injury. That was the start of the friendship between Eskay and Anwar.[268]

Of course, there was much controversy as to why the Attorney General Gani Patail chose to prosecute the three with a lighter offence and the fact that AG Patail decided to use a special team lead by Kamaludin bin Mohd Said, the head of the Appellate and Trial Division in the Attorney General's Chambers, instead of the head of the Wilayah Persekutuan prosecution section, Puan Raja Rozela binti Raja Toran, or Datuk Tun Abd Majid bin

---

[268] 'Proof lies in the sex video, Anwar! Whistle-blower seen in sex tape: The 3 Datuks', Rightways, 25 Mar 2011, accessed at: https://rightways.wordpress.com/2011/03/25/proof-lies-in-the-sex-video-anwar/.

Tun Hamzah, the head of prosecution of the AGC, who would normally handle such prosecutions.

There was also much outrage given that since the three had already pleaded guilty, the Deputy Public Prosecutor should have only read out very brief facts regarding the case, which would normally only outline the place, date, and time of the offence.

Instead, the prosecutor went on to state that not only was the pornographic video authentic but that experts from Dartmouth College also carried out a facial recognition analysis on the man in the video and found that it resembled Anwar.

As opposition leaders noted, who was in the video was immaterial to the charge of displaying/exhibiting pornography and whether the video was tampered or not was also irrelevant. What was of relevance was only the fact that sex had occurred in the video. So, it was obvious that even though the three were found guilty, there was still a bid from persons unknown to still try and use the tape to smear Anwar.

Sitting down with my friend over a beer one evening after the case was over, he turned to me and asked, 'Now do you understand the silence of your seniors and how the game is played?'

I said, 'No, I don't.'

'I'm even more confused by the connections and the powerplay going on.'

'But I can see that it is not so black and white and there is so much history and connections that if you figure it out, it ends up showing who is really pulling the strings. The old man has friends in powerful places, people he put there and those who share his agenda and are willing to carry it out.'

'Well then,' he said, holding up his glass, 'you're definitely on the way to understanding Malaysian politics.'

Appendix 2

Interfering with the Judiciary

I suppose the Malaysian judiciary has never been the same after Mahathir neutered it with the removal of Tun Salleh Abas as Lord President back in 1988[269] and then appointed many new judges who were viewed as loyal to Mahathir, some of whom now occupy senior posts across the land. As Mahathir's Attorney General Tommy Thomas—in Mahathir's second run as PM—noted:

> The lord President and the two most senior of the puisne judges were removed from office. The three remaining judges were reinstated, but psychologically scarred. The immediate beneficiaries of the vacancies caused by these dismissals were Hamid Omar and Hashim Yeop Sani, becoming Lord President and Chief Justice respectively. All the High Court judges who assisted the Hamid Omar cause in any way were promoted to the Federal Court. The message to the Bench and Bar was loud and clear. The clarion call was reward for those who wished to play the game. Merit, competence and integrity did not matter. Apple-polishing was the only qualification. The decline in standards in the next decade, during the leadership

---

[269] 'Behind closed doors: Mahathir's 1988 showdown with Salleh Abas', *Aliran*, accessed at: https://m.aliran.com/towering-msians/mahathirs-1988-showdown-with-salleh-aba.

of Hamid Omar and Eusoff Chin, undoubtedly the darkest days in the nation's judicial history, was directly caused by the removal of Salleh, and his replacement by Hamid.

The hopes of the Bar that any semblance of independence on the part of the senior judiciary to rule against the Executive branch, and indeed any governmental agency, disappeared upon the taking of office of Hamid Omar as Lord President in late 1988.[270]

And of course, let's not forget Mahathir's involvement in the fourteen-minute video of the VK Lingam affair. Lingam, a senior lawyer very close to Mahathir, allegedly, in 2001, brokered a deal with the then Chief Judge of Malaya Ahmad Fairuz Sheikh Abdul Hamid to make him the next Chief Justice. Mahathir then made Fairuz Chief Justice shortly after, choosing Fairuz over a more senior candidate favoured by the outgoing Chief Justice. When asked in 2008 by a Royal Commission of Inquiry (RCI)—set up to investigate the interference in judicial appointments—as to his rationale, Mahathir quipped, 'I don't have to explain to anybody the reasons why.'[271]

In its 2008 report, the RCI recommended that action be taken against Mahathir, Fairuz, and four others for misconduct while in office[272].

In 2015, Lingam was struck off the rolls of advocates and solicitors by the Bar Council who brought complaints against him, which included interfering in or influencing judicial appointments. However, Mahathir and Fairuz were not prosecuted.

---

[270] Thomas, Tommy, *My Story*, pp. 121–122.

[271] '"I don't have to explain why", says Dr Mahathir', *Bernama*, accessed at: https://www.malaysianbar.org.my/article/news/bar-news/news/-i-don-t-have-to-explain-why-says-dr-mahathir.

[272] Lingam Tape Report, Scribd, accessed at: https://www.scribd.com/document/60920700/Lingam-Tape-Report#.

Fairuz was the country's presiding Chief Justice before Mahathir stepped down in 2003, and Fairuz had long retired before the entire scandal blew up in 2008. Interestingly, a young judicial officer named Tengku Maimun Tuan Mat was Fairuz's special officer when he served as Chief Justice.

And, of course, when he again became prime minister in 2018, Mahathir was back at it.

Within days of PH1.0 winning GE14, Daim Zainuddin, Mahathir's former Finance Minister and Chairman of Mahathir's Council of Eminent Persons (CEP), summoned Chief Justice Tun Md Raus Sharif and Court of Appeal President Tan Sri Zulkefli Ahmad Makinudin and allegedly ordered them to resign.

A Chief Justice is not a political appointee who should resign if the government during which period he was appointed is defeated in a general election.

Nonetheless, Mahathir defended Daim's actions saying, 'Otherwise, the government may take action to remove them because we believe that the extension of their office as senior judges was not right.'[273]

This appeared to be a replay of the Tun Salleh Abas episode, which was so galling that even a staunch Democratic Action Party (DAP) member like senior lawyer Ramkarpal Singh—son of the late DAP Chairman Karpal Singh—spoke out:

> Prime Minister Dr Mahathir Mohamad's defence of the Council of Eminent Persons for summoning the top two judges to demand their resignations was ill-advised and against the rule of law ... When it summons judges and demands their resignations, it will be seen as the government demanding their resignations which is in complete disregard for the principle

---

[273] 'Dr M defends CEP over summoning of judges', *The Sun*, 12 Jun 2018, accessed at: https://www.thesundaily.my/archive/dr-m-defends-cep-over-summoning-judges-MUARCH554906.

of separation of powers (. . .) It is a basic hallmark of any
democracy that the executive does not interfere in the affairs
of the judiciary.[274]

Singh said that criticizing the appointments of Raus and Zulkefli
was not wrong but it was 'quite another matter to summon them
and demand their resignations'.[275]

The two senior judges had asked to retire on 31 July 2018, but
Mahathir's newly appointed AG, Tommy Thomas took offence:

> When I assumed office on 6 June 2018, the continued tenure
> of the two highest judicial officers in the land required
> my immediate attention. I wrote an opinion to the Prime
> Minister, advising him that since both judges had tendered
> their resignations in writing, the government was not bound
> to accept their last date of 31 July 2018, which was chosen by
> them unilaterally for their own convenience. I further advised
> that the government should accept their resignations with
> immediate effect, rather than waiting for 31 July. The Prime
> Minister agreed. The resignations were then brought forward
> to early July 2018.[276]

So, instead of focusing on key legal issues affecting the country and
in learning the ropes in his first month at the Attorney General's
Chambers, Thomas was busy writing opinions on how to make
the country's two former senior judges retire at the beginning of
the month instead of at the end of it.

---

[274] 'Ramkarpal says Council of Eminent Persons overstepped boundaries',
Malay Mail, 13 Jun 2018, accessed at: https://www.malaymail.com/
news/malaysia/2018/06/13/ramkarpal-says-council-of-eminent-persons-
overstepped-boundaries/1641672.

[275] Ibid.

[276] Thomas, Tommy, *My Story*, p. 337.

Was there a need to be so petty?

It would appear that this was the start of a vendetta against supposedly pro-Barisan Nasional judicial and legal officers.

And there was more to come.

But the biggest irony was that the Judicial Appointments Commission (JAC) had been set up following Mahathir and his crony shenanigans in the VK Lingam affair. The RCI had noted that:

> The Commission find sufficient cause to invoke the Sedition Act 1948, the Legal Profession Act 1976, the Official Secrets Act 1972, and the Penal Code against various individuals mentioned in the video clip which we have elaborated in the Report. We do not discount the possibility of other laws being contravened. We leave it to the Attorney General Malaysia and the Malaysian Bar Council, to take appropriate actions against the personalities implicated. Additionally, we are proposing to the Government for the necessary reforms including the establishment of **a Judicial Appointments Commission.**[277]

The Government accepted the RCI's recommendation on the act and enacted the Judicial Appointments Commission Act 2009. Section 2 of the JAC Act required all prime ministers to uphold the 'independence of the judiciary'. The principal function and power of the JAC was 'to select suitably qualified persons who merit appointment as judges of the superior court for the prime minister's consideration'.[278]

Under the JAC Act, a prime minister does not have the power to select candidates for the appointment of judges of the superior courts.

---

[277] Laporan Pasukan Petugas Khas, p. 37.

[278] Ibid.

It states that the prime minister 'does not select candidates for the appointment to the highest judicial offices; the advice he tenders to the Yang di-Pertuan Agong on the appointment to these high judicial offices must be based on the selection and recommendation made by the JAC'.

And most importantly,

> . . . the Attorney General is not a member of the JAC and has no right or power under the JAC Act or Article 122B of the Federal Constitution, to select or recommend to the Prime Minister, or be consulted on, any candidate for the appointment to the high judicial offices. The Attorney General's advice is not constitutionally required to enable the Prime Minister to tender his advice to the Yang di-Pertuan Agong for appointment of judges.

And despite the JAC Act, Mahathir yet again allegedly subverted the independence of the judiciary. Not once, but twice, during his twenty-two months as prime minister.

And this time, with the knowing help of Thomas, who—as noted in the task force report on Thomas' book—as the government's top legal officer, was duty bound to 'advise the prime minister to act according to Article 122B(1), (2) and (3) of the Federal Constitution and comply with sections 26, 27 and 28 of the JAC Act in order to uphold the continued independence of the Judiciary'.

What was worse, Thomas himself also appears to have ridden roughshod over the Constitution and the JAC Act.

On 24 May 2018, a few weeks after GE14, the JAC at its meeting came up with a list of top judicial officials that should replace Raus and Zulkefli and other positions that would become vacant shortly.

On 13 June, the then Chief Justice conveyed in writing the JAC's decision to Mahathir. The JAC had recommended Tan Sri Dato' Sri Azahar bin Mohamed as Chief Justice of Federal Court,

Dato Rohana binti Yusuf as President Court of Appeal and Dato'
Abdul Rahman bin Sebli as Chief Judge of High Court in Sabah
and Sarawak.

But as Thomas confessed in his book, in reality, it was
Mahathir and him who decided on who would be proposed as the
country's top judges:

> I was pleasantly surprised during my discussion with the Prime
> Minister as to Chief Justice Raus's successor, when he mentioned
> Tan Sri Richard Malanjum. Tun had heard good things about
> Richard Malanjum. **We also agreed** (emphasis added) on the
> other three appointments caused by the retirement of Raus and
> Zulkefli. Tan Sri Dato' Sri Ahmad Maarop was promoted from
> Chief Judge of Malaya to President of the Court of Appeal,
> Tan Sri Zaharah Ibrahim became Chief Judge of Malaya and
> Tan Sri David Wong Dak Wah, the Chief Judge of Sabah
> and Sarawak.[279]

Regardless of whatever 'good things' Mahathir had heard about
Malanjum, the fact remains that Malanjum, Ahmad Maarop,
Zaharah Ibrahim and David Wong were NOT recommended
by the JAC.

If Mahathir disagreed with the JAC's recommendations,
under the JAC Act, he could ask the JAC for additional names.

This did not appear to have happened.

As the task force reporting on Thomas' book noted, 'the
names submitted by the Prime Minister when he tendered his
advice to the Yang di-Pertuan Agong under Article 122B were the
names discussed and agreed upon between the Prime Minister
and the Attorney General'.[280]

---

[279] Thomas, Tommy, *My Story*, p. 338.

[280] Laporan Pasukan Petugas Khas, p.43.

It was even worse when it came to the candidate for the post of Chief Judge of the High Court in Sabah and Sarawak.

Under Article 122B(3) of the Federal Constitution, the Chief Ministers of Sabah and Sarawak had to be consulted regarding the appointment, and they would then issue certificates indicating their approval. It would appear that Mahathir never consulted the chief ministers as no certificates were issued and Mahathir and Thomas' candidate for the post was pushed through in violation of the Constitution.[281]

And it did not stop there.

In 2019, Thomas and Mahathir were at it again when there were about to be vacancies again for the country's top judicial position.

Once again, the JAC had on 17 January made recommendations, namely Tan Sri Dato' Sri Ahmad bin Haji Maarop as Chief Justice, Datuk Seri Panglima David Wong Dak Wah as President of the Court of Appeal, Dato' Tengku Maimun binti Tuan Mat as Chief Judge of High Court in Malaya, and Dato' Abang Iskandar bin Abang Hashim as Chief Judge of High Court in Sabah and Sarawak.

On 18 March, Mahathir sent a letter approving the JAC's recommendations to the Cabinet department responsible for proposing the names of judges to the Council of Rulers.

The department duly prepared the appointment papers for the approval of the rulers but without any explanation, on 21 March, the Chief Secretary ordered the department to withdraw and cancel the paper.

It was clear that the prime minister, for whatever reason, was unhappy with the choices at that late stage.

Was the withdrawal made because Thomas was unhappy with the JAC's list although Mahathir was ok with it? Did he then urge the PM to cancel the appointments and seek more names from

---

[281] Ibid.

the JAC? And why was Thomas involved, given that he, as a senior lawyer and the Government's top legal officer, must have known that his involvement would be a violation of the Constitution and laws of the land?

It is not clear from Thomas' book when the following meeting took place, but his description of it makes clear his involvement in what transpired:

> The Prime Minister and I discussed filling the four offices as all the incumbents would be retiring within a year of each other. Having regularly appeared in the courts, I was familiar with all the judges of the Federal Court.
>
> Seniority was not relevant. **Our criteria** (emphasis added) was integrity, competence, temperament, independence and a proven track record on written judgements . . .
>
> **It was agreed** (emphasis added) there was only one candidate who satisfied the tests: Justice Tan Sri Tengku Maimun Tuan Mat.
>
> I shared with the Prime Minister my experiences of appearances before her as a judicial commissioner and judge of the High Court, and subsequently, in the Court of Appeal and the Federal Court. Justice Rohana Yusuf was the standout candidate for the President of the Court of Appeal. Justice Dato' Abang Iskandar Abang Hashim was essentially the only contender for the office of the Chief Judge of Sabah and Sarawak. Justice Tan Sri Dato' Sri Azahar Mohamed was chosen as Chief Judge of Malaya.[282]

Thomas also noted that the 'Chief Justice must also be ever vigilant to protect and preserve the supreme law of the land, the Federal Constitution'[283] but by dismissing the JAC's (who presumably

---

[282] Thomas, Tommy, *My Story*, p. 342.

[283] Ibid.

would have used similar criteria in making their decision) recommendations and in involving himself in the decision to appoint the country's top judges, was he not subverting the independence of the Judiciary and violating the Constitution he claimed to be protecting?

So, the JAC met again to draw up a new list of candidates. On 5 April 2019, a letter to the prime minister from Mahathir and Thomas' handpicked Chief Justice Richard Malanjum, recommended new candidates to fill each judicial position.

Chief Justice

i.   YA Dato' Tengku Maimum binti Tuan Mat;
ii. YA Tan Sri Dato' Sri Azahar bin Mohamed.

President of Court of Appeal

i.   YA Tan Sri Dato' Sri Azahar bin Mohamed;
ii. YA Dato' Rohana binti Yusuf.

Chief Judge of the High Court in Malaya

i.   YA Dato' Rohana binti Yusuf;
ii. YA Tan Sri Dato' Sri Azahar bin Mohamed.[284]

It was clear from the list that the JAC felt that Azahar bin Mohamed was the preferred candidate for the country's top, or at least one of the top, judicial positions, as he was nominated for all three posts.

However, three days later, Mahathir informed the Cabinet department preparing the proposal for appointments of the top judges that Tengku Maimum binti Tuan Mat would be proposed

---

[284] Laporan Pasukan Petugas Khas, p. 31.

for Chief Justice, Rohana binti Yusuf would be proposed for President of Court of Appeal, and Abang Iskandar bin Abang Hashim would be proposed for Chief Judge Malaya.[285]

Azahar and Ahmad Haji Maarop, who had both been nominated by the JAC for the CJ's post, had been dumped in favour of Tengku Maimun. Abang Iskandar's name had also suddenly appeared as the candidate for the position of Chief Judge of Malaya.

The Attorney General's deep involvement was obvious when it was he who informed Tengku Maimun of the proposed names for the post of President of Court of Appeal, Chief Justice Malaya, and Chief Justice of Sabah and Sarawak.

> I paid a courtesy call to Chief Justice Tengku Maimum soon thereafter. She warmly received me in her spacious chamber in the Palace of Justice in Putrajaya. I showed the names of the Prime Minister's choices for the other three names. She was happy with each of them, saying that she could work with them, and that they could work together as an effective team.[286]

Any reasonable person would understand that the JAC was set up to ensure that judges, especially the Chief Justice and the country's top judges, would not end up being beholden and/or bound to act on the whims of a Prime Minister—whether current or former—because he had chosen them specifically for the post while he was in power.

The fact that Mahathir totally ignored the JAC, violated the constitution, and instead decided on the positions in collusion with his Attorney General—who, as a senior lawyer, must have been fully aware that he had no power or role in such decisions—would make anyone question the independence of the judiciary given that some of these individuals are still in post.

---

[285] Ibid.

[286] Thomas, Tommy, *My Story*, p. 342.

The fact that it was Thomas, rather than the PM, who informed the Chief Justice of the other top judicial appointments would give the perception of his high-level involvement and influence with the prime minister with regard to the judiciary.

As such, many would come to this irresistible conclusion. Given that the Attorney General is the head of prosecutions, it is unacceptable that he was not only involved in deciding on which top judges would be in key future positions to decide on cases which he or his chamber would prosecute on, but also by being the messenger to the Chief Justice, he showed, in no uncertain terms, to the judiciary to whom these top judges owed their new positions.

So, after getting rid of Raus, Mahathir appointed former Chief Judge of Sabah and Sarawak, Richard Malanjum, as the ninth Chief Justice—who, it then transpired, was a supporter of staunch Mahathir loyalist Shafie Apdal's Warisan party, campaigning for Pakatan Harapan in the Sabah state elections after his retirement in 2019.

Mahathir replaced him with Fairuz's former special officer Tengku Maimun Tuan Mat as the country's tenth Chief Justice. She ended up being the presiding—and remains the current—Chief Justice when Mahathir stepped down for the second time.

Appendix 3

The Implosion of PH1.0: A Chronology of Events

Many have asked how the implosion of PH1.0 came about and it really began with Mahathir's unwillingness, following his win at GE14, to hand over power to Anwar and the Democratic Action Party (DAP). As part of his machinations, he had tasked Muhyiddin with the challenge to build a Grand Malay Alliance, or coalition of parties, that would include the Malaysian United Indigenous Party (BERSATU), United Malays National Organization (UMNO), and Parti Islam Se-Malaysia (PAS), in a bid to ensure that Mahathir would have enough seats to form a government without Anwar, his supporters within Parti Keadilan Rakyat (PKR), and the DAP. However, Mahathir quickly lost control of the situation when the movement began to take a life of its own, as pro-Mahathir and pro-Anwar factions began openly fighting on the date of transition of power and whether such a transition would even take place.

Friday, 21 February 2020

In a heated Pakatan Harapan (PH) Presidential Council meeting, both Mahathir and Anwar's factions agree that Mahathir would choose the date on which to resign after the APEC meetings in November 2020.

Mahathir also finally decides in his mind that he will actually hand over power to Anwar.

Saturday, 22 February 2020

Parti Islam Se-Malaysia (PAS) announces that it was cancelling its move to table a parliamentary motion of confidence in Mahathir as the Pakatan Harapan Presidential Council had decided to leave it to the chairman to decide on when the succession will take place.

However, Muhyiddin and Azmin, along with several other future Perikatan Nasional coalition partners, are unhappy with Mahathir's hand being forced on a succession date and believe they have to act quickly to stop Mahathir from handing power to Anwar.

Sunday, 23 February 2020

BERSATU and all its other future coalition partners hold separate party supreme council meetings.

At BERSATU's meeting, Muhyiddin and other leaders attempt to convince Mahathir to form the new Perikatan Nasional coalition on that day itself, following reports that Anwar is trying to meet the King to form a government.

Mahathir is reluctant to form Perikatan Nasional despite Muhyiddin telling him that he has the numbers as Mahathir doesn't want to work with UMNO. He asks for an appointment with the King and orders Muhyiddin to deliver the 134 statutory declarations in support of Mahathir, while Mahathir himself monitors things from home. The BERSATU Supreme Council agree to give Mahathir until the end of the week to decide on when to announce the party's pull out from PH1.0

Leaders of the future Perikatan Nasional coalition, namely Muhyiddin, Azmin, Zahid, Hadi, Abang Johari Openg, and Shafie Apdal, then turn up at Mahathir's home to try and convince him to set up the new coalition. Mahathir still demurs.

At the Istana, Muhyiddin again tries to convince Mahathir over the phone but to no avail, and Muhyiddin then leaves with the other PN leaders. However, the momentum to form the coalition is great and some of these leaders agree that they will head to the Sheraton Hotel, where they will announce the formation of the new coalition regardless.

Mahathir gets wind of the plan through Syed Saddiq, Mukhriz, and Rina Harun. He then despatches Syed Saddiq and Rina Harun to the Sheraton Hotel to get the plotters to stand down. Syed Saddiq gets to the hotel with minutes to spare and stops the plan.

But Muhyiddin and the plotters are unhappy, especially the BERSATU leadership, who want Mahathir to pull out of PH1.0 immediately.

Monday, 24 February 2020

First thing in the morning, Anwar, Wan Azizah, Mohamad Sabu, and Lim Guan Eng meet Mahathir at his home, and Mahathir assures them he has nothing to do with the plot.

Once they leave, Muhyiddin meets Mahathir, telling him that the BERSATU leaders are adamant that they want to leave PH1.0 and that Muhyiddin would be drafting a statement to that effect and releasing it that afternoon. The pull out would only cause the PH1.0 coalition to collapse while Mahathir would still have the confidence of the majority of the lawmakers to carry on as prime minister.

However, realizing that he had been outmanoeuvred and has lost control of BERSATU and of his grand plan, and believing that he still had the support of the majority of lawmakers who would eventually clamour for his return, Mahathir resigns as prime minister, BERSATU chairman, and chairman of PH1.0

He meets the King and is appointed as caretaker prime minister. BERSATU announces its pull out from the coalition, as does Azmin, along with several other Parti Keadilan Rakyat (PKR) lawmakers, and this now results in the total collapse of the PH1.0 Government.

Tuesday, 25 February 2020

The King interviews ninety lawmakers to determine who has the support of the majority of Parliamentarians. UMNO and PAS withdraw their support for Mahathir and call for fresh elections as they cannot agree to Mahathir's idea of a unity government that would include DAP and Anwar's PKR faction.

The remaining PH coalition partners are also unable to accept Mahathir's unity government plan as Mahathir wants the sole say on who would be in Cabinet, thus eliminating any influence the parties would have on the government.

Wednesday, 26 February 2020

In a televised speech, Mahathir announces his plan for a unity government. Pakatan Harapan now announces Anwar as its candidate for Prime Minister.

Thursday, 27 February 2020

The King tells Mahathir that he is unable to find anyone with a distinct majority to form the government and Mahathir orders a special sitting of the Parliament on 2 March 2020 to determine who holds the confidence of the majority of MPs, failing which he hints at snap elections.

Friday, 28 February 2020

The Conference of Rulers holds a special session at Istana Negara to address the ongoing political crisis, and they are joined by the heads of the country's military and security services. The Palace then announces that the King will meet with leaders of the various political parties the next day in a bid to nominate their prime ministerial candidate, to settle the issue.

The Speaker of Parliament rejects Mahathir's order for a special sitting, noting that it does not adhere to parliamentary standing orders.

Meanwhile, Muhyiddin and his team are working behind the scenes with the PN coalition leaders to determine if they will support him as Prime Minister instead of Mahathir. They agree to Muhyiddin's plan as it means a new government that does not include Anwar or the Democratic Action Party.

Muhyiddin goes to see Mahathir out of 'respect' and asks for Mahathir's support. He says that Mahathir is willing to support him if he has the majority of support from MPs.

That evening, BERSATU, along with Azmin's Parti Keadilan Rakyat faction, UMNO, PAS, Malaysian Chinese Association, and the Malaysian Indian Congress announce their support for Muhyiddin as the country's eighth prime minister.

Saturday, 29 February 2020

The Pakatan Harapan Presidential Council leaders scramble to hold a meeting in the morning and announce the reversal of support for Anwar and their decision to now back Mahathir as PM.

Meanwhile, leaders from BERSATU, UMNO, PAS, Gabungan Parti Sarawak, Parti Bersatu Rakyat Sabah, and Homeland Solidarrity Party (STAR) meet with the King and pledge their support for Muhyiddin. Muhyiddin announces the formation of the new Perikatan Nasional Coalition and that they have the numbers to form the government and elect a new prime minister.

In the evening, the Palace announces that Muhyiddin would be sworn in as the country's next prime minister.

Sunday, 1 March 2020

Muhyiddin Yassin becomes Malaysia's eighth prime minister.

Index